THE VIRGIN BOOK OF BABY NAMES

Emily Wood

To my beloved children,
Lucy and Katie,
and wonderful husband, Keith

This revised and updated edition first published
in Great Britain in 2006 by
Virgin Books Ltd
Thames Wharf Studios
Rainville Road
London W6 9HA

A catalogue record for this book is available from the British
Library.

ISBN 0 7535 1054 5

Typeset by TW Typesetting, Plymouth, Devon

Printed and bound in Great Britain by Clays Ltd, St Ives PLC

Contents

Acknowledgements

There are so many people who have helped along the way with this book. When you say you are researching a 'themed' book on baby names, it's amazing how many people offer suggestions. When you are also trying to do it with two young children and while moving house, it's equally amazing how many people are prepared to help out. The support, patience and kindness of everyone have made a real difference. There are too many to mention individually but they know who they are and I hope they know just how very grateful I am.

Some people, though, must be mentioned: Liza Edelshain for her help with Welsh names; Myrtle Parker for her help with Celtic names; my parents, John and Daphne Rae, for their constant support and depth of knowledge on almost any subject; my mother-in-law, Janet McErlain, for keeping things running in a crisis; Sally Lewis for her readiness to have the children at her house; Nicky Mockford, without whose help, optimism and occasional glass of wine this would never have been finished.

Last, but certainly not least, thanks, apologies and eternal gratitude to my long-suffering husband, Keith, who probably never wants to see or hear another word about baby names and who has regularly been on 'children duty' over entire weekends; and to Anna Cherrett, the kindest and most patient editor who has put up with so much over the last few months without once raising her voice – even when I inadvertently crashed her system with a virus!

INTRODUCTION

Anyone who has ever been expecting a baby will know that this gives friends and strangers alike the inalienable right to ask you hundreds of questions. After 'When is it due?' and 'Boy or girl?' is almost certain to come 'Have you got a name for it yet?'

This high level of interest in the name of even an unborn baby reflects our need to identify everything around us. We also often make immediate associations about character simply from a name. If someone told you they were thinking of Sky or River as a name for their baby, you might well associate that with the Swinging 60s and hippies. If, on the other hand, someone decided on Bruno or Amelia, you might link the parents to a particular social class.

We also make associations based on other people we have known with the same name, transposing their characteristics onto their namesake. This might work in favour of the child, bringing back memories of a much-loved relative or friend. Unfortunately, it might have the opposite effect. I am as prone to this as anyone else in that I cannot think of the name Lucinda without picturing a girl at school who excelled at netball while I was humiliatingly left in line as the last one picked for a team.

As parents, we can't do anything about the weird and wonderful associations people might make based on someone else's character, but we can do an awful lot to protect our child from negative assumptions or indeed future ridicule by really thinking carefully about what to call our child.

I was told about a group of parents in one particular primary school recently who had chosen names with the starting point that no other child might have the same name in school. Why not?! This is a dangerous route because by definition it means that the child will be given a deliberately obscure name with which it is saddled for the rest of its life. Can you imagine a thirty-year-old man still having to explain why his parents called him Disney?

This trend has been growing, particularly with girls' names. The fact that this book contains almost 300 more entries for girls than for boys is indicative of how much more adventurous parents are inclined to be when naming daughters. The Victorians led the charge with their fashion for naming girls after flowers and gemstones while boys' names remained largely traditional. Yet common sense tells us that the bank of possible names is finite and the reason some names have been favourites for decades and centuries is that they are good names.

What you call your child says more about you than it does about the child. Attention-seekers beware – more often than not, your child will ditch the fanciful name you thought so amusing in favour of a more traditional one when he or she reaches an age when they can assert their own opinion.

The fact is that there are hundreds of names to choose from; too many to include in any one book. Choosing just one of these for you child is a daunting prospect but I believe one that is made easier if parents begin from the standpoint of what a name actually means and how that relates to them.

It may be as simple as going back to your roots. It may mean delving into the rich world of Greek or Roman mythology or the romantic tales of King Arthur for inspiration. It could be a biblical name or one taken from a favourite song. It might be a colour, a description, a place . . . the list is almost endless and the choice is wide.

Hopefully, this book will inspire parents to revive what have been regarded as old-fashioned or ancient names, on the basis of what they mean or the stories that surround them. The fact is that most of us will at some point look up the meaning of our own names. How wonderful it would be for our children if they were to find that their name means 'sunbeam' or 'peace-lover' or that they were named after the goddess of the moon because they were born at midnight? Or perhaps find that their name was associated with the sea and chosen because that's where their parents shared their first romantic walk?

If you're after a unique name, you don't need this book or, for that matter, any other book. If, on the other hand, you want to explore the rich and wonderful diversity of meanings, legends and backgrounds to the vast array of so-called 'traditional' names to find one that means something to you and yours, read on.

A name is about the most personal thing you can give a child. It's worth thinking about what that name should be. One day, you can be sure that your child will ask you why you chose it.

1. NAMES BY CATEGORY

If you start looking for a name for your child on the basis of its meaning or association, it is far easier to get some ideas by looking under various headings. None of these lists is exhaustive – that would be an almost impossible task and the end result would be more like an encyclopedia! Also, many names have more than one possible meaning, so don't be surprised if the same name appears in more than one list. For additional information about each name, refer to the entry in the relevant A to Z section.

Hopefully what this will do is encourage you to think about the meaning and perhaps be a little more adventurous than you might otherwise have been. The name you choose has got to last a lifetime, after all!

Jewels and other precious things

Giving a name based on something that is rare, precious or priceless reflects your own feelings about your child. There are many to choose from although they are almost exclusively female.

Amber
Beryl
Ceinlys (meaning 'jewels')
Christelle (associated with crystal)
Chrystal (based on crystal)
Coral
Crystal
Diamond
Emerald

Esmeralda (based on emerald)
Gemma (meaning 'jewel')
Jade
Jewel
Margaret (meaning 'pearl')
Myron (based on myrrh)
Opal
Pearl
Ruby
Sapphire
Silver
Topaz

Nature

Names taken from nature are always popular, particularly those based on the names of flowers. Flower names became especially popular in the nineteenth century and many of them continue to be used today. Other 'natural' names are based on surnames that developed as descriptions of where someone lived or worked. Others still have been used much more recently, simply to be different. Whatever the reason, there are some lovely associations.

General nature

Aamor (meaning 'sunbeam')
Aaron (meaning 'high mountain')
Bryn (meaning 'hill')
Chantal (meaning 'stone')
Douglas (meaning 'black water')
Dunstan (meaning 'dark stone')
Dylan (meaning 'sea')
Echo
Eirwen (meaning 'white snow')
Gaia (meaning 'earth')
Glenda (possibly meaning 'valley')
Glynis (possibly meaning 'valley')
Guy (meaning 'wood')
Heulwen (meaning 'sunshine')
Iris (meaning 'rainbow')

Jordan (meaning 'flowing down')
Keith (meaning 'wood')
Llew (possibly meaning 'radiant light')
Lucia (meaning 'light')
Lucilla (meaning 'light')
Lucinda (meaning 'light')
Lucius (meaning 'light')
Lucy (meaning 'light')
Lynette (possibly meaning 'waterfall')
Marina (possibly meaning 'of the sea')
Melody
Morgan (possibly meaning 'bright sea')
Muriel (possibly meaning 'bright sea')
Neil (possibly meaning 'cloud')
Peter (meaning 'stone' or 'rock')
Rainbow
River
Rosemary (meaning 'sea dew')
Samson (meaning 'sun')
Selene (meaning 'moon' or 'bright light')
Silvester (meaning 'of the woods')
Silvia (possibly meaning 'wood')
Sita (meaning 'furrow')
Sky
Sorcha (meaning 'brightness' or 'light')
Storm
Tallulah (meaning 'running water')
Tara (meaning 'hill')
Theresa (possibly meaning 'to harvest')

Flowers, trees and fruit

Aerona (meaning 'berries')
Alma (meaning 'apple' in Turkish)
Amaryllis
Anthea (meaning 'flowery')

Avalon (probably meaning 'apple')
Azalea
Berry
Blodwen (meaning 'white flower')
Blossom
Briar
Bryony
Cerise (possibly based on 'cherry')
Cherry
Chloe (meaning 'young green shoot')
Clematis
Clover
Columbine
Daffodil
Dahlia
Daisy
Dalia
Daphne (meaning 'laurel')
Delphine (associated with the delphinium)
Ebony
Edna (meaning 'kernel' in Irish)
Enya (possibly meaning 'nut kernel')
Euan (possibly meaning 'yew tree')
Evadne (meaning 'fair flowering')
Evelyn (possibly meaning 'hazelnut')
Fabia (meaning 'bean')
Fabian (meaning 'bean')
Fabiola (meaning 'bean')
Fern
Fflur (meaning 'flower')
Fleur (meaning 'flower')
Flora (Roman goddess of flowers)
Florence (meaning 'blossoming')
Gladys (meaning 'delicate flower')
Hazel
Heather

Holly
Hortense (possibly meaning 'garden')
Hyacinth
Iris
Ivy
Jasmine
Jonquil
Juniper
Laura (from laurel)
Laurel
Laurence (from laurel)
Lavender
Lilac
Lilian (from lily)
Lily
Lindford (meaning 'lime tree')
Marguerite
Marigold
Myrtle
Nana (possibly after the ancient Irish goddess of flowers)
Nigella
Olive
Oliver (possibly based on olive)
Olivia (possibly based on olive)
Pansy
Perry (based on pear tree)
Petal
Phyllida (meaning 'leafy')
Phyllis (meaning 'leafy')
Poppy
Posy (as in bunch of flowers)
Primrose (from the Latin meaning 'first rose')
Prunella (based on plum)
Rhoda (probably based on rose)
Rosa (based on rose)
Rosalie (based on rose)

Rosalind (possibly meaning 'lovely rose')
Rosamund (possibly meaning 'rose of the world')
Rose
Saffron
Sorrel
Susanna (meaning 'lily')
Tamara (meaning 'date tree')
Thalia (meaning 'to bloom')
Valma (meaning 'mayflower')
Viola (meaning 'violet' or 'pansy')
Violet
Willow
Yasmin (based on jasmine)
Yvette (meaning 'yew')
Yvonne (meaning 'yew')
Zara (possibly meaning 'flower')

Animals and birds

Most of the names based on animals and birds are intended
to give the bearer of the name the associated characteristics. A
dove, for example, indicates peace while a lion is strong and
regal. This might be the reason you choose one of these names
or it might simply be that you like the animal or bird
concerned.

Altair (meaning 'bird')
Arlette (possibly meaning 'eagle')
Arthur (meaning 'strong as a bear')
Aslan (meaning 'lion')
Ava (possibly meaning 'bird')
Bernard (meaning 'brave as a bear')
Bran (meaning 'raven')
Bunty (indicating a lamb)
Cal(l)um (meaning 'dove')
Columbine (meaning 'dove')

Dorcas (meaning 'doe' or 'gazelle')
Emmet (meaning 'ant')
Everard (meaning 'brave boar')
Fauna (collective name for animals)
Gavin (meaning 'white hawk of battle')
Giles (meaning 'young goat')
Jay (based on the bird)
Jemima (meaning 'dove')
Jonah (meaning 'dove')
Kestrel (based on the bird)
Lark (based on the bird)
Leah (meaning 'gazelle')
Leander (meaning 'lion man')
Leo (meaning 'lion')
Leonard (meaning 'strong lion')
Linda (possibly meaning 'serpent')
Lionel (meaning 'lion')
Llew (possibly meaning 'lion')
Llewellyn (possibly meaning 'lion')
Lyall (probably meaning 'wolf')
Mavis (meaning 'song thrush')
Melissa (meaning 'bee')
Mena (possibly meaning 'nightingale')
Merle (possibly meaning 'blackbird')
Ophrah (meaning 'fawn')
Orson (meaning 'bear cub')
Philip (meaning 'lover of horses')
Portia (meaning 'pig')
Rachel (meaning 'ewe')
Ramsay (possibly meaning 'raven's island')
Ray (possibly meaning 'roe deer')
Rhona (possibly meaning 'seal')
Robin (based on the bird)
Ronan (meaning 'little seal')
Rosalind (possibly meaning 'tender horse')
Rosamund (from words meaning 'horse' and 'protector')

Rose (meaning 'horse')
Ross (possibly meaning 'horse')
Tabitha (meaning 'doe' or 'roe')
Teal (based on the duck)
Todd (meaning 'fox')
Una (possibly meaning 'lamb')
Ursula (meaning 'she-bear')

Time, date and season

Why not choose a name based on the time, day, month or season that your child was born?

Aamor (meaning 'sunbeam', so for children born during the day)
April
Augustus (from August)
Aurora (the Roman goddess of the dawn)
Avril (from April)
Beltane (May Day)
Cecil (possibly meaning 'sixth', so for children born in the sixth month, day or hour perhaps)
Dawn
Eirwen (meaning 'white snow', so for children born during the winter)
Eos (the Greek goddess of the dawn)
Ersa (meaning 'dew', so for children born at daybreak perhaps)
Gabriel (often given to children born at Christmas)
Hafwen (meaning 'fair summer')
Holly (a plant often associated with Christmas)
Juliet (often given to children born in July)
June
Jupiter (the Roman god of the day)
Lark (the bird that sings at dawn)
Leila (meaning 'night')

Lilith (meaning 'night')

Luna (the Roman goddess of the moon)

Mae (May)

Maia (May)

Matuta (a Roman goddess of the dawn)

May

Mena (possibly meaning 'daughter of light')

Nana (possibly based on nine, so for children born in the ninth month or hour perhaps)

Natalie (meaning 'birthday' and often given to children born at Christmas)

Noel (Christmas)

Nona (meaning 'nine', so for children born in the ninth month, day or hour perhaps)

Nyx (a Greek goddess of the night)

Octavia (meaning 'eight', so for children born in the eighth month, day or hour perhaps)

Oriana (meaning 'to rise', so for children born at sunrise perhaps)

Quintin (meaning 'fifth', so for children born in the fifth month, day or hour perhaps)

Rhiannon (a Welsh goddess of the moon)

Roxana (meaning 'dawn')

Samson (meaning 'sun', so for children born during the day)

Selene (meaning 'moon', so for children born at night)

Summer

Theresa (possibly meaning 'to harvest', so for children born in the autumn)

Tiffany (based on Epiphany, so often given to children born on 6 January)

Zara (possibly meaning 'brightness of the dawn')

Descriptive

There are many names that describe how someone looks or something else about them. Most are complimentary but one or two certainly began as nicknames that were less than flattering!

Algernon (meaning 'with whiskers')
Aline (possibly meaning 'lovely')
Astrid (meaning 'divinely beautiful')
Aveline (meaning 'longed-for child')
Barbara (meaning 'foreign woman')
Barry (meaning 'fair headed')
Belinda (meaning 'pretty')
Bella (meaning 'beautiful')
Belle (meaning 'beautiful')
Bonita (meaning 'pretty')
Bonnie (meaning 'pretty')
Boris (meaning 'small')
Bronwen (meaning 'white breast')
Cale (meaning 'beautiful')
Calvin (meaning 'little bald one' – appropriate for most babies!)
Cameron (meaning 'crooked nose')
Campbell (meaning 'crooked mouth')
Cecilia (meaning 'blind')
Celeste (meaning 'heavenly')
Charles (meaning 'free man')
Charon (meaning 'bright eyes')
Ciara (meaning 'dark')
Claud(e) (meaning 'crippled')
Cole (meaning 'black as coal')
Courtney (meaning 'short nose')
Crispin (meaning 'curly hair')
Curtis (possibly meaning 'short person')
Darcy (possibly meaning 'dark haired')
Darius (meaning 'he who is rich')
Donovan (meaning 'brown or black featured')
Drusilla (meaning 'soft eyed')
Duane (meaning 'little dark one')

Eilwen (meaning 'beautiful')
Electra (meaning 'radiant')
Europa (meaning 'wide eyed' or 'broad browed')
Fenella (meaning 'white shouldered')
Flavia (meaning 'fair haired')
Francis (meaning 'French')
Franklin (meaning 'free man')
Gaynor (meaning 'fair and beautiful')
Geraint (meaning 'old man')
Ginger (meaning 'red hair')
Grant (meaning 'tall')
Guinevere (meaning 'fair and beautiful')
Gwenllian (meaning 'blond')
Hebe (meaning 'young')
Ingrid (meaning 'fair and beautiful')
Iseult (meaning 'beautiful one')
Julian (possibly meaning 'fair skinned')
Kane (possibly meaning 'dark')
Kayley (possibly meaning 'slender')
Kenneth (meaning 'handsome')
Kevin (meaning 'handsome' or 'beautiful')
Kieran (meaning 'dark one')
Leda (meaning 'woman')
Linda (meaning 'pretty' or 'neat')
Mabel (meaning 'lovely' or 'my beautiful one')
Maeve (meaning 'bringing joy' or 'intoxicating')
Malvina (possibly meaning 'smooth brow')
Martha (meaning 'lady')
Maurice (meaning 'dark skinned')
Maximilian (meaning 'greatest')
Melanie (meaning 'black' or 'dark')
Mildred (meaning 'gentle giant')
Mirabelle (meaning 'lovely')
Miranda (meaning 'fit to be wondered at')
Morag (meaning 'great young one')
Rory (meaning 'red haired' or 'red king')

Rowan (meaning 'little red one')
Roy (meaning 'red haired' or 'ruddy')
Rufus (meaning 'red haired' or 'ruddy')
Russell (meaning 'red haired')
Sandy (meaning 'sandy-coloured hair')
Selma (meaning 'beautiful')
Shayna (possibly meaning 'beautiful')
Sheila (possibly meaning 'longed for')
Silas (possibly meaning 'snub nosed')
Spike (meaning 'spiky haired')
Taliesin (meaning 'shining brow')
Talitha (meaning 'little girl')
Talulla (meaning 'princess')
Tamsin (meaning 'female twin')
Tawny (meaning 'light brown haired')
Tegan (meaning 'beautiful')
Tegwen (meaning 'beautiful and blessed')
Thomas (meaning 'twin')
Todd (meaning 'cunning as a fox' or 'fox-featured')
Unity (implies 'unique')
Vaughan (meaning 'small')
Wynford (meaning 'fair lord')
Wynn (meaning 'fair')
Yseult (meaning 'fair one')
Zita (probably meaning 'girl')

Characteristics

These are names that describe something about a person, not their physical looks but their virtues or outward attitude. Many of these were popular among the Puritans of the seventeenth century who gave them, as anyone would today, as aspirational names.

Agatha (meaning 'good')
Agnes (meaning 'pure')

Aida (possibly meaning 'modesty')
Allegra (meaning 'cheerful')
Alma (meaning 'kind')
Amanda (meaning 'fit to be loved')
Amelia (meaning 'hard working')
Amena (meaning 'pure')
Andromache (meaning 'she who fights against men'!)
Andromeda (meaning 'fit to rule over men'!)
Angelica (meaning 'angelic')
Angharad (meaning 'much loved')
Annabel (meaning 'loveable')
Arabella (possibly meaning 'someone who can be entreated')
Archibald (meaning 'brave')
Arene (meaning 'manly')
Ariadne (meaning 'very pure')
Arthur (meaning 'strong as a bear')
Aude (possibly meaning 'blessed')
Augustine (meaning 'great')
Augustus (meaning 'great')
Beatrice (meaning 'she who brings joy')
Benedict (meaning 'blessed')
Bernard (meaning 'brave as a bear')
Bertha (meaning 'famous')
Bertram (meaning 'famous and wise')
Caelia (meaning 'heavenly')
Caleb (meaning 'bold')
Cara (meaning 'beloved')
Carey (meaning 'well loved')
Cary (meaning 'well loved')
Cassandra (meaning 'entangler of men'!)
Catherine/Katherine (possibly meaning 'pure')
Celeste (meaning 'heavenly')
Charis (meaning 'grace')
Charity (one of the three Christian virtues)
Clemence (meaning 'merciful')
Clemency (meaning 'merciful')

Clementine (meaning 'merciful')
Constance (meaning 'steadfast')
Constantine (meaning 'steadfast')
Curtis (possibly meaning 'courteous')
Deborah (meaning 'sweet and diligent')
Declan (meaning 'full of goodness')
Dulcie (meaning 'sweet')
Ellis (probably meaning 'benevolent')
Elwin (meaning 'kind and fair')
Ernest (meaning 'serious')
Ethan (meaning 'strong')
Faith (one of the three Christian virtues)
Felicity (meaning 'lucky')
Felix (meaning 'lucky' or 'happy')
Fergal (meaning 'brave man')
Gareth (meaning 'gentle')
Glynis (possibly meaning 'pure')
Grace
Hilary (meaning 'joyful')
Honesty
Honey (meaning 'sweet')
Honour
Hope (one of the three Christian virtues)
Hubert (meaning 'understanding and kind')
Hywel (meaning 'eminent')
Ira (meaning 'watchful')
Irene (meaning 'peace')
Jezebel (meaning 'domination'!)
Joy
Justin (meaning 'just' or 'fair')
Lara (meaning 'chatterer')
Letitia (meaning 'joy')
Madoc (meaning 'generous')
Manfred (possibly meaning 'peaceful man')
Marcus (possibly meaning 'virile')
Mark (possibly meaning 'virile')

Mary (probably meaning 'strong' or 'fertile')
Mercy
Merry
Miles (possibly meaning 'grace')
Millicent (meaning 'strong worker')
Miriam (probably meaning 'strong' or 'fertile')
Mohammed (meaning 'praiseworthy')
Mona (possibly meaning 'noble')
Mungo (meaning 'dearest friend')
Olga (meaning 'healthy' or 'holy')
Patience
Pax (meaning 'peace')
Pia (meaning 'dutiful')
Pius (meaning 'dutiful')
Polydora (meaning 'many gifts')
Prudence (meaning 'cautious')
Rebecca (possibly meaning 'to be gentle')
Rhianwen (meaning 'pure maiden')
Riley (meaning 'courageous')
Roderick (sometimes meaning 'strength')
Ruth (possibly meaning 'friend', sometimes 'compassion')
Salome (meaning 'peace')
Serena (meaning 'calm')
Solomon (meaning 'peace')
Sophia (meaning 'wisdom')
Tacey (meaning 'be silent')
Tacita (meaning 'silent')
Valentine (meaning 'healthy' or 'strong')
Valene (meaning 'healthy' or 'strong')
Verity (meaning 'true')
Wilfred (meaning 'peace lover')

Colours

Colour is another area from which to draw inspiration for naming your child. Whether because of the colour of their hair (in which case you should also check the descriptive names) or because you simply like a particular colour or for any other personal reason, there are several to choose from. Many of the names below will be based on words meaning 'white', which often have the additional meaning of purity.

Alban (meaning 'white')
Aurelia (meaning 'golden')
Auryn (meaning 'gold')
Bianca (meaning 'white')
Blaine (possibly meaning 'white')
Blake (meaning 'black' or 'pale', the complete opposite)
Blanche (meaning 'white')
Boyd (meaning 'yellow')
Bruno (meaning 'brown')
Candida (meaning 'white')
Cerise (meaning 'light red')
Cole (meaning 'black')
Cressida (possibly meaning 'golden')
Cyane (meaning 'blue')
Donovan (meaning 'brown' or 'black')
Eurwen (meaning 'golden girl')
Eurwyn (meaning 'golden fair')
Fiona (meaning 'white')
Flavia (meaning 'yellow')
Gwen (meaning 'white')
Hazel
Iole (meaning 'violet')
Lilac (from the Persian meaning 'bluish')
Livia (possibly meaning 'bluish')
Lloyd (meaning 'grey')
Nigel (meaning 'black')
Oriel (probably meaning 'golden')
Phineas (meaning 'black')
Phoenix (meaning 'blood red')

Rama (meaning 'black' or 'dark')
Roy (meaning 'red')
Ruby (meaning 'red')
Rufus (meaning 'red')
Scarlett
Viola (meaning 'violet')
Violet
Xanthe (meaning 'yellow')

Astrological names

Look up to the heavens for inspiration! There are some lovely names given to stars, for example. Only a few can be listed here but they give an idea. Others are based on the moon, the sun and the sky.

Aamor (meaning 'sunbeam')
Alcyone (the brightest star in Pleiades)
Altair (the brightest star in Aquila)
Antares (the brightest star in Scorpius)
Caelia (meaning 'heavenly')
Celeste (meaning 'heavenly')
Celia (meaning 'sky' or 'heaven')
Estella (meaning 'star')
Heulwen (meaning 'sunshine')
Iris (meaning 'rainbow')
Luna (meaning 'moon')
Neil (possibly meaning 'cloud')
Rigel (the brightest star in Orion)
Samson (meaning 'sun')
Selene (meaning 'moon')
Sky
Star
Stella (meaning 'star')
Sterling (possibly meaning 'little star')
Tara (meaning 'star')

Regal names

There are many names that have been closely associated with royalty. Several became increasingly popular simply because of this association. Albert, for example, took on a whole new life after Prince Albert married Queen Victoria. Other names simply have literal royal meanings. This is not an exhaustive list by any means but it should give pause for thought!

Adelaide (wife of King William IV)
Albert (husband of Queen Victoria)
Alberta (daughter of Queen Victoria)
Alexandra (including the wife of Tsar Nicholas II)
Alexis (son of Tsar Nicholas II)
Amelia (daughter of King George III)
Anastasia (daughter of Tsar Nicholas II)
Andrew (second son of Queen Elizabeth II)
Annabella (mother of King James I of Scotland)
Anne (daughter of Queen Elizabeth II)
Arlette (mother of William the Conqueror)
Augusta (mother of King George III)
Basil (meaning 'royal')
Beatrice (including the daughter of Queen Victoria and the granddaughter of Queen Elizabeth II)
Brenda (possibly meaning 'royal')
Brendan (meaning 'royal')
Bruce (after Robert the Bruce)
Caesar (from the Roman title)
Candace (title of several queens of Ethiopia)
Charles (including Charlemagne and the Prince of Wales)
Charlotte (wife of King George III)
Edgar (a tenth-century king)
Edith (daughter of King Edgar)
Edward (including Edward the Confessor and the third son of Queen Elizabeth II)
Eleanor (wife of King Henry II)

Elizabeth (including Queens Elizabeth I and II)
Eric (meaning 'royal')
Eugenie (granddaughter to Queen Elizabeth II)
George (including six Kings of England)
Harry (grandson to Queen Elizabeth II)
Henry (including eight Kings of England)
Isabel (including the wife of King John and King Richard II)
Jane (including Lady Jane Grey)
Louis (including no less than eighteen French Kings)
Margaret (including the eleventh-century Margaret of Scotland
    and the sister of Queen Elizabeth II)
Mary (including Queen Mary I and Mary, Queen of Scots)
Matilda (wife of William the Conqueror)
Peter (grandson of Queen Elizabeth II)
Philip (husband of Queen Elizabeth II)
Raine (possibly meaning 'queen')
Ray (possibly meaning 'king')
Regan (possibly meaning 'queen')
Regina (meaning 'queen')
Reine (meaning 'queen')
Rex (meaning 'king')
Richard (including three Kings of England)
Robert (from Robert the Bruce)
Roy (meaning 'king')
Ryan (possibly meaning 'king')
Sarah (meaning 'princess')
Talulla (meaning 'princess')
Victoria (nineteenth-century Queen of England)
William (including four Kings and the grandson of Queen
    Elizabeth II)
Zara (granddaughter of Queen Elizabeth II)

Biblical names

The Bible has been a source of names for children for
centuries. With a wealth of characters, male and female, to

choose from, the list is almost endless. It is impossible to give a full history of every character so the list below is a taster, not a definitive 'who's who'!

Aaron (brother of Moses)
Abel (son of Adam and Eve)
Abigail (wife of King David)
Abner (commander of King Saul's army)
Abraham (father of the Hebrew nation)
Ada (the second woman, after Eve, mentioned in the Bible)
Adam (the first man)
Amos (after whom an Old Testament book is named)
Andrew (an apostle)
Asa (a King of Judah)
Barnabas (a friend of Paul)
Bartholomew (an apostle)
Benjamin (son of Jacob)
Berenice (sister of Herod Agrippa II)
Bethany (a village near Jerusalem)
Cain (brother of Abel)
Caleb (who survived 40 years in the wilderness)
Christian (generic name for a follower of Christ)
Claudia (a friend of Paul)
Daniel (the interpreter of dreams)
David (a King of Israel)
Deborah (a Judge of Israel)
Dinah (a victim of rape)
Drusilla (wife of a governor of Jerusalem)
Edna (mother of Sarah)
Eli (a high priest)
Elijah (a prophet)
Elizabeth (mother of John the Baptist)
Enoch (son of Cain)
Esther (wife of Xerxes of Persia)
Eunice (mother of Timothy)
Eve (the first woman)

Ezra (a prophet)
Gabriel (an archangel)
Gideon (an Israelite)
Hannah (mother of Samuel)
Ira (one of King David's officers)
Isaac (son of Abraham)
Jacob (son of Isaac)
James (the name of two apostles)
Jemima (daughter of Job)
Jesse (father of David)
Jesus (son of God)
Jethro (father-in-law of Moses)
Jezebel (wife of King Ahab)
Joanna (wife of the manager of King Herod's household)
Job (faithful follower of God)
Joel (a prophet)
John (several characters including John the Baptist)
Jonah (a reluctant prophet)
Jonathan (son of King Saul)
Joseph (several characters including the husband of Mary)
Joshua (leader of the Israelites after Moses)
Josiah (a King of Judah)
Judas (a disciple and betrayer of Christ)
Judith (wife of Esau)
Keren (daughter of Job)
Lazarus (raised from the dead by Jesus)
Leah (first wife of Jacob)
Levi (son of Jacob)
Lois (grandmother of Timothy)
Luke (friend of Paul)
Mara (name Naomi asks to be called)
Mark (author of the second Gospel)
Martha (sister of Lazarus)
Mary (several characters including the Virgin Mary)
Matthew (an apostle)
Matthias (the disciple who replaced Judas)

Michael (an archangel)
Miriam (sister of Moses and Aaron)
Moses (leader of the Israelites)
Naomi (mother-in-law of Ruth)
Nathan (a prophet)
Nathaniel (a disciple)
Noah (builder of the Ark)
Paul (one of the founders of the Christian Church)
Peter (an apostle)
Philip (an apostle)
Priscilla (wife of Aquila)
Rachel (second wife of Jacob)
Raphael (an angel)
Rebecca (wife of Isaac)
Reuben (son of Jacob)
Rhoda (a maidservant)
Ruth (daughter-in-law of Naomi)
Samson (betrayed by Delilah)
Samuel (a prophet)
Sarah (wife of Abraham)
Saul (original name of Paul)
Seth (son of Adam and Eve)
Silas (friend of Paul)
Simeon (old man who saw the infant Jesus)
Simon (original name of Peter and name of another of the
   apostles)
Solomon (son of King David)
Stephen (the first martyr)
Susanna (follower of Jesus)
Tabitha (brought back to life by Peter)
Tamara (several characters including King David's
   daughter)
Thaddeus (an apostle)
Thomas (an apostle)
Timothy (companion of Paul)
Uriah (warrior killed on King David's orders)

Zachary (father of John the Baptist)
Zebedee (father of James and John)

Saints' names

It probably comes as no surprise that there is actually a Saint Valentine, or indeed a Saint Peter or Saint Paul. Some saints' names, however, are more surprising. Would you have known of a Saint Hyacinth? What about a Saint Rita or a Saint Silas? They're all there, although there are far too many others for an exhaustive list. Those included here are the names that already appear in the full listing of this book and in the calendar.

Aaron	Benedict	David
Abraham	Bernadette	Denis
Adelaide	Blaise	Dominic
Adrian	Brendan	Donald
Agatha	Bridget	Dorothy
Agnes	Bruno	Dunstan
Aidan	Camillus	Edith
Alban	Catherine/	Edmund
Albert	Katherine	Edward
Alexander	Cecilia	Egbert
Alexis	Celestine	Elijah
Ambrose	Charity	Emily
Anastasia	Charles	Eric
Andrew	Christina	Eugenia
Angela	Christopher	Fabian
Anne	Clare	Fabiola
Anthony	Columbia	Faith
Apollonia	(Columba)	Felicity
Augustine	Cornelius	Felix
Barbara	Cuthbert	Ferdinand
Barnaby	Cyril	Flora
Bartholomew	Damian	Frances
Basil	Daria	Francis

Gemma	Kevin	Paul
George	Laurence	Paula
Gerald	Leander	Peter
Gerard	Leo	Philip
Germaine	Leonard	Pius
Gertrude	Leopold	Raphael
Gilbert	Louis	Raymond
Giles	Louisa	(Raymund)
Gregory	Lucy	Richard
Guy	Ludmila	Rita
Harvey	Luke	Robert
Helena	Madoc (Maedoc)	Rose
Henry	Magnus	Rupert
Herbert	Marcella	Samson
Hilary	Margaret	Sebastian
Hilda	Marina	Siegfried
Hope	Marion	Silas
Hubert	Mark	Simeon
Hugh	Martha	Simon
Hyacinth	Martin	Stephen
Irene	Martina	Susanna
Isaac	Mary	Tatiana
Isidora (Isidore)	Matilda	Theodore
James	Matthew	Theresa
Jane	Matthias	Thomas
Jerome	Maximilian	Timothy
Joan	Melanie	Ursula
John	Mercury	Valentine
Jonah	Michael	Veronica
Joseph	Mildred	Victor
Julia	Natalia	Vincent
Julian	Nicholas	Vivian
Justin	Odile (Odilia)	Wilfrid
Justina	Olga	William
Kenelm	Oswald	Zachary
Kentigern	Patrick	Zita

Names from other cultures

A huge number of names used normally today actually derive from other cultures. Those listed here, therefore, are only the tip of the iceberg, but do represent names that have perhaps come into more common use in recent years.

Aamor (Breton meaning 'sunbeam')

Aida (possibly Arabic meaning 'reward', or French meaning 'save')

Altair (Arabic meaning 'bird')

Ananda (Sanskrit meaning 'joy')

Aslan (Turkish meaning 'lion')

Astrid (Norse meaning 'divinely beautiful')

Ayesha (Arabic meaning 'flourishing')

Beau (French meaning 'handsome')

Bonita (Spanish meaning 'pretty')

Boris (Tartar meaning 'small', or Slavonic meaning 'glorious in battle')

Candace (possibly Ethiopian, of uncertain meaning)

Celeste (French meaning 'heavenly')

Chantal (French meaning 'stone')

Cherie (French meaning 'darling')

Cosmo (Italian meaning 'order' or 'beauty')

Darius (Persian meaning 'he who is rich')

Darcy (French meaning 'fortress')

Desirée (French meaning 'desired')

Dolores (Spanish, based on 'Mary of the Sorrows')

Elvira (Spanish, of uncertain meaning)

Esmeralda (Spanish meaning 'emerald')

Estella (French meaning 'star')

Fatima (Arabic meaning 'weaner')

Fleur (French meaning 'flower')

Freya (Norse meaning 'noble')

Gudrun (Norse meaning 'god' and 'secret')

Heidi (Swiss, a pet form of Adelheid)

Igor (Russian, based on 'Ing', a fertility god, and 'careful')
Indra (Hindu, from a god of thunder and lightning)
Ingrid (Norse meaning 'fair' or 'beautiful')
Ivor (Scandinavian, ultimately meaning 'archer')
Jolene (American origin, of uncertain meaning)
Katya (Russian, a form of Katherine)
Kylie (Australian, of uncertain origin)
Leila (Arabic meaning 'night')
Lewis (German, ultimately meaning 'famous warrior')
Lia (Italian, probably a short form of Rosalia)
Lonnie (possibly a pet form of the Spanish Alonso)
Louis (German, ultimately meaning 'famous warrior', but now
    more closely associated with France)
Lourdes (from the French place name)
Ludmila (Russian/Czech meaning 'people' and 'grace')
Madonna (Italian meaning 'my lady')
Marcel (French, possibly meaning 'virile')
Mercedes (Spanish, based on the Virgin Mary)
Mia (Danish/Swedish, pet form of Maria)
Mohammed (Arabic meaning 'praiseworthy')
Nadia (Russian meaning 'hope')
Odette (French, ultimately meaning 'prosperity')
Odile (French, ultimately meaning 'prosperity')
Olga (Russian meaning 'healthy' or 'holy')
Orson (French meaning 'bear cub')
Phineas (Egyptian meaning 'black')
Pia (Italian meaning 'dutiful')
Raine (possibly French meaning 'queen')
Rama (Sanskrit meaning 'black' or 'dark')
Rigel (Arabic meaning 'foot')
Romeo (Italian, based on Rome)
Roxana (Persian meaning 'dawn')
Saskia (Dutch, of uncertain meaning)
Sigrid (Norse meaning 'victory' and 'beautiful')
Sigurd (Norse meaning 'victory' and 'guardian')
Sita (Sanskrit meaning 'furrow')

Sky (Norse meaning 'cloud')
Tatiana (Russian, of uncertain meaning)
Travis (French meaning 'to cross')
Verena (Swiss, of uncertain meaning)
Vernon (French meaning 'place of alders')
Yvette (French meaning 'yew')
Zara (possibly Arabic meaning 'flower' or 'brightness of the dawn')
Zina (Russian, of uncertain meaning)
Zita (probably Italian meaning 'girl')

Literary names

Several names have been invented or certainly first used by authors for characters in their novels, plays and poems. Many have become commonly used names. In a different 'literary' association, how about naming your children after characters in favourite books? You could, for example, use Edmund, Peter, Susan and Lucy, from C. S. Lewis's *The Lion, The Witch and The Wardrobe* (1950); Amy, Beth, Jo and Meg from Louisa M. Alcott's *Little Women* (1868–9); Cordelia, Julia and Sebastian from Evelyn Waugh's *Brideshead Revisited* (1945) or even Roberta, Peter and Phyllis from E. Nesbit's *The Railway Children* (1906). And that's just for starters!

Aelita (invented by Alexei Tolstoy)
Allegra (probably first used by Lord Byron, not in one of his poems but as the name for his daughter)
Cedric (probably first used by Sir Walter Scott)
Christabel (probably invented by Samuel Taylor Coleridge)
Clarinda (first used by Sir Edmund Spenser)
Cora (possibly first used by James Fenimore Cooper)
Cordelia (possibly first used by William Shakespeare)
Dorian (probably invented by Oscar Wilde)
Geraldine (invented by Henry Howard)
Imogen (first used by William Shakespeare)

Jancis (first used by Mary Webb)
Janice (probably first used by Paul Leicester Ford)
Jessica (probably invented by William Shakespeare)
Lara (probably invented by Ovid)
Lorna (invented by R. D. Blackmore)
Luana (first used in a King Vidor film!)
Malvina (invented by James Macpherson)
Miranda (invented by William Shakespeare)
Myra (invented by Fulke Greville)
Norma (probably first used by Felice Romani)
Olivia (first used by William Shakespeare)
Ophelia (first used by Jacopo Sannazzaro)
Orville (invented by Fanny Burney)
Pamela (invented by Sir Philip Sidney)
Perdita (invented by William Shakespeare)
Regan (first used by William Shakespeare)
Rowena (probably first used by Sir Walter Scott)
Stella (probably first used by Sir Philip Sidney)
Thelma (probably first used by Marie Corelli)
Vanessa (invented by Jonathan Swift)
Wendy (invented by J. M. Barrie)

Pop names

Why not give your child a name based on a favourite song title? There are hundreds to choose from but this list might give you some ideas.

Alfie (Cilla Black: 'Alfie')
Alice (Smokie: 'Living Next Door to Alice')
Angie (The Rolling Stones: 'Angie')
Annie (John Denver: 'Annie's Song')
Avalon (Roxy Music: 'Avalon')
Barbara (The Beach Boys: 'Barbara Ann')
Billie Jean (Michael Jackson: 'Billie Jean')
Carol (Neil Sedaka: 'Oh Carol')

Carolina (Shaggy: 'Oh Carolina')
Caroline (Status Quo: 'Caroline')
Cathy (Everly Brothers: 'Cathy's Clown')
Cecilia (Simon and Garfunkel: 'Cecilia')
Daniel (Elton John: 'Daniel')
Debora (Marc Bolan and T-Rex: 'Debora')
Delilah (Tom Jones: 'Delilah')
Diana (Paul Anka: 'Diana')
Eileen (Dexy's Midnight Runners: 'Come on Eileen')
Eleanor (The Beatles: 'Eleanor Rigby')
Eloise (Damned: 'Eloise')
Frankie (Sister Sledge: 'Frankie')
Georgy (The Seekers: 'Georgy Girl')
Jolene (Dolly Parton: 'Jolene')
Jack (The Rolling Stones: 'Jumpin' Jack Flash')
Jane (Rod Stewart: 'Baby Jane')
Joe (Jimmy Hendrix: 'Hey Joe')
Johnny (Chuck Berry: 'Johnny B Goode')
Jude (The Beatles: 'Hey Jude')
Julie (Ali G. feat. Shaggy: 'Me Julie')
Laura (Scissor Sisters: 'Laura')
Layla (Eric Clapton: 'Layla')
Lizzy (The Beatles: 'Dizzy Miss Lizzy')
Lucille (Kenny Rogers: 'Lucille')
Lucy (The Beatles: 'Lucy in the Sky with Diamonds')
Madonna (The Beatles: 'Lady Madonna')
Maggie (Rod Stewart: 'Maggie May')
Mandy (Barry Manilow: 'Mandy')
Matthew (Cat Stevens: 'Matthew and Son')
Maxwell (The Beatles: 'Maxwell's Silver Hammer')
Michelle (The Beatles: 'Michelle')
Mickey (Toni Basil: 'Mickey')
Oliver (Elvis Costello: 'Oliver's Army')
Rita (The Beatles: 'Lovely Rita')
Pearl (Elkie Brooks: 'Pearl's a Singer')
Peggy (Buddy Holly: 'Peggy Sue')

Prudence (The Beatles: 'Dear Prudence')
Rhonda (The Beach Boys: 'Help me Rhonda')
Roxanne (Police: 'Roxanne')
Sally (Little Richard: 'Long tall Sally')
Sam (T-Rex: 'Telegram Sam')
Sandy (John Travolta: 'Sandy')
Suzanne (Leonard Cohen: 'Suzanne')
Sylvia (Dr Hook: 'Sylvia's Mother')
Vincent (Don McLean: 'Vincent')

Place names

Many names in use today developed from place names, frequently describing where someone lived or worked. These in turn often became surnames. It was fairly usual to give a child its mother's maiden name as a given name and this is how many such names have developed into modern given names.

Adrian (from the Adriatic)
Africa (from the continent)
Ailsa (from the island in the Clyde estuary)
Ainsley (meaning 'one meadow')
Alma (from the River Alma)
Alun (from the River Alun)
Ashley (meaning 'ash wood')
Bethany (a village near Jerusalem)
Beverley (meaning 'beaver stream')
Blair (meaning 'field')
Bradley (meaning 'broad clearing')
Brandon (meaning 'gorse hill')
Branwell (meaning 'raven's well')
Brent (meaning 'hill')
Brett (possibly meaning 'man of Brittany')
Byron (meaning 'at the cattlesheds')
Carmel (a range of hills in Israel)
Cary (from the River Cary)

Charlton (meaning 'settlement of free peasants')
Chelsea (from the area of London)
Chester (meaning 'legionary camp')
Clive (meaning 'cliff' or 'riverbank')
Courtney (from Courtenay in France)
Craig (meaning 'rock')
Dale (meaning 'dale' or 'valley')
Darcy (meaning 'fortress')
Darryl (from Airelle in France)
Dean (meaning either 'valley' or 'dean')
Delia (from the Greek island of Delos)
Delphine (meaning 'woman from Delphi')
Demelza (from a place in Cornwall)
Denzil (from a place in Cornwall)
Desmond (from South Munster in Ireland)
Douglas (from the River Douglas)
Dudley (meaning 'Dudda's wood')
Dustin (possibly meaning 'Thor's stone')
Elton (meaning 'Ella's enclosure')
Errol (from a Scottish place name)
Fraser (from La Fraseliere in France)
Garth (meaning 'enclosure')
Gladstone (from words meaning 'kite' and 'rock')
Glen (meaning 'valley')
Gordon (meaning 'spacious fort')
Graham (meaning 'Granta's or gravelly village')
Granville (meaning 'large settlement')
Hayley (meaning 'hay clearing')
Hope (meaning 'small valley')
India (from the continent)
Iona (from the island in the Hebrides)
Irving (meaning 'green water')
Isla (from the island of Islay)
Jordan (from the River Jordan)
Judith (meaning 'woman of Judea')
Keith (meaning 'wood')

Kelly (meaning 'church')

Kelvin (from the River Clyde)

Kendall (from either Kendal in Cumbria or Kendale in Humberside)

Kent (meaning 'border')

Kerry (from the Irish county)

Killian (meaning 'church')

Kimberley (from the city in South Africa)

Kingsley (meaning 'king's wood')

Kirk (meaning 'church')

Kyle (meaning 'church' or 'narrow')

Lachlan (meaning 'land of the lochs')

Larissa (from an ancient Greek town)

Laurence (meaning 'man of Laurentum')

Lee (meaning 'clearing in a wood')

Lena (from a river in Siberia)

Lennox (meaning 'grove of elms')

Leslie (from an uncertain place name)

Lester (from Leicester)

Lincoln (meaning 'lake' or 'settlement')

Lindford (possibly meaning 'lime-tree')

Lindsay (meaning 'the wetland belonging to Lincoln')

Lorraine (meaning 'kingdom of Lothair')

Lourdes (from the place in France)

Luke (meaning 'man from Lucania')

Lydia (meaning 'woman of Lydia')

Lyle (meaning 'from the island')

Lyndon (meaning 'lime-tree hill')

Marvin (meaning 'sea fort')

Maxwell (meaning 'Magnus's or Maccus's stream')

Melville (meaning 'bad town')

Merlin (meaning 'sea fort')

Murray (meaning 'settlement beside the sea')

Neville (meaning 'new town')

Norman (meaning 'man from the north')

Norris (meaning 'from the north')

Percy (from a place in France)
Perry (meaning 'pear tree')
Preston (meaning 'priest's enclosure')
Ramsay (meaning either 'wild garlic island' or 'raven's island')
Randall (meaning 'edge', such as of a village)
Riley (meaning either 'courageous' or 'rye clearing')
Rodney (meaning 'Hroda's island')
Ross (possibly meaning 'clearing' or 'headland')
Sabina (meaning 'Sabine woman')
Sabrina (from the River Severn)
Scott (meaning 'from Scotland')
Sebastian (meaning 'man from Sebastia')
Seymour (from Saint-Maur in Normandy)
Shannon (from the River Shannon)
Sharon (from a plain mentioned in the Bible which ran from
    Joppa to Caesarea)
Sheldon (from various place names)
Shelley (meaning 'wood near a slope')
Shirley (meaning 'bright clearing')
Sidney (either from Saint-Denis in France or meaning 'wide
    land by the marsh')
Sidony (meaning 'woman from Sidon')
Sinclair (from Saint-Clair in northern France)
Skye (from the island in the Hebrides)
Stanley (meaning 'stone clearing')
Stirling (from the town in Scotland)
Tara (from a fort in Meath, Ireland)
Theresa (possibly from the Greek island of Thera)
Tracy (meaning 'man of Thrace')
Tremaine (meaning 'stone homestead')
Trevor (meaning 'big village')
Troy (from either Troyes in France or the ancient city)
Ultan (meaning 'Ulsterman')
Vernon (meaning 'place of alders')
Verona (possibly from the city in Italy)
Warren (from Larenne in Normandy)

Wesley (meaning 'western wood' or 'clearing')
Whitney (meaning 'by the white island')
Winston (possibly meaning 'friend's farm')
Xavier (meaning 'new house')

Occupational names

Several names were originally based on the occupation of the bearer.

Aaron (possibly meaning 'mountaineer')
Alexander (meaning 'defender of men')
Angel (meaning 'messenger')
Asa (meaning 'doctor' or 'healer')
Cain (possibly meaning 'blacksmith')
Campion (meaning 'champion')
Colin (possibly meaning 'chieftain')
Cyril (meaning 'lord')
Dean (meaning 'dean'!)
Donald (meaning 'ruler of the world')
Edryd (possibly meaning 'storyteller')
Enoch (meaning 'teacher')
Fletcher (meaning 'arrow-maker')
George (meaning 'farmer')
Idris (meaning 'ardent lord')
Ifor/Ivor (meaning 'archer')
Illtud (meaning 'lord of all')
Ithel (meaning 'generous lord')
Jasper/Caspar/Gaspard (meaning 'treasurer')
Joyce (meaning 'lord')
Kay (possibly meaning 'key-maker')
Lysander (meaning 'liberator of men')
Maia (meaning 'mother' or 'nurse')
Martha (meaning 'lady')
Melody (meaning 'singer of songs')
Meredith (meaning 'great lord')

Monica (possibly meaning 'giver of advices')
Neil (possibly meaning 'champion')
Nicholas (probably meaning 'conqueror')
Peregrine (meaning 'wanderer' or 'pilgrim')
Persephone (meaning 'bearer of death')
Priam (probably meaning 'chief')
Riordan (meaning 'king's poet')
Scarlett (meaning 'a dyer or seller of bright cloth')
Spencer (meaning 'someone who works in a pantry')
Stewart/Stuart (meaning 'steward')
Taylor (meaning 'tailor')
Travis (meaning 'toll collector')
Victor (meaning 'conqueror')
Walter (meaning 'military leader')
Wayne (meaning 'cartwright')
Webster (meaning 'weaver')
Wynford (meaning 'fair lord')

Female versions of male names

Many girls' names developed simply as feminine versions of
boys' names. Others are based on the same root meaning.

Adriana (Adrian)
Alana (possibly Alan)
Alberta (Albert)
Alexandra (Alexander)
Aloise (Aloysius)
Amanda (Amandus)
Andrea (probably Andreas)
Angela (Angel)
Antoinette/Antonia (Anthony)
Augusta (Augustus/Augustine)
Bernadette (Bernard)
Briana (Brian)
Carla (Carl)

Caroline (Charles)
Cecilia (Cecil)
Charlotte (Charles)
Christiana/Christina (Christian)
Claudia/Claudette (Claud)
Clemency/Clementine (Clement)
Colleen (Colin)
Cornelia (Cornelius)
Cosima (Cosmo)
Daniela/Danielle (Daniel)
Daria (Darius)
Davina (David)
Dena (Dean)
Denise (Denis)
Dominique (Dominic)
Edwina (Edwin/Edward)
Emily (Emlyn)
Erica (Eric)
Eugenia/Eugenie (Eugene)
Eurwen (Eurwyn)
Fabia/Fabiola (Fabian)
Felicia/Felicity (Felix)
Frances/Francesca (Francis)
Freda/Frederica (Frederick)
Gabriella/Gabrielle (Gabriel)
Georgette/Georgia/Georgina (George)
Geraldine (Gerald)
Glenda/Glynis (possibly Glen)
Henrietta (Henry)
Horatia (Horatio)
Jacqueline (James/Jacob/Jack)
Jane (John)
Josephine/Josette (Joseph)
Julia/Juliet (Julian)
Justina/Justine (Justin)
Kyla (Kyle)

Laura/Lauren (possibly Laurence)
Leonie (Leo)
Lesley (Leslie)
Louisa/Louise (Louis)
Marcella (Marcel)
Marcia (Marcus)
Martina (Martin)
Michaela/Michelle (Michael)
Nicola/Nicole (Nicholas)
Nigella (Nigel)
Norma (possibly Norman)
Patrice/Patricia (Patrick)
Paula/Pauline (Paul)
Peta/Petra (Peter)
Philippa (Philip)
Quinta (Quintin)
Richelle (Richard)
Roberta (Robert)
Samantha (Samuel)
Shauna (Shaun)
Simone (Simon)
Stephanie (Stephen)
Tamsin (Thomas)
Theodora (Theodore)
Valerie (Valentine)
Victoria (Victor)
Vivien/Vivienne (Vivian)
Xaviera (Xavier)
Yvette/Yvonne (Yves)

Names from the Arthurian legends

The romantic and chivalrous tales of King Arthur and his Knights of the Round Table are steeped in legend. The tales have come down through the centuries, told and retold, until fact and fiction merge into one. There are countless sources of the stories and some characters appear in several, some in just one. Other characters go by different names depending on the source. The names given here, therefore, are simply a collection taken from across the board. It doesn't matter – all or none of these characters may or may not have existed but they are part of the various tales that are as much a part of our history as any definite event.

Alcina (sister to Morgan Le Fay)
Aldan (possibly Merlin's mother)
Alice (the 'beautiful pilgrim')
Amene (a queen whose kingdom was saved by King Arthur)
Andred (a cousin of Tristan)
Angelica (mother of King Arthur's son, Tom a'Lincoln)
Angharad (lover of Sir Perceval)
Anna (a sister of King Arthur)
Antony (a secretary to Merlin)
Ardan (an uncle of King Arthur)
Aron (a Knight of the Round Table)
Arthur (King)
Avalon (where King Arthur was taken to die)
Beatrice (wife of Carduino)
Blaise (a magician)
Blasine (a sister of King Arthur)
Caelia (a lover of Tom a'Lincoln)
Camille (a sorceress)
Carl (a Knight of the Round Table)
Cerdic (possibly the founder of Wessex)
Claire (sister of Sir Sagremor)
Clarine (possibly mother of Sir Lancelot)
Claris (a Knight of the Round Table)
Clarisse (a sister of Sir Gawain)
Coel (a King of Colchester)
Conan (an ancestor of King Arthur)
Conrad (a bishop)
Constance (possibly mother of Sir Lancelot)

Daniel (brother of Sir Dinadan)
Elaine (the Lady of Shalott)
Eliabella (a cousin of King Arthur)
Ellen (daughter of King Arthur)
Elsa (daughter of the Duke of Brabant)
Elyzabel (a cousin of Queen Guinevere)
Emmeline (daughter of a Duke of Cornwall)
Felix (a King of Cornwall)
Fergus (a Knight of the Round Table)
Florence (sister of Sir Gawain)
Galahad (a Knight of the Round Table)
Gareth (nephew of King Arthur)
Gawain (a Knight of the Round Table)
Geraint (a Knight of the Round Table)
Gracia (niece of King Arthur)
Guinevere (wife of King Arthur)
Gwen (grandmother of King Arthur)
Gwendolina (wife of Merlin)
Illtud (cousin of King Arthur)
Inogen (daughter of Merlin)
Iseult (lover of Tristan)
Lancelot (a Knight of the Round Table and lover of Queen
    Guinevere)
Laurel (wife of Sir Agravain)
Lionel (King of Gaul)
Lotta (a Queen of Ireland)
Madoc (brother-in-law of King Arthur)
Marc (grandson of Tristan)
Mark (King of Cornwall and husband of Iseult)
Marrion (sister to Morgan Le Fay)
Melora (daughter of King Arthur)
Merlin (King Arthur's magician)
Mordred (nephew or son of King Arthur)
Morgan (Le Fay) (half-sister of King Arthur)
Orlando (lover of Melora)
Padarn (founder of a church in Wales)

Percival (a Knight of the Round Table)
Rowland (son of King Arthur)
Tristan (lover of Iseult)
Vivienne (mistress of Merlin)

Names from Greek and Roman mythology

Just as the Arthurian legends give some lovely stories behind names, so too do the tales and legends from Greek and Roman mythology. Some names are commonly used today; others are more unusual and could be adapted to create a unique name for your child that can be traced back to the ancient gods and the tales of the mortals they ruled.

Greek

Alcyone (wife of Ceyx who was turned into a kingfisher)
Alexander (the alternative name for Paris)
Althea (mother of Meleager)
Ambrose (from Ambrosia, the food of the gods)
Andromache (a Trojan princess)
Anthea (a byname of the goddess Hera)
Antigone (daughter of Oedipus)
Aphrodite (goddess of love)
Apollo (god of song and music)
Ares (god of war)
Ariadne (lover of Theseus)
Artemis (goddess of the hunt)
Atalanta (huntress)
Athene/Athena (goddess of wisdom and crafts)
Boreas (god of the north wind)
Cassandra (daughter of King Priam)
Cilla (sister of King Priam)
Clio (Muse of history)
Cyane (nymph)
Cynthia (a byname of Artemis)
Daphne (nymph)

Delia (a byname of Artemis)
Demeter (goddess of fertility)
Denis (based on Dionysus, god of wine)
Dia (byname of Hera)
Dione (earth goddess)
Doris (a goddess of the sea)
Echo (nymph)
Electra (daughter of Agamemnon)
Elissa (original name of Dido)
Enyo (goddess of battle)
Eos (goddess of the dawn)
Eris (goddess of discord)
Eros (god of love)
Ersa (daughter of Zeus)
Europa (wife of the King of Crete)
Evadne (daughter of Poseidon)
Evander (original name of Pan)
Gaia (goddess of the earth)
Hebe (personification of youth)
Hector (son of King Priam)
Helen (daughter of Zeus)
Helios (god of the sun)
Hera (Queen of heaven)
Hercules (famous warrior)
Hermes (messenger of the gods)
Hermione (daughter of Helen)
Hestia (goddess of hearth and home)
Hyacinth (boy loved by Apollo)
Ida (mountain where Zeus was brought up)
Iliona (daughter of King Priam)
Iole (daughter of the King of Oechalia)
Irene (goddess of peace)
Iris (messenger of the gods)
Jason (leader of the Argonauts)
Jocasta (mother of Oedipus)
Lamia (daughter of Hecate)

Larissa (the possible birthplace of Achilles)
Leander (lover of Hero)
Leda (Queen of Sparta)
Linus (son of Apollo)
Lucretia (wife of Tarquinius Collatinus)
Magnes (son of Zeus)
Maia (daughter of Atlas)
Medea (lover of Jason)
Melissa (daughter of the King of Crete)
Nerissa (from 'Nereids', the name of beautiful sea-nymphs)
Nestor (the oldest Greek in the Trojan war)
Nike (goddess of victory)
Notus (god of the south wind)
Nyx (goddess of the night)
Pan (god of fields, shepherds and flocks)
Pandia (daughter of Zeus and Selene)
Pandora (the first woman)
Paris (son of King Priam)
Penelope (wife of Odysseus)
Persephone (daughter of Zeus)
Phaedra (wife of Theseus)
Philomela (sister of Procne)
Phoebe (daughter of heaven and earth)
Phyllis (wife of Demophon)
Pluto (god of the Underworld)
Poseidon (god of seas and water)
Priam (King of Troy)
Rhea (earth goddess)
Rhode (daughter of Poseidon)
Selene (goddess of the moon)
Thalia (Muse of comedy and pastoral poetry)
Themis (goddess of justice and order)
Tyche (goddess of luck)
Zephyrus (god of the west wind)
Zeus (ruler of the gods)

Roman

Aurora (goddess of the dawn)
Bellona (goddess of war)
Ceres (goddess of the harvest)
Diana (goddess of the moon and hunting)
Dido (princess of Tyre)
Flora (goddess of flowers and the spring)
Fortuna (goddess of good luck)
Ilia (mother of Romulus and Remus, also known as Rhea
    Silvia)
Janus (god of beginnings)
Juno (goddess of womanhood and childbirth)
Jupiter (god of the day)
Juventas (goddess of youth)
Lara (nymph)
Laverna (goddess of thieves)
Liber (god of fertility)
Luna (goddess of the moon)
Lupercus (god who protected flocks)
Marcus (possibly based on Mars, god of war)
Marina (possibly based on Mars, god of war)
Mark (probably based on Mars, god of war)
Mars (god of war)
Martin (probably based on Mars, god of war)
Matuta (goddess of dawn)
Mercury (messenger of the gods)
Minerva (goddess of household arts)
Moneta (goddess of money)
Neptune (god of the sea)
Ops (goddess of plenty)
Pomona (goddess of fruit)
Saturn (god of agriculture)
Silvanus (god of agriculture)
Somnus (god of sleep)
Terminus (god of boundaries and frontiers)

Uranus (god of the sky)
Venus (goddess of fertility and gardens)
Vertumnus (god of fertility)
Vesta (goddess of victory)
Vulcan (god of fire)

Celtic names

There is certainly a revival of interest in Celtic names. The Celts themselves were an ancient race who were once found all over Europe. Today the surviving Celtic languages are Welsh, Irish, Breton and Scottish Gaelic. The names listed here represent only a fraction of the vast range of Celtic names there is to choose from and, indeed, most of these names have variations in spelling and pronunciation.

Aerona	Bethan	Cecil
Aileen	Blaine	Ceinlys
Ailsa	Blaise	Ceridwen
Aindrias	Blodwen	Cerwyn
Aine	Boyd	Ciara
Ainsley	Bran	Colin
Aisling	Brenda	Colleen
Alan	Brendan	Connor
Alana	Brett	Craig
Alasdair	Brian	Dana
Aled	Brice	Dara
Amena	Bridget	Darcy
Aneurin	Bronwen	Declan
Angharad	Bryn	Deidre
Angus	Caitlin	Denzil
Arthur	Callum	Dermot
Aude	Cameron	Dilys
Auryn	Carey	Donald
Barry	Cary	Dougal
Bernard	Carys	Drew

Duane	Guinevere	Llewellyn
Duncan	Gwen	Lloyd
Dwynwen	Gwendolen	Lynette
Dylan	Gwenllian	Madoc
Eamon	Gwilym	Maeve
Edryd	Gwyneth	Magnus
Eileen	Hafwen	Malcolm
Eilwen	Hamish	Marvin
Eirwen	Harvey	Maura
Ellis	Heulwen	Maureen
Eluned	Hywel	Megan
Elwin	Ian	Mena
Emlyn	Idris	Meredith
Enid	Ifor	Merlin
Enya	Illtud	Mervyn
Epona	Inira	Moira
Erin	Iona	Mona
Euan	Iseult	Morag
Eurwen	Ithel	Morgan
Eurwyn	Jago	Myfanwy
Evan	Jarred	Nana
Fenella	Jennifer	Neil
Fergal	Kane	Nerys
Fergus	Kathleen	Niall
Ffion	Kenneth	Olwen
Fflur	Kent	Oscar
Fiona	Kentigern	Owen
Gavin	Kermit	Padarn
Gaynor	Kevin	Patrick
Geraint	Kieran	Ramsay
Gerwyn	Killian	Rees
Gildas	Kyle	Regan
Gladys	Lachlan	Rhiannon
Glen	Lennox	Rhianwen
Glenda	Liam	Rhona
Glynis	Llew	Riordan

Rogan	Sian	Tristram
Ronan	Sinclair	Ultan
Rory	Sinead	Una
Rowan	Siobhan	Valma
Roy	Sorcha	Vaughan
Ryan	Taliesin	Wallace
Seamus	Tara	Winifred
Sean	Tegan	Wynford
Selma	Tegwen	Wynn
Sheena	Tremaine	Yestin
Sheila	Trevor	

Names from the past

Some names have survived the years, the decades and even the centuries and are still unchanged in popular use today. For example:

10 popular seventeenth-century Puritan names

Abel	Grace	Prudence
Abraham	Hope	Reuben
Eli	Noah	Ruth
Faith		

10 popular names from the eighteenth century

Benjamin	Joseph	Rebecca
Charlotte	Lydia	Samuel
George	Phoebe	William
Hannah		

10 popular names from the nineteenth century

Alice	Emma	James
Amy	Frederick	Oliver
Elizabeth	Jack	Thomas
Emily		

10 popular names from the twentieth century

Arthur	Florence	Linda
Daniel	Jack	Margaret
David	John	Mary
Dorothy		

The 10 most popular names at the end of the twentieth century

Charlotte	James	Matthew
Daniel	Jessica	Rebecca
Hannah	Lauren	Thomas
Jack		

10 most popular names by country

England

Boys		*Girls*	
Jack	Samuel	Emily	Lucy
Joshua	Oliver	Ellie	Olivia
Thomas	William	Jessica	Charlotte
James	Benjamin	Sophie	Katie
Daniel	Joseph	Chloe	Megan

Scotland

Boys		*Girls*	
Lewis	Liam	Emma	Katie
Jack	Jamie	Sophie	Erin
James	Ben	Ellie	Emily
Cameron	Kyle	Amy	Lucy
Ryan	Callum	Chloe	Hannah

Wales

Boys		*Girls*	
Joshua	Rhys	Megan	Ffion
Jack	Daniel	Ellie	Katie
Thomas	Morgan	Chloe	Jessica
Dylan	James	Emily	Caitlin
Ethan	Benjamin	Sophie	Lucy

Northern Ireland

Boys		*Girls*	
Jack	Ben	Katie	Sarah
Matthew	Ryan	Emma	Chloe
James	Dylan	Ellie	Niamh
Adam	Connor	Sophie	Aimee
Daniel	Jamie	Amy	Rachel

Ireland

Boys		*Girls*	
Sean	Daniel	Emma	Sophie
Jack	Michael	Sarah	Rachel
Adam	Cian	Aoife	Chloe
Connor	David	Ciara	Amy
James	Dylan	Katie	Leah

United States

Boys		*Girls*	
Jacob	Andrew	Emily	Abigail
Michael	Daniel	Emma	Isabella
Joshua	William	Madison	Ashley
Matthew	Joseph	Olivia	Samantha
Ethan	Christopher	Hannah	Elizabeth

Canada

Boys		*Girls*	
Ethan	Ryan	Emily	Olivia
Matthew	Alexander	Emma	Jessica
Joshua	Michael	Sarah	Hayley
Jacob	Nathan	Madison	Julia
Nicholas	Daniel	Hannah	Grace

Australia

Boys		*Girls*	
Jack	James	Emily	Charlotte
Joshua	Ethan	Chloe	Ella
Lachlan	Samuel	Olivia	Isabella
Thomas	Daniel	Sophie	Sarah
William	Ryan	Jessica	Emma

New Zealand

Boys		*Girls*	
Joshua	Jacob	Emma	Hannah
Jack	Ethan	Sophie	Olivia
Benjamin	James	Ella	Grace
Samuel	Thomas	Emily	Charlotte
Daniel	Matthew	Jessica	Georgia

'Celebrity baby' names

Alexandria	daughter of David Bowie and Iman
Anaïs	daughter of Noel Gallagher and Meg Mathews
Apple	daughter of Gwyneth Paltrow and Chris Martin
Brooklyn	son of David and Victoria Beckham
Carys	daughter of Michael Douglas and Catherine Zeta-Jones
Connor	son of Tom Cruise and Nicole Kidman
Cruz	son of David and Victoria Beckham

Dylan	son of Michael Douglas and Catherine Zeta-Jones
Ella	daughter of John Travolta and Kelly Preston and daughter of Warren Beatty and Annette Bening
Gaia	daughter of Greg Wise and Emma Thompson
Gene	son of Liam Gallagher and Nicole Appleton
Iris	daughter of Jude Law and Sadie Frost
Isabella	daughter of Tom Cruise and Nicole Kidman
Jaden	son of Will Smith and Jada Pinkett Smith
Jaz Elle	daughter of Andre Agassi and Steffi Graff
Jett	son of John Travolta and Kelly Preston
Junior	son of Peter Andre and Jordan
Lennon	son of Liam Gallagher and Patsy Kensit
Leo	son of Tony and Cherie Blair
Lily-Rose	daughter of Johnny Depp and Vanessa Paradis
Mia	daughter of Jim Threapleton and Kate Winslet
Paris	son of Pierce Brosnan and Keely Shaye-Smith
Rocco	son of Guy Ritchie and Madonna
Romeo	son of David and Victoria Beckham
Rory	son of Bill and Melinda Gates
Rumer	son of Bruce Willis and Demi Moore
Scout	son of Bruce Willis and Demi Moore
Tallulah	daughter of Bruce Willis and Demi Moore
Willow	daughter of Will Smith and Jada Pinkett Smith
Woody	son of Norman Cook and Zoë Ball
Zola	daughter of Eddie Murphy and Nicole Mitchell

Names to avoid

This is probably the most important list of all! Of course, if someone really loves a particular name, nothing and no one is going to dissuade them from using it. Cameron, for example, is an attractive name; in fact it was one of the most popular boys' names at the end of the twentieth century. It's just a pity that it means 'crooked nose'! So it really is worth double-checking here just to be sure.

Agrippa (meaning 'sick' or 'painful')
Andromache (meaning 'she who fights against men')
Audrey (closely associated with the word 'tawdry')
Bertha (has come to be associated with 'Big Bertha')
Calvin (meaning 'little bald one')
Cameron (meaning 'crooked nose')
Campbell (meaning 'crooked mouth')
Cassandra (meaning 'entangler of men')
Claud(e) (meaning 'crippled')
Deidre (possibly meaning 'brokenhearted')
Desdemona (meaning 'ill fated')
Electra (has come to be associated with Freud's 'Electra complex')
Emily (meaning 'rival')
Emlyn (meaning 'rival')
Jezebel (meaning 'domination')
Job (meaning 'persecuted')
Jocasta (possibly meaning 'woe adorned')
Kennedy (meaning 'ugly head')
Mara (meaning 'bitter')
Melville (meaning 'bad town')
Patsy (means a 'homosexual' in Australia)
Persephone (meaning 'bearer of death')
Sorrel (probably meaning 'sour')
Tristram (probably meaning 'sad')
Uranus (simply because of how some people pronounce it!)

2. NAMES FOR EACH DAY OF THE YEAR

Why not look up a famous person born on your child's birthday, or perhaps use the name of the relevant saint, or use some other connection to the day? The list here is by no means exhaustive – to include all the many hundreds of saints alone would take a whole book, if not more, and many have names that simply would not be used today! What is included here is meant to give you more inspiration.

1 January

Odilo (11th century): The fifth abbot of Cluny who originated All Souls Day on 2 November when, in 998, he ordered all Clunac monks to pray for the dead on that day.

2 January

David Bailey, photographer (1938); Christy Turlington, model (1969)

Gregory of Nazianzus (4th century): Called 'The Theologian', he was an eloquent orator who followed his friend St Basil to a life of solitude before being chosen as Bishop of Constantinople in 381.
Basil the Great (4th century): A learned man who began a life of solitude before becoming Bishop of Caesarea. Here he had to combat the Arian heresy (which denied the full

divinity of Christ) and wrote monastic rules that are still followed today.

Seraphim of Sarov (18/19th century): A recluse priest who lived for sixteen years in a shack in a forest living self-sufficiently and praying. Having been attacked by robbers, he recuperated in a monastery before returning to his solitary life, this time on a rock. Here he stayed until old age forced him back to the monastery. It is claimed that he had several visions of the Virgin Mary.

3 January

John Thaw, actor (1942); Victoria Principal, actress (1946); Mel Gibson, actor (1956)

Genevieve (4th century): From a young age she dedicated her life to God and was credited, among other things, with preventing Attila and his Huns from storming Paris.

Dionysus, the god of wine, honoured in Ancient Greece

4 January

Jane Wyman, actress (1914); Dyan Cannon, actress (1937)

Elizabeth Seton (19th century): The first native American to be canonised.

5 January

Robert Duvall, actor (1931); Diane Keaton, actress (1946)

Simeon the Stylite (5th century): Lived on a platform at the top of a 60-foot pillar for the last 36 years of his life. He was trying to avoid those who came to him for advice but, in the end, the very fact that he was living on a pillar drew even more people to him, from sightseers to emperors.

John Nepomucene Neumann (19th century): Worked among the German-speaking immigrants in North America and became Bishop of Philadelphia in 1851.

6 January

St Joan of Arc, French heroine (1412); Rowan Atkinson, comedian (1955)

7 January

St Bernadette of Lourdes (1844); Gerald Durrell, author (1925)

Lucian of Antioch (3th century): A priest of Antioch who was put to death for refusing to denounce Christ. Legend has it that he was drowned at sea and his body returned by a dolphin, but it is more likely he was killed with a sword.

Raymund of Penafort (13th century): Joined the Dominican Order and was commanded by Gregory IX to edit the Book of Decretals. He wrote the *Summary of Cases*.

Charles of Sezza (17th century): A Franciscan friar noted for his holiness.

8 January

Elvis Presley, singer (1935); Shirley Bassey, singer (1937); David Bowie, singer/actor (1947)

Gudule (7th century): Patron saint of Brussels, Belgium, in whose honour Charlemagne founded a nunnery.

Pega (8th century): The sister of a hermit who followed a solitary life herself. After her brother's death she went on a pilgrimage to Rome and died about five years later.

9 January

Gracie Fields, singer (1898); Joan Baez, singer (1941); Susannah York, actress (1941)

Adrian of Canterbury (8th century): Twice declined the Archbishopric of Canterbury but agreed to accompany the new candidate, Theodore, to England and supported his work there.

Philip of Moscow (16th century): Primate of the Russian Church at the time of Ivan the Terrible and famously protested against the tsar's massacres of innocent people. Tsar Ivan eventually had him deposed on charges of sorcery. He was dragged in chains to prison and eventually suffocated on Ivan's orders.

10 January

Rod Stewart, singer (1945)

Peter Orseolo (10th century): A doge of Venice. After two years in the post he joined a monastery in the Pyrenees, leaving his unsuspecting wife and son behind. He ended his days living as a hermit.

11 January

Theodosius (6th century): Founder of a community near Bethlehem whose members cared for the mentally and physically sick.

12 January

Des O'Connor, singer (1932); Anthony Andrews, actor (1948); Kirstie Alley, actress (1955)

Benedict Biscop (7th century): Founder of a monastery at Wearmouth, Northumbria, and a sister house at Jarrow.
Tatiana (dates unknown): Very little is known about Tatiana except that she was probably a deaconess who was martyred in the early part of the third century.

13 January

Hilary of Poitiers (4th century): A bishop of Poitiers who was exiled by Emperor Constantine for opposing the Arian heresy. St Hilary gives his name to the 'Hilary' term of universities and law courts.

Kentigern (6th century): His nickname is Mungo, Celtic for 'most dear'. St Kentigern was a missionary in Scotland. After suffering persecution, he worked in north-west England and Wales before eventually returning to Scotland.

14 January

Richard Briers, actor (1934); Faye Dunaway, actress (1941)

Felix of Nola (3rd century): A priest arrested during the persecutions of the Christians. Having escaped from prison he rescued the bishop, carrying him to safety on his back.
Macrina the Elder (4th century): Grandmother of Macrina the Younger (19 July). She and her husband suffered for their faith during a persecution of the Christians.

15 January

Martin Luther King, champion of black civil rights (1929)

Paul the First Hermit (4th century): Lived in a cave in the Theban desert for most of his 100 years and is regarded as the first Christian hermit.
Macarious the Elder (4th century): Lived most of his life in the wilderness.
Ita (6th century): Head of a community of women in County Limerick who is said to have performed several miracles.

16 January

Sade, singer (1960); Kate Moss, model (1974)

Fursey (7th century): He was known for falling into long trances during which he saw visions of good and evil.
Berard and companions (13th century): Sent by St Francis of Assisi to preach to the Muslims. They preached in the streets of Morocco and at first the Moors simply thought they were mad. However, their staying power proved too

much and they were supposedly killed by the sultan himself, making them the first Franciscan martyrs.

17 January

Benjamin Franklin, American statesman (1706); Anne Brontë, author (1820); David Lloyd George, statesman (1863); Al Capone, gangster (1899); Paul Young, singer (1956); Jim Carrey, actor (1962)

Antony of Egypt (4th century): Patron saint of pigs and basket makers. A hermit who is regarded by many as the founder of monasticism. When his parents died, he gave away everything to the poor and went to live in the desert.

18 January

Oliver Hardy, comic actor (1892); Cary Grant, actor (1904); Danny Kaye, actor (1913); Kevin Costner, actor (1955)

Prisca (dates unknown): Also known as Priscilla. Very little is known about her except that she was a virgin martyr.
Margaret of Hungary (13th century): A Hungarian princess who entered a convent built by her father and refused to leave, even for marriage to the King of Bohemia.

19 January

Edgar Allan Poe, author (1809); Paul Cézanne, artist (1839); Michael Crawford, actor (1942); Janis Joplin, singer (1943); Dolly Parton, singer/actress (1946)

Canute (11th century): King of Denmark who led raids on England before being murdered in a church.
Henry of Finland (12th century): An Englishman who became patron saint of Finland.
Marius and Martha (dates unknown): Along with their two sons, they were martyred for their faith in Rome.

20 January

George Burns, actor (1896)

Fabian (3rd century): Legend has it that he was a layman, appointed as pope after a dove landed on his head as the clergy met in Rome. He was martyred during the persecution under Emperor Decius.

Sebastian (3rd century): Patron saint of archers and athletes. Tradition claims that he was a Roman officer who was discovered to be a Christian and then sentenced to death by arrows. Having survived this, he was then bludgeoned to death.

St Agnes Eve: If young girls fast for the day, they are said to dream tonight about their future husbands.

21 January

Telly Savalas, actor (1924); Benny Hill, comedian (1925); Jack Niklaus, golfer (1940); Martin Shaw, actor (1945); Michael Hutchence, singer (1960)

Agnes (3rd century): Patron saint of girls. Little is known about her, but she is traditionally thought to have been a young girl of just twelve years who refused marriage, preferring to give herself to God, and was stabbed to death. According to one account: 'You could see the executioner shaking . . . you could see his right hand shaking, his face growing pale, though the child had no fear of her own.'

Meinrad (9th century): A hermit monk murdered by thieves whose place of solitude became the famous Abbey of St Meinrad in Switzerland.

22 January

Lord Byron, poet (1788); John Hurt, actor (1940)

Vincent Zaragoza (3rd century): A martyr who endured many tortures including, it is said, roasting, during persecutions in Valencia, Spain.

Anastasius (7th century): Patron saint of goldsmiths. He was a soldier before converting to Christianity and becoming a monk. He went to preach in Persia where he was arrested and tortured. When he still refused to renounce his faith, he was strangled.

Vincent Pallotti (19th century): A priest in Rome and founder of the Society of Catholic Apostolate and the Pallottine Missionary Sisters.

23 January

Humphrey Bogart, actor (1899)

John the Almsgiver (6/7th century): As patriarch of Alexandria, he founded hospitals for the old and sick and helped those driven out of Jerusalem after the city was attacked by the Persians in 614.

24 January

Neil Diamond, singer (1941)

Francis of Sales (17th century): Patron saint of authors, writers and journalists.

25 January

Robert Burns, poet (1759); Virginia Woolf, author (1882)

The Conversion of St Paul the Apostle: As a young man, Paul persecuted the Christians and was on the road to Damascus to do just that when he had a vision of Christ and was duly converted.

Burns Night in Scotland, in celebration of the birth of the great Scottish poet Robert Burns.

26 January

Paul Newman, actor (1925); Eartha Kitt, singer (1928); Jacqueline du Pre, cellist (1945)

Timothy (1st century): Converted by St Paul and became his helper and first Bishop of Ephesus.

Titus (1st century): A convert of St Paul who became the first Bishop of Crete.

Paula (4th century): Patron saint of widows.

Alberic (11th century): A co-founder of the Cistercian monastic order.

27 January

Angela Merici (15/16th century): Founder of the Company of St Ursula, the first women's order devoted to teaching young girls.

28 January

Acker Bilk, musician (1929); Alan Alda, actor (1936)

Peter Nolasco (13th century): Founder of the Order of Our Lady of Ransom, which was devoted to rescuing captives of the Moors in Spain.

Thomas Aquinas (13th century): Patron saint of students and theologians. A writer and teacher of theology. His body was reburied at Toulouse.

29 January

Sacha Distel, singer (1933); Germaine Greer, author (1939); Tom Selleck, actor (1945); Katharine Ross, actress (1942); Oprah Winfrey, talk-show host/actress (1954)

Gildas (6th century): Known as 'the Wise', Gildas was the monk who wrote the famous work, *Concerning the Ruin and Conquest of Britain*.

30 January

Gene Hackman, actor (1930); Vanessa Redgrave, actress (1937); Phil Collins, singer/actor (1951)

Bathild (7th century): An Englishwoman who was stolen by pirates as a child and later married King Clovis II of the Western Franks. As regent for her son, she opposed the slave trade and encouraged monasticism before ending her days in a nunnery.

Martina of Rome (3rd century): Little is known about her except that she was a virgin martyr.

31 January

Anna Pavlova, ballerina (1882); Tallulah Bankhead, actress (1903); Jean Simmons, actress (1929); Johnny Rotten, singer (1956)

John Bosco (19th century): Patron saint of editors, schoolboys and youth. He was brought up in poverty before becoming a priest. He devoted much of his life to the education of young people.

Marcella (4th century): Established a religious group of Roman ladies at her home after the death of her husband. When Alaric the Goth attacked Rome, the invaders tried to force Marcella to hand over her wealth. The attack was so severe that she died from her wounds.

1 February

Clark Gable, actor (1901); Lisa Marie Presley (1968)

Bridget (Bride) of Ireland (6th century): Patron saint of scholars and dairymaids. She is considered by many to be the founder of the first religious community for women in Ireland.

2 February

Nell Gwyn, royal mistress (1650); James Joyce, author (1882); Les Dawson, comedian (1933); David Jason, actor (1940); Farrah Fawcett, actress (1947); Christie Brinkley, model (1953)

Joan de Lestonnac (17th century): Founded the sisters of Notre Dame of Bordeaux, dedicated to the education of girls.

3 February

Frankie Vaughan, singer (1928); Val Doonican, singer (1929); Morgan Fairchild, actress (1950)

Blaise (4th century): Patron saint of throat sufferers.
Ia (dates unknown): According to tradition, Ia travelled from Ireland to Cornwall on a leaf and landed at Porth Ia, now St Ives.
Laurence of Canterbury (6th century): Chosen by St Augustine to be his successor at Canterbury.
Ansgar (9th century): He was born in France but went to preach in Denmark and Sweden. He eventually became Bishop of Hamburg before being made legate of Denmark and Sweden by Gregory IV.

4 February

Norman Wisdom, actor (1920)

Phileas (3rd century): A bishop martyred for his faith in Alexandria.
Gilbert of Sempringham (12th century): Patron saint of the paralysed. He founded the Gilbertine Order, the only specifically English order. It ended when all its houses were suppressed under King Henry VIII.
John de Britto (17th century): A Jesuit beheaded in India during a persecution of Christians.
Andrew Corsini (14th century): A Carmelite friar and reluctant bishop of Fiesole.
Joan of France (15th century): As a hunchback and unattractive daughter of King Louis XI of France, she was swiftly married off to the Duke of Orleans. She was later publicly humiliated when her husband had the marriage annulled for non-consummation so that he could marry someone

else. She took it all quietly and spent the rest of her life doing good works and founding a small religious order of women.

5 February

Sir Robert Peel, statesman (1788); Charlotte Rampling, actress (1946)

Agatha (dates unknown): Patron saint of bell-founders, nurses, firefighters, Malta and breast diseases. According to legend, she was tortured, including having her breasts cut off, as a Christian. In many paintings, she is pictured carrying her breasts on a plate. Since they look like bells, she is now the patron saint of bell-founders . . . and as they equally look like round loaves, there is a custom of breaking bread on her feast day!

6 February

Ronald Reagan, actor/US President (1911); Zsa Zsa Gabor, actress (1915); Leslie Crowther, comedian (1933); Jimmy Tarbuck, comedian (1940); Bob Marley, singer (1945); Natalie Cole, singer (1950); Axl Rose, singer (1962)

Dorothy (3rd century): Patron saint of florists. She was sentenced to death for her Christianity. According to the story, on her way to execution she was mocked by a lawyer who called to her to send flowers from the heavenly garden. When these actually arrived, he too was converted and he too was martyred.

Paul Miki and companions (16th century): He was born in Japan and preached there successfully before the country was swept by persecution of Catholics. Paul and twenty-five others were arrested and tortured before being crucified at Nagasaki in 1597.

7 February

Sir Thomas More, statesman (1478); Charles Dickens, author (1812)

8 February

Lana Turner, actress (1920); Jack Lemmon, actor (1925); James Dean, actor (1931); Nick Nolte, actor (1940)

Cuthman (8th century): Built a church in Steyning, having travelled there pulling his widowed mother in a cart.

Jerome Emilian (16th century): Began adult life as a soldier before devoting his life to helping orphan children and the poor.

John of Matha (12/13th century): Founded an order of friars whose work was to free those taken prisoner by the Muslims.

9 February

Carole King, singer (1942); Mia Farrow, actress (1945)

Apollonia (3rd century): Patron saint of dentists and toothache sufferers. Her teeth were knocked out during a riot against Christians. She was then threatened with being burned alive but she astounded her attackers by saying a prayer and walking into the fire.

10 February

Joyce Grenfell, actress/writer (1910); Larry Adler, musician (1914); Robert Wagner, actor (1930); Roberta Flack, singer (1940); Greg Norman, golfer (1958)

Scholastica (6th century): Patron saint of convulsive children and nuns. Regarded as the 'mother' of Benedictine nuns.

11 February

Mary Quant, fashion designer (1934); Burt Reynolds, actor (1936)

Benedict of Aniane (8th century): The supreme abbot over all monasteries in Charlemagne's empire.

12 February

Abraham Lincoln, US President (1809); Charles Darwin, naturalist (1809)

Julian the Hospitaller (dates unknown): Patron saint of ferrymen and innkeepers.
Marina (dates unknown): She lived as a monk, not revealing her sex even when accused of fathering the child of the innkeeper's daughter!

13 February

George Segal, actor (1934); Oliver Reed, actor (1938); Peter Gabriel, musician (1950)

Catherine dei Ricci (16th century): A nun in Tuscany, famous for her religious experiences.

14 February

Kevin Keegan, footballer/manager (1951)

Valentine (3rd century): Patron saint of lovers.
Cyril (9th century): Invented the Cyrillic alphabet in order to be able to translate the liturgical books into Slavonic.
Methodius (9th century): The brother of St Cyril (above) who preached with him in Monravia. After Cyril died, he became a bishop in Hungary.

St Valentine's day, when lovers send cards and gifts to each other.

15 February

Claire Bloom, actress (1931); Jane Seymour, actress (1951)

Claude La Colombiere (17th century): A Jesuit priest who worked in the household of the Duchess of York and the future James II. He was arrested and imprisoned after the false discovery of a 'popish plot' and deported back to France.

16 February

Barry Humphries, comedian (1934); John McEnroe, tennis player (1959)

Elias and companions (3/4th century): Went with a group of Christians sentenced to hard labour in the quarries. They were arrested on their return and beheaded.

17 February

Alan Bates, actor (1934)

Fintan of Cloneenagh (6th century): Lived an austere life as an abbot, eating only stale bread and drinking dirty water.
The Seven Servite Founders (13th century): Lived as hermits on Monte Senario before founding the Order of Servites. The day is chosen as that on which *St Alexis Falconieri*, one of the seven, died.

18 February

Yoko Ono, singer (1933); Cybill Shepherd, actress (1950); John Travolta, actor (1954); Matt Dillon, actor (1964)

Colman of Lindisfarne (7th century): Bishop of Lindisfarne. He retired after he lost his argument about the date of Easter.

19 February

David Garrick, actor (1717); Merle Oberon, actress (1911); Lee Marvin, actor (1924); Margaux Hemingway, actress (1955); Prince Andrew (1960); Holly Johnson, singer (1960)

The birthday of Athena, goddess of war, wisdom and arts in Ancient Greece and that of her equivalent, Minerva, in Ancient Rome was celebrated today.

20 February

Sidney Poitier, actor (1924); Cindy Crawford, model (1966)

21 February

Peter Damian (11th century): A theologian and one of the doctors of the Church.

22 February

George Washington, US President (1732); John Mills, actor (1908); Julie Walters, actress (1950); Drew Barrymore, actress (1975)

Margaret of Cortona (13th century): Patron saint of repentant prostitutes, she lived for 10 years as a mistress before her lover was killed. After this, she repented and devoted herself to good works.

23 February

Samuel Pepys, diarist (1633); Peter Fonda, actor (1939)

Polycarp (2nd century): A bishop of Smyrna who was martyred for his faith by being burned alive in Rome's stadium.
Mildburga (7th century): A sister of St Mildred (13 July) and founder of Wenlock Abbey in Shropshire.

24 February

Dennis Waterman, actor (1948)

25 February

Zeppo Marx, comic actor (1901); Leslie Thomas, actor (1914); David Puttnam, producer (1941); George Harrison, singer and ex-Beatle (1943)

Ethelbert of Kent (6th century): The king who gave his encouragement to St Augustine when he arrived in Kent. He built the first St Paul's Cathedral in London.

26 February

Victor Hugo, author (1802); 'Fats' Domino, musician (1928); Johnny Cash, singer (1932); Sandie Shaw, singer (1947); Michael Bolton, singer (1953)

Porphyry (5th century): Bishop of Gaza.

27 February

John Steinbeck, author (1902); Lawrence Durrell, author (1912); Joanne Woodward, actress (1930); Elizabeth Taylor, actress (1932)

Leander (6th century): A bishop of Seville responsible for the conversion of many Visigoths from Arianism.
Gabriel Possenti (19th century): Known as St Gabriel of Our Lady of Sorrows.

28 February

Brian Jones, musician with the Rolling Stones (1942)

Oswald of Worcester (10th century): He was both Bishop of Worcester and Archbishop of York.

29 February

William Wellman, director (1896); Jimmy Dorsey, musician (1904); Jack Lousma, astronaut (1936)

1 March

Glenn Miller, band leader (1904); David Niven, actor (1910); Harry Belafonte, singer (1927); Roger Daltrey, singer (1944); Nik Kershaw, singer (1958)

David (6th century): Patron saint of Wales. Consecrated a bishop in Jerusalem and became Primate of Wales.

St David's day celebrated in Wales.

2 March

Lou Reed, musician (1944); Karen Carpenter, singer (1950); Jon Bon Jovi, singer (1962)

Chad (7th century): A pupil of St Aidan, he eventually became Bishop of the Mercians.

3 March

Alexander Graham Bell, inventor of the telephone (1847); Jean Harlow, actress (1911)

Ailred of Rievaulx (12th century): An Englishman who became abbot of the Cistercian monastery at Rievaulx, Yorkshire.
Cunegund (11th century): Wife of the Holy Roman Emperor, Henry II.

4 March

Kenny Dalglish, footballer/manager (1951)

Casimir (15th century): Patron saint of Poland. He was son of the King of Poland and at his tomb miracles were reported.

5 March

Rex Harrison, actor (1908); Elaine Page, singer (1952)

Piran (6th century): Patron saint of Cornwall. He established a monastery in Cornwall, and until the nineteenth century his feast day was a holiday for tin miners there.

6 March

Elizabeth Barrett Browning, poet (1806); Frankie Howerd, comedian (1922)

Colette (15th century): Acted on a vision of St Francis of Assisi in which he asked her to reform the Poor Clare nuns.

7 March

Viv Richards, cricketer (1952); Rik Mayall, comedian (1958)

Perpetua and Felicity (2nd century): Martyrs, condemned to death-by-wild-animals. While in prison, Perpetua had several visions of heaven and they emerged defiant into the arena. The women helped each other in their ordeal before finally being stabbed in the throat. According to a report of their deaths: 'If they were trembling at all, it was from joy, not fear.'

Paul the Simple (4th century): An Egyptian peasant who endured several tests before being accepted as a disciple of St Anthony.

8 March

Cyd Charisse, actress (1923); Lynn Seymour, actress (1939); Lynn Redgrave, actress (1943); Gary Numan, singer (1958)

Felix of Dunwich (7th century): A missionary bishop. He gave his name to Felixstowe.

John of God (16th century): Patron saint of booksellers, heart patients, hospitals, nurses, printers and the sick. He spent many years as a soldier before devoting himself to looking after the sick. He founded a hospital in Spain and set up the Order of Hospitallers of Saint John of God.

Julian of Toledo (7th century): A bishop of Toledo.

9 March

Micky Dolenz, singer (1945); Bill Beaumont, rugby player (1952)

Gregory of Nyssa (4th century): A brother of St Basil (2 January) and Bishop of Nyssa.

Frances of Rome (15th century): Patron saint of motorists. Frances was an aristocrat who founded the Oblates of Tor de' Specchi.

Catherine of Bologna (15th century): Abbess of a convent in Bologna, said to have experienced many visions.

Dominic Savio (19th century): One of the pupils of St John Bosco (31 January) noted for his goodness.

10 March

Sharon Stone, actress (1958); Prince Edward (1964)

John Ogilvie (17th century): A Jesuit arrested in his native Scotland. Despite torture, he refused to acknowledge the spiritual supremacy of the crown and was tried and executed for high treason.

11 March

Eulogius of Cordoba (9th century): A priest in Cordoba when the African Muslim occupiers began to persecute the Christians. Eulogius was arrested but later released. For seven years, he kept a record of all those who were killed, the 'Memorandum of the Saints', before being arrested again for sheltering Leocritia, a young converted Muslim girl, and beheaded.

12 March

Liza Minnelli, singer/actress (1946)

Maximilian (3rd century): Tried and beheaded for refusing to become a soldier on account of his Christianity.

Paul Aurelian (6th century): Founded several churches in Brittany and was Bishop of Saint-Pol-de-Leon, which was named after him.

13 March

Neil Sedaka, singer (1939)

Gerald of Mayo (8th century): Succeeded St Colman as Abbot of Mayo.

14 March

Albert Einstein, physicist (1879); Michael Caine, actor (1933); Jasper Carrott, comedian (1946); Billy Crystal, actor (1947)

Matilda of Quedlinburg (10th century): The wife of King Henry I, 'the Fowler' of Germany.

15 March

Terence Trent d'Arby, singer (1961)

Leocritia (9th century): A Muslim converted to Christianity and given shelter by St Eulogius (11 March). Both were arrested. Leocritia was beheaded four days after her friend and they are buried together.
Louise de Marillac (17th century): Co-founder, with St Vincent de Paul, of the Daughters of Charity.
Clement-Mary Hofbauer (18th century): Worked as a priest in Poland before Napoleon closed the religious communities there. He then moved to Vienna, and from there fought against state control of the Church.

The festival of the goddess Cybele, and her consort, Attis, was celebrated in Ancient Rome.

16 March

Jerry Lewis, comedian (1926)

Julian of Antioch (dates unknown): He was tied in a sack and thrown into the sea for his faith.

17 March

Nat 'King' Cole, musician (1919); Patrick Duffy, actor (1949); Rob Lowe, actor (1964)

Joseph of Arimathaea (1st century): One of the disciples. Legend has it that he also founded the first British church at Glastonbury.
Patrick (4th century): Patron saint of Ireland. Born in England but taken as a slave to Ireland. When he escaped, he became a priest and was made Bishop of Ireland. He organised the Irish Church and was responsible for converting many people to the faith.
Gertrude of Nivelles (7th century): Patron saint of the recently dead.

St Patrick's Day is celebrated by Irish people everywhere.

18 March

Wilfred Owen, poet (1893)

Cyril of Jerusalem (4th century): Bishop of Jerusalem and a tireless fighter against the Arian heresy, for which he was exiled several times.
Edward the Martyr (10th century): King of England in 975 who was murdered while travelling to see his half-brother, Ethelred.

19 March

Dr David Livingstone, explorer (1813); Ursula Andress, actress (1936); Glenn Close, actress (1947); Bruce Willis, actor (1955); Courtney Pine, singer (1964)

Joseph (1st century): Patron saint of bursars, carpenters, the dying, fathers, holy death and workers. Husband of the Blessed Virgin Mary.

20 March

Sir Isaac Newton, scientist (1727); Dame Vera Lynn, singer (1917)

Martin of Braga (6th century): Founded the Abbey of Dumium and was Archbishop of Braga.
Cuthbert (7th century): Patron saint of shepherds.
Herbert of Derwentwater (7th century): A hermit on the island of Derwentwater and a friend of St Cuthbert.

21 March

Timothy Dalton, actor (1944)

Nicholas of Flue (15th century): Credited with saving Switzerland from civil war.

22 March

Marcel Marceau, mime artist (1923); William Shatner, actor (1931); Leslie Thomas, author (1931); Andrew Lloyd Webber, composer (1948)

Zacharias (8th century): Elected pope in 741.

23 March

Joan Crawford, actress (1908); Donald Campbell, land speed record holder (1921); Roger Bannister, athlete (1929); Chaka Khan, singer (1953)

Gwinear (6th century): Said to have travelled as a missionary from Ireland to Cornwall, only to be killed by the local ruler, Teudar.

Turibius of Mogroveio (16th century): Patron saint of
  missionary bishops and Bishop of Lima. He went to
  America where he spent a lot of time working for the good
  of the native Indian population.

24 March

Harry Houdini, escape artist (1874); Steve McQueen, actor
(1930)

Catherine of Sweden (14th century): A daughter of St Bridget
  (23 July).

25 March

David Lean, director (1908); Simone Signoret, actress (1921);
Aretha Franklin, singer (1942); Paul Michael Glaser, actor
(1943); Sir Elton John, singer (1947)

The Annunciation of the Blessed Virgin Mary (1st century):
  Patron saint of mothers, nuns and virgins.
Dismas the Good Thief (1st century): Patron saint of prisoners
  and thieves. He was crucified with Christ.

26 March

Tennessee Williams, playwright (1911); Leonard Nimoy, actor
(1931); James Caan, actor (1939); Diana Ross, singer (1944)

William of Norwich (12th century): Popularly thought to have
  been murdered by Jews at the age of 12 years, although this
  story was never substantiated.

27 March

Gloria Swanson, actress (1899); Michael York, actor (1942);
Quentin Tarantino, director (1963); Mariah Carey, singer
(1970)

John the Egyptian (4th century): Worked as a carpenter before deciding to live as a hermit in the mountains. He was said to have the gift of foretelling the future.

Rupert (7th century): A missionary and founder of a church in Salzburg.

28 March

Dirk Bogarde, actor/author (1921)

29 March

Eric Idle, comedian (1945); Julie Goodyear, actress (1945); Elle MacPherson, model (1963)

Jonah and Berikjesu (4th century): They refused to denounce their Christianity, for which Jonah was dismembered and crushed to death and Berikjesu had burning pitch poured down his throat.

Mark of Arethusa (4th century): Martyred for his faith, supposedly by being stabbed to death.

30 March

Vincent van Gogh, artist (1853); Tom Sharpe, author (1928); Rolf Harris, singer/presenter (1930); Warren Beatty, actor (1937); Eric Clapton, singer (1945); Celine Dion, singer (1968)

John Climacus (7th century): Little is known about him except that he was Abbot of the monastery at Mount Sinai and author of the book *Ladder to Paradise*.

31 March

Joseph Haydn, composer (1732); Richard Chamberlain, actor (1935); Christopher Walken, actor (1943); Rhea Perlman, actress (1946)

The Feast of Luna, goddess of the moon, was celebrated in Ancient Rome.

1 April

Debbie Reynolds, actress (1932); Ali McGraw, actress (1938)

Hugh of Grenoble (11th century): Bishop of Grenoble for 52 years.

2 April

Émile Zola, author (1840); Sir Alec Guinness, actor (1914); Marvin Gaye, singer (1939); Emmy Lou Harris, singer (1947)

Mary of Egypt (5th century): Patron saint of repentant prostitutes. A prostitute who converted to Christianity and repented for the rest of her life.
Francis of Paola (15th century): Patron saint of sailors. Founded a congregation of hermits that developed into the Order of Minims. He was supposed to be able to read minds.

3 April

Leslie Howard, actor (1893); Marlon Brando, actor (1924); Doris Day, actress (1924); Eddie Murphy, actor (1961)

Agape, Irene and Chione (3rd century): Sisters martyred after they refused to eat food that was sacrificed to the gods.
Richard of Chichester (13th century): Patron saint of coachmen. He followed St Edmund into exile, and on his return became Bishop of Chichester.

This day marks Persephone's annual return from the Underworld and the start of spring in Greek mythology.

4 April

Anthony Perkins, actor (1932)

Isidore of Seville (6th century): Succeeded his brother, St Leander, as Archbishop of Seville, and is a doctor of the Church.

Benedict the Black (16th century): Joined the Franciscans as a laybrother and eventually became leader of a friary in Palermo.

5 April

Spencer Tracy, actor (1900); Bette Davis, actress (1908); Gregory Peck, actor (1916); Nigel Hawthorne, actor (1929)

Vincent Ferrer (14th century): Patron saint of builders.

6 April

Sir John Betjeman, poet (1906)

William of Aebelholt (12th century): An abbot tasked with reforming the Abbey of Aebelholt in Denmark.

7 April

William Wordsworth, poet (1770); Billie Holliday, singer (1915); James Garner, actor (1928); Andrew Sachs, actor (1930)

Jean-Baptist de la Salle (17th century): Patron saint of teachers. Became a priest and devoted himself to teaching and founding schools for the poor.

8 April

Sir Adrian Boult, composer (1889); Hywel Bennett, actor (1944)

9 April

Charles Baudelaire, poet (1821); Hugh Hefner, entrepreneur (1926)

10 April

Joseph Pulitzer, publisher (1847); Omar Sharif, actor (1932)

11 April

Stanislaus of Cracow (11th century): Bishop of Cracow. He was
   murdered by King Boleslav II in 1097 while celebrating
   Mass after rebuking and excommunicating him for his
   behaviour.
Gemma Galgani (19th century): A devout woman who
   experienced several visions. For eighteen months, the
   stigmata of Christ's crucifixion appeared on her hands and
   feet. Occasionally, though, she also had fits, which she said
   were caused by being possessed by the devil.

12 April

Alan Ayckbourn, playwright (1939); Bobby Moore, footballer
(1941); David Cassidy, singer (1950)

Teresa of the Andes (20th century): Made her vows as a
   Carmelite novice when she found she was suffering from
   typhus. She died, aged nineteen, just three months later.

13 April

Thomas Jefferson, statesman (1743); Samuel Beckett,
playwright (1906); Edward Fox, actor (1937); Ricky Schroder,
actor (1970)

Martin I (7th century): Made Pope in 649. Four years later, he
   was imprisoned by Constans II, Emperor of Byzantium, and
   died in the Crimea.

14 April

Sir John Gielgud, actor (1904); Rod Steiger, actor (1925); Julie
Christie, actress (1940)

Tiburtius, Valerian and Maximus (dates unknown): Valerian was the man to whom St Cecilia was betrothed (22 November). He, his brother Tiburtius, and another man named Maximus, were martyred for their faith.

15 April

Henry James, author (1843); Emma Thompson, actress (1959)

16 April

Charlie Chaplin, actor/comedian (1889); Spike Milligan, comedian/writer (1918); Peter Ustinov, actor/writer (1921); Kingsley Amis, author (1922)

Magnus (11th century): Patron saint of fishermen. The son of the joint ruler of Orkney who was known for his devotion to the faith. He was murdered by his cousin and, according to the story, died praying for his murderers.

Benedict Joseph Labre (18th century). Patron saint of beggars, the homeless and tramps. Having been rejected by several religious orders, he went on a pilgrimage to Rome, begging his way. He then spent several years wandering around western Europe, praying and living as a beggar before collapsing in a church in Rome.

Bernadette (19th century): The famous Bernadette Soubirous. She had eighteen visions of the Virgin Mary, who showed her an unknown stream. Many people refused to believe her but she did not give in to their persecution. She joined the Sisters of Charity, some of whom also did not live up to their name in their dealings with Bernadette, and died at the age of 35. The scene of her visions at Lourdes has become one of the most famous pilgrimage sites in the world.

17 April

William Holden, actor (1918); Clare Francis, author/yachtswoman (1946); Olivia Hussey, actress (1951)

Donnan (7th century): Founded a community of monks on the island of Eigg in the Inner Hebrides. They were all massacred by armed men after Mass, possibly at the instigation of local chieftains who did not want the monks there.

Robert of Chaise-Dieu (11th century): Founded an abbey in Auvergne.

Stephen Harding (12th century): One of the three original founders of Cistercian reform. William of Malmesbury wrote of him that he was 'approachable, good-looking, always cheerful in the Lord – everyone liked him.'

18 April

Hayley Mills, actress (1946)

19 April

Jayne Mansfield, actress (1933); Dudley Moore, actor (1935); Paloma Picasso, actress (1949)

Leo IX (11th century): Elected Pope in 1048.

Today is Primrose Day, which marks the death of British Prime Minister Benjamin Disraeli in 1881. At his funeral, Queen Victoria sent a wreath of primroses, which were, she said, 'his favourite flower'.

20 April

Ryan O'Neal, actor (1941); Jessica Lange, actress (1949); Luther Vandross, musician (1951); Nicholas Lyndhurst, actor (1961)

Agnes of Montepulciano (13th century): Established a Dominican nunnery at Montepulciano.

21 April

Charlotte Brontë, author (1816); Anthony Quinn, actor (1915); Queen Elizabeth II of Great Britain (1926)

Beuno (6th century): Patron saint of sick animals.
Anselm (11th century): Made Archbishop of Canterbury and fought for the freedom of the church.

22 April

Yehudi Menuhin, violinist (1916); Jack Nicholson, actor (1937)

Theodore of Sykeon (7th century): The son of a prostitute, he became a monk and was later elected Bishop of Anastasiopolis.
Conrad of Parzham (19th century): A laybrother with the Capuchin Franciscans.

23 April

William Shakespeare, playwright (1564); Shirley Temple, actress/ambassador (1928); Roy Orbison, singer (1936)

George (3rd century): Patron saint of England, archers, husbandmen, knights, soldiers and those suffering from syphilis. Very little is known about him. He was supposedly a knight who was martyred in Palestine by being beheaded. His fame spread when crusaders brought back his story to England.

St George's Day is celebrated in England.

24 April

Anthony Trollope, author (1815); Shirley MacLaine, actress (1934); Barbra Streisand, actress/singer (1942)

Ivo (dates unknown): Patron saint of St Ives, England.
Egbert (8th century): He spent the last years of his life living as a hermit on the island of Iona.
Fidelis of Sigmaringen (17th century): Martyred by heretics in Switzerland.

25 April

Oliver Cromwell (1559); Walter de la Mare, poet/novelist (1873); Ella Fitzgerald, singer (1918); Al Pacino, actor (1939)

Mark the Evangelist (1st century): Patron saint of secretaries. A disciple of St Peter who is supposed to have founded the Church of Alexandria.
William of Monte Vergine (12th century): Lived as a hermit on Mont Vergine, eventually establishing a community of monks there.

26 April

Charlie Chester, comedian/actor (1914); Duane Eddy, musician (1938); Roger Taylor, musician (1960)

Stephen of Perm (14th century): Worked as a missionary among the Zyrians, west of the Urals. He created an alphabet for them and was eventually made Bishop of Perm.

27 April

Anouk Aimée, actress (1932); Sheena Easton, singer (1959)

Zita (13th century): Patron saint of bakers and servants.

28 April

Louis Grignion de Montfort (17th century): Founded the Daughters of Wisdom in Poitiers and the Company of Mary (the Montfort Missionaries).
Peter Chanel (19th century): Born a peasant's son in 1803, he was one of the first members of the missionary Society of Mary. He was sent as a missionary to the island of Futuna in the Pacific, where he came to be called 'Great-heart'. Although he was successful in converting many, including the son of the local ruler, it was this very success that led to jealousy and, three years after he arrived, he was clubbed to death.

Paul of the Cross (18th century): Founded the first Passionist house in Tuscany and an enclosed convent of Passionist nuns.

29 April

Arthur Wellesley, Duke of Wellington (1769); Duke Ellington, musician (1899); Lonnie Donegan, singer (1931); Daniel Day Lewis, actor (1957); Michelle Pfeiffer, actress (1957)

Hugh of Cluny (11th century): Abbot of Cluny and a deeply respected religious man.
Robert of Molesme (11th century): One of the founders of the Cistercian order.
Catherine of Siena (14th century): One of the doctors of the Church.

30 April

Willie Nelson, singer (1933)

Marion and James (3rd century): Thrown into prison in Algeria because of their Christianity. When they refused to denounce their faith, they were lined up with many others and an executioner walked down each row, slashing off the heads of the prisoners as he went.
Joseph of Cottolengo (19th century): Founded the Little House of Divine Providence to care for the sick and needy.

1 May

Rita Coolidge, singer (1944); Joanna Lumley, actress (1946)

Joseph (1st century): Patron saint of bursars, carpenters, the dying, fathers, holy death and workers.

Maia, the goddess of spring, was honoured in Ancient Rome.

2 May

Bianca Jagger, first wife of Rolling Stone Mick (1945)

Mafalda of Portugal (13th century): A sister of St Sanchia (17 June) and St Teresa (17 June), she also founded a Cistercian abbey.

3 May

Bing Crosby, singer/actor (1904); James Brown, singer (1928); Henry Cooper, boxer (1934); Engelbert Humperdinck, singer (1936)

Philip (1st century): A disciple of John the Baptist before becoming one of the Apostles.
James the Less (1st century): A cousin of Christ and one of the Apostles.

4 May

Eric Sykes, comedian/actor (1923); Audrey Hepburn, actress (1929)

Florian (3rd century): Patron saint of fire brigades.

5 May

Karl Marx, socialist author (1818); Tammy Wynette, singer (1942); Michael Palin, comedian/presenter (1943)

Hilary of Arles (5th century): Succeeded St Honoratus as Bishop of Arles.

6 May

Sigmund Freud, psychoanalyst (1856); Ruldolph Valentino, actor (1895); Stewart Granger, actor (1913); Orson Welles, actor (1915); George Clooney, actor (1961)

7 May

Robert Browning, poet (1812); Gary Cooper, actor (1901); Maria Eva Peron, 'Evita' (1919)

Apollo, the god of the sun, song and music, was honoured in Ancient Greece.

8 May

David Attenborough, wildlife expert/presenter (1926); Jack Charlton, footballer/manager (1936); Gary Glitter, singer (1944)

Victor (3rd century): Very little is known about this saint.
Peter of Tarentaise (12th century): A Cistercian monk who became Bishop of Tarentaise. However, on one occasion he disappeared, only to be found hiding in a remote abbey.

9 May

Alan Bennett, playwright (1934); Albert Finney, actor (1936); Glenda Jackson, actress/politician (1936); Candice Bergen, actress (1946); Billy Joel, singer (1949)

10 May

Fred Astaire, actor/dancer (1899); Donovan, singer (1946); Maureen Lipman, actress (1946); Sid Vicious, singer (1957); Paul Hewson, 'Bono', singer (1960)

Antonino of Florence (15th century): Founded the friary of San Marco and later became Archbishop of Florence.
Isidore the farm servant (11/12th century): Patron saint of Madrid. He worked on a farm just outside Madrid all his life. King Philip III insisted that he be canonised because he believed that Isidore had helped him recover from a serious illness.

11 May

Irving Berlin, producer (1888); Margaret Rutherford, actress (1892); Salvador Dali, artist (1904); Phil Silvers, comedian (1912); Ian Dury, singer (1942)

Francis di Girolamo (17/18th century): Spent most of his life in Naples and the surrounding area. An effective preacher, he went into prisons and brothels and on to street corners in order to spread the word. He also rescued many children. At his funeral, his coffin was surrounded by the poor people of the town he served.

12 May

Edward Lear, author (1812); Florence Nightingale, Crimean nurse (1820); Tony Hancock, comedian (1924); Burt Bacharach, composer (1929); Steve Winwood, singer (1948)

Nereus and Achilleus (2nd century): Roman soldiers. Having converted to Christianity, they refused to serve any longer and were martyred.
Pancras of Rome (4th century): Little is known about Pancras save that he was martyred. His name lives on, however, as he gave his name to one of London's main railway stations!
Leopold Mandic (19/20th century): He was of frail health with a speech defect but worked tirelessly as a Franciscan friar in Italy for over 50 years.

13 May

Daphne du Maurier, author (1907); Stevie Wonder, singer (1950)

Andrew Fournet (18/19th century): A priest in France at the time of the French Revolution. He continued his ministry in secret and was arrested in 1792. At one point, he escaped the police by pretending to be a dead body. After the

Revolution, he collaborated with St Elizabeth Bichier in setting up the Daughters of the Cross.

14 May

Eric Morecambe, comedian (1926); Chay Blyth, yachtsman (1940)

Matthias (1st century): Chosen by the Apostles to take the place of Judas.
Maria-Domenica Mazzarello (19th century): Worked with St John Bosco (31 January) to set up the Daughters of Mary.
Michael Garicoits (19th century): Founded a missionary society known as the Priests of the Sacred Heart of Betharram.

15 May

James Mason, actor (1909); Mike Oldfield, musician (1953)

Dympna (7th century): Patron saint of epileptics and the mentally ill. According to legend she fled with a priest to escape her father's advances. She and the priest were murdered when her father eventually caught up with them.

16 May

Henry Fonda, actor (1905); Pierce Brosnan, actor (1953); Debra Winger, actress (1955); Janet Jackson, singer (1966)

Brendan the Navigator (6th century): Founded the monastery of Clonfert in Galway. *Brendan's Voyage*, his story of how he and a group of monks set sail to find a Land of Promise in the Atlantic, was translated into many languages.
Simon Stock (13th century): Prior General of the Carmelite Order.
John of Nepomuk (14th century): Patron saint of bridgebuilders.
Andrew Bobola (17th century): A Polish Jesuit murdered by Cossacks.

17 May

Maureen O'Sullivan, actress (1911); Dennis Potter, playwright (1935)

Paschal Baylon (16th century): A Franciscan laybrother.

18 May

Perry Como, singer (1912); Margot Fonteyn, ballerina (1919); Nobby Stiles, footballer (1942)

John I (6th century): Elected Pope in 523 and sent, against his wishes, by the Arian King Theodoric on a mission to the Emperor of Constantinople, who was actively anti-Arian. The King was unhappy with John's close relations with the Emperor and, on his return to Italy, had him imprisoned. He died a few days later.
Eric (12th century): A Christian king of Sweden, who was murdered by a Danish prince.
Felix of Cantalice (16th century): A Capuchin laybrother.

19 May

Pete Townshend, musician (1945); Grace Jones, model/actress (1952); Victoria Wood, comedian (1953)

Dunstan (10th century): Patron saint of blacksmiths, goldsmiths and the blind.
Peter Celestine (13th century): At the age of 80 he was elected pope through a lack of any other agreeable choice. He lasted in office just five months.
Yves of Brittany (13th century): Patron saint of judges and lawyers.

20 May

James Stewart, actor (1908); Joe Cocker, singer (1944); Cher, actress/singer (1946)

Bernardine of Siena (15th century): Patron saint of advertisers, preachers and weavers.

Athena, goddess of war, wisdom and arts, was honoured in Ancient Greece.

21 May

Alexander Pope, poet (1688); Raymond Burr, actor (1917)

Godric (11th century): Gave up his life as a trader to live as a hermit near Durham.

22 May

Richard Wagner, composer (1813); Sir Arthur Conan Doyle, author (1859); Sir Laurence Olivier, actor (1907); George Best, footballer (1946)

Rita of Cascia (15th century): Patron saint of desperate causes and unhappily married women who, having lost her husband and son, became a nun. It is said that she developed the marks of Christ's crown of thorns on her forehead.

23 May

Douglas Fairbanks, actor (1883); Joan Collins, actress (1933)

William of Rochester (12th century): He is said to have been murdered while on pilgrimage to Jerusalem.

Flora, goddess of flowers and the spring, and Venus, goddess of fertility, were honoured today in Ancient Rome with the rose festival, Rosalia.

24 May

Bob Dylan, singer (1941); Priscilla Presley, actress (1945)

David of Scotland (12th century): A king of Scotland and a son of St Margaret (16 November), he was a deeply religious monarch.

The birthday of Artemis, goddess of the hunt, was celebrated in Ancient Greece.

25 May

Ian McKellen, actor (1939); Paul Weller, singer (1958)

Gregory VII (12th century): Elected Pope in 1173, he took on the might of Emperor Henry IV in his attempts to reform the Church, at one point excommunicating him. After Henry besieged Rome, Gregory fled to Salerno and died there. His famous last words were: 'I have loved righteousness and hated iniquity and therefore I die in exile'.
Mary Magdalene of Pazzi (16th century): A Carmelite nun.

The birthday of Apollo, god of the sun, song and music, was celebrated in Ancient Greece.

26 May

Al Jolson, singer (1886); John Wayne, actor (1907); Sir Matt Busby, football manager (1909); Peter Cushing, actor (1913); Stevie Nicks, singer (1948)

Philip Neri (16th century): Founded the Congregation of the Oratory and came to be called 'the apostle of the city of Rome'.

27 May

Isadora Duncan, dancer (1878); Vincent Price, actor (1911); Christopher Lee, actor (1922)

Augustine of Canterbury (6th century): Sent from Rome by Pope Gregory the Great to preach the gospel in England. He eventually became the first Archbishop of Canterbury.
Julius the Veteran (3rd century): A Roman soldier martyred for his faith.

28 May

Gladys Knight, singer (1944); Sondra Locke, actress (1947);
Kylie Minogue, singer (1968)

Bernard of Aosta (11th century): Patron saint of mountaineers.
He built two resthouses for travellers at the top of two
passes. The breed of dog is named after him.

29 May

Bob Hope, actor/comedian (1903); John F. Kennedy, US
President (1917)

Bona of Pisa (12th century): Patron saint of guides and air
hostesses. Aged just fourteen, she set off to see her father
who was fighting in the crusades near Jerusalem. She was
captured by Muslim pirates on the way home and had to be
rescued. This episode did not put her off travelling. During
her life, she took large numbers of pilgrims on the
thousand-mile journey to Compostela. It was said of her
that she was 'full of energy, helpful and unselfish, ready to
reassure with her smile those who were sick'.

30 May

Ferdinand III (13th century): Patron saint of engineers.
Joan of Arc (15th century): Patron saint of France. The famous
'Maid of Orleans', who followed the heavenly voices she had
heard since a young child that told her to save France from
the forces of England and Burgundy. At the age of just
seventeen, she persuaded the French dauphin and
churchmen to allow her to join the army. The French
witnessed several successes before Joan was captured by the
Burgundians and accused of witchcraft. At less than twenty
years old, Joan of Arc was sentenced to death and was
burned at the stake in Rouen. Twenty-five years later, her
conviction was quashed.

31 May

Denholm Elliott, actor (1922); Clint Eastwood, actor (1930); Brooke Shields, actress (1965)

The Visitation of the Blessed Virgin Mary (1st century): Patron saint of mothers, nuns and virgins.

1 June

Marilyn Monroe, actress (1926); Edward Woodward, actor (1930); Robert Powell, actor (1944); Jonathan Pryce, actor (1947); Ron Wood, musician (1947); Alanis Morissette, singer (1974)

Justin (2nd century): Patron saint of philosophers and travellers. Born to a pagan family but converted to Christianity at the age of 33. Having refused to sacrifice to the gods on a visit to Rome, he was taken away, flogged and beheaded.

2 June

Thomas Hardy, author (1840); Sir Edward Elgar, composer (1857); Johnny Weissmuller, actor (1904); Charlie Watts, musician (1941)

Marcellinus and Peter (3rd century): Martyred under the persecution of Diocletian and buried on the Via Labicana 'at the two laurels'.

3 June

Tony Curtis, actor (1925); Suzi Quatro, singer (1950)

Kevin (7th century): Founded a monastery at Glendalough.
Charles Lwanga and companions (19th century): Christians martyred in Uganda under King Mwanga. In one episode, the King had 32 men and boys burned alive, among them Charles Lwanga, the King's head of household. The

youngest was just thirteen years old. Today, their feast day is a public holiday in Uganda.

4 June

Geoffrey Palmer, actor (1927)

Francis Caracciolo (16th century): Founded the Lesser Clerks Regular.

5 June

Boniface (8th century): Born in England, he went to Germany to preach the faith and became Bishop of Mainz. When he was over 70 years of age, he tried to take the gospel to Holland and was killed by heathens as he sat reading in a tent.

6 June

Captain Robert Falcon Scott, explorer (1868); Billie Whitelaw, actress (1932)

Norbert (12th century): Founded the Premonstratensian Canons and was later made Archbishop of Magdeburg.

7 June

'Beau' Brummell, 'dandy' (1778); Paul Gauguin, artist (1848); Virginia McKenna, actress (1931)

Robert of Newminster (12th century): A Cistercian abbot of Newminster, Northumberland.

8 June

Joan Rivers, comedian (1933); Nancy Sinatra, singer (1940)

William of York (12th century): His election as Archbishop of York was vigorously opposed by Cistercian monks. He was probably poisoned by his enemies.

Melania the Elder (4/5th century): Grandmother of Melania the Younger (31 December).

9 June

Patrick Steptoe, physician (1913); Bonnie Tyler, singer (1951); Michael J. Fox, actor (1961); Johnny Depp, actor (1963)

Columba of Iona (6th century): Patron saint of poets.

10 June

Prince Philip, Duke of Edinburgh (1921); Judy Garland, actress (1922); Elizabeth Hurley, model (1966)

11 June

Ben Jonson, poet/dramatist (1572); John Constable, artist (1776); Richard Strauss, composer (1864); Gene Wilder, actor (1935)

Barnabus (1st century): Born in Cyprus and became one of the first converts. He became a companion of St Paul.

12 June

Anne Frank, diarist (1929)

John of Sahagun (15th century): A friar who was probably poisoned in 1479 by a woman unhappy that her lover had been converted.

Zeus, the king of the gods, honoured in Ancient Greece.

13 June

Basil Rathbone, actor (1892); Dorothy L. Sayers, author (1893)

Antony of Padua (13th century): Patron saint of lost articles, the poor and the starving.

14 June

Che Guevara, revolutionary leader (1928); Boy George, singer (1961)

15 June

Nicola Pagett, actress (1945); Simon Callow, actor (1949); Helen Hunt, actress (1963); Courteney Cox, actress (1964)

Vitus (dates unknown): Patron saint of dancers and epileptics.
Germaine of Pibrac (16th century): Born disabled and sickly, she was badly treated by her stepmother, fed on scraps, made to sleep in a stable and sent out every day to tend the sheep. She ignored the taunts that her religious devotion brought. She died at just 22 years old and, soon afterwards, miracles of healing were reported at her grave. It is now a place of pilgrimage.

16 June

Stan Laurel, comedy actor (1890); Erich Segal, actor (1937)

Cyricus and Julitta (3rd century): A mother and son martyred for their faith; Cyricus was just three years old.
John Regis (17th century): A Jesuit home missioner in Auvergne and Languedoc.

17 June

Dean Martin, actor/singer (1917); Barry Manilow, singer (1946)

Harvey (6th century): Little is known about Harvey save that he was blind from birth and, after living as a hermit, he became Abbot of Plouvien. He is known as Herve in Brittany, where he is widely venerated. There was a chapel that claimed to have the cradle in which the baby Harvey was rocked but this was destroyed during the French Revolution.

Sanchia and Teresa (12/13th century): Daughters of King
  Sancho of Portugal. Sanchia founded an abbey of Cistercian
  nuns at Cellas while Teresa founded a similar abbey in
  Lorvao. The sisters are buried side by side at Lorvao.

18 June

Ian Carmichael, actor (1920); Paul Eddington, actor (1927);
Sir Paul McCartney, singer and ex-Beatle (1942); Isabella
Rossellini, actress (1952); Alison Moyet, singer (1961)

Mark and Marcellian (3rd century): According to legend, they
  were twins beheaded for their faith.
Elizabeth of Schonau (12th century): A friend of St Hildegard.

19 June

Wallis Simpson, Duchess of Windsor (1896); Kathleen
Turner, actress (1954)

Bruno of Querfurt (10/11th century): A Polish bishop
  murdered for his faith.
Juliana Falcoieri (14th century): Regarded as the foundress of
  the Servite nuns.

20 June

Errol Flynn, actor (1909); Lionel Richie, singer (1949); Cyndi
Lauper, singer (1953); Nicole Kidman, actress (1967)

Adalbert of Magdeburg (10th century): The first archbishop of
  Magdeburg.

21 June

Jane Russell, actress (1921); Prince William (1982)

Aloysius Gonzaga (16th century): Patron saint of youth. He
  dedicated himself to a religious life and was killed by the
  plague while working among the sick in a hospital in 1591.

22 June

Prunella Scales, actress (1932); Kris Kristofferson, actor/singer (1936); Meryl Streep, actress (1949); Lindsay Wagner, actress (1949)

Alban (2nd century): The first martyr in Britain. He lived in what is now St Albans during a persecution of Christians. He gave shelter to one man fleeing the persecution and was himself arrested and beheaded.

John Fisher (16th century): Opposed King Henry VIII's divorce from Catherine of Aragon and his claim to be head of the Church of England, and was therefore imprisoned in the Tower of London. When Pope Pius III named him a cardinal while he was still a prisoner, it made the King furious. He was charged with treason and sentenced to death. He was so ill that he had to be carried to his execution on a chair.

Thomas More (16th century): Like John Fisher (above) he opposed King Henry VIII's claim to be head of the Church of England. He was imprisoned in the Tower of London and found guilty on a charge of treason. He was beheaded on Tower Hill.

23 June

Edward, Duke of Windsor (1894); Adam Faith, singer (1940)

Joseph Cafasso (19th century): A priest in Turin and teacher of St John Bosco (31 January).

24 June

Mick Fleetwood, singer (1947)

Birthday of John the Baptist (1st century): Patron saint of monks.

Fortuna, the goddess of good luck, was honoured in Ancient Rome.

25 June

George Orwell, author (1903); Carly Simon, singer (1945); George Michael, singer (1963)

Febronia (dates unknown): A beautiful Christian, offered her freedom during Diocletian's persecution if she renounced her faith and married the prefect's son. When she refused, she was tortured, mutilated and battered to death. Many of those who witnessed the martyrdom were converted.

26 June

Laurie Lee, author (1914)

John and Paul (4th century): Martyrs about whom very little is known.

Alexandra Rose Day, instigated by Queen Alexandra, wife of King Edward VII, to mark the fiftieth anniversary of her arrival in England.

27 June

Helen Keller, blind, deaf and mute scholar (1880)

Cyril of Alexandria (5th century): Made a doctor of the Church in 1882.

28 June

Mel Brooks, actor/director (1926); Kathy Bates, actress (1948)

Austell (6th century): Travelled to Brittany with St Meen.

29 June

Peter (1st century): Patron saint of fishermen and popes. The leader of the Apostles. His original name was Simon, but Jesus renamed him Peter, meaning 'rock'. Although he denied Jesus three times, the resurrected Jesus appeared to Peter and told him: 'Feed my lambs. Feed my sheep.' This is what St Peter went on to do, continuing the work started by Jesus until he, too, was crucified, head down at his own request.

Paul (1st century): Patron saint of missionary bishops. He started life as Saul, taking a new name after his dramatic conversion on the road to Damascus (where he had intended to continue his persecution of Christians). After this, he preached the gospel until he was arrested in Rome and beheaded. According to legend, his head bounced three times on the ground and at each place a fountain of water appeared.

30 June

Susan Hayward, actress (1918)

1 July

Charles Laughton, actor (1899); Amy Johnson, aviator (1903); Olivia de Havilland, actress (1916); Dan Aykroyd, actor (1952); Diana, Princess of Wales (1961); Pamela Anderson, actress (1967)

Oliver Plunket (17th century): An archbishop of Armagh and primate of all Ireland. He was arrested and martyred for his faith by being hanged at Tyburn.

Simeon Salus (6th century): Left his life as a hermit to return home to Syria and live among the most wretched people there. He was called 'the crazy' because of his eccentric behaviour, which he supposedly put on so as to really understand the contempt his 'flock' endured. However, it is possible that he was, in fact, sometimes actually off the rails!

2 July

Cheryl Ladd, actress (1951); Jerry Hall, model (1960)

The Visitation of the Blessed Virgin Mary (1st century): Patron saint of mothers, nuns and virgins.

3 July

Tom Stoppard, playwright (1937); Tom Cruise, actor (1962)

Aaron and Julius (dates unknown): Martyrs about whom very little is known.

Thomas the Apostle (1st century): Patron saint of architects and blind people. Known as 'doubting Thomas' because he did not believe in the resurrection until Christ appeared in front of him.

4 July

Gertrude Lawrence, actress (1898); Gina Lollobrigida, actress (1927); Neil Simon, playwright (1927)

Andrew of Crete (7th century): An archbishop of Crete and author of many hymns.

Elizabeth of Portugal (14th century): Married to King Denis of Portugal at the age of twelve, she spent much of her life acting as peacemaker between members of the royal family. As a widow, she retired to a Poor Clare convent she had founded and devoted herself to the service of God and good works. Her last act as peacemaker occurred when her son went to war with her son-in-law, Alfonso of Castile. She died before returning home.

The day of Pax (peace) was celebrated in Ancient Rome.

5 July

Phineas Barnum, showman (1810); Cecil Rhodes, politician (1853)

Antony Mary Zaccaria (16th century): Founded the Congregation of St Paul.

6 July

Bill Haley, singer (1925); Dave Allen, comedian (1936); Sylvester Stallone, actor (1946)

Moninne (6th century): An abbess of Killeavy said to have been veiled by St Patrick.

Maria Goretti (19th century): A devoted, religious young girl who was just twelve years old when she was raped and murdered. Her murderer spent 27 years in prison, during which time he converted to Christianity. On Christmas Day 1937, he and Maria's mother took Holy Communion together.

7 July

Ringo Starr, musician and ex-Beatle (1940); Bill Oddie, comedian (1941); Shelley Duval, actress (1949)

Hedda of Winchester (7th century): The first bishop of Winchester.

8 July

Anjelica Huston, actress (1951)

Juno, goddess of women and marriage, was honoured in Ancient Rome.

9 July

Michael Williams, actor (1935); David Hockney, artist (1937); Tom Hanks, actor (1956); Kelly McGillis, actress (1959); Courtney Love, singer (1964)

Veronica Giuliani (17th century): An abbess of a convent of Capuchin nuns in Umbria.

10 July

Arthur Ashe, tennis player (1943); Virginia Wade, tennis player (1945)

Alexander (3rd century): A martyr about whom little is known.
Antony of the Caves (10/11th century): A hermit and founder of the first Russian monastery.

11 July

Robert the Bruce of Scotland (1274); Yul Brynner, actor (1915); Debbie Harry, singer (1945); Suzanne Vega, singer (1959)

Benedict (6th century): Patron saint of monks. Regarded as the founder of monasticism in the West.
Olga (10th century): The widow of the ruler of Kiev, and one of the first of her line to be converted.

12 July

Bill Cosby, actor (1937)

Veronica (1st century): Supposed to have wiped Jesus's face as he struggled to Calvary. The image of his features is said to have appeared on the cloth she used.
John the Iberian (10th century): Established the Iviron monastery at Mount Athos.
John Gualbert (11th century): Founded a community of monks in Tuscany.

13 July

Harrison Ford, actor (1942)

Silas (1st century): A companion of St Paul.
Henry the Emperor (11th century): A Holy Roman Emperor and strong supporter of Benedictine monasticism.
Francis Solano (16/17th century): A Franciscan friar and missionary, he worked among the Indians in South America.

14 July

Emmeline Pankhurst, champion of women's rights (1858); Terry-Thomas, actor (1911)

Phocas of Sinope (4th century): Patron saint of agricultural workers, gardeners and sailors.

Camillus of Lellis (16th century): Patron saint of hospitals, nurses and sick people. A soldier who dedicated himself to the care of the sick after his conversion.

15 July

Linda Ronstadt, singer (1946)

James of Nisibis (4th century): The first Bishop of Nisibis in Mesopotamia.
Donald (8th century): A Scotsman who, after the death of his wife, formed a religious community together with his nine daughters.
Edith of Polesworth and Edith of Tamworth (10th century): Very little is known about these saints.

Today is St Swithin's Day when, according to tradition, if it rains, it will rain for 40 days.

16 July

Ginger Rogers, actress (1911); Stewart Copeland, musician (1952)

Helier (6th century): Lived as a hermit on Jersey and gave his name to the town of St Helier.
Mary Magdalen Postel (19th century): Founded the Sisters of the Christian Schools of Mercy.

17 July

James Cagney, actor (1899); Donald Sutherland, actor (1934); Diahann Carroll, actress (1935); David Hasselhoff, actor (1952)

Alexis of Rome (dates unknown): Died a homeless beggar. Only after his death was he found to be the son of a Roman noble. He had deserted his fiancée on their wedding day to live a life of poverty.

Kenelm (9th century): A son of the King of Mercia. Some believed that he was killed by his sister after succeeding his father at a young age, others that he died in battle.

18 July

William Makepeace Thackeray, author (1811); Nelson Mandela, statesman (1918); Richard Branson, entrepreneur (1950)

19 July

Macrina the Younger (4th century): Granddaughter of Macrina the Elder (14 January). She became head of a community on the river Iris.

20 July

Sir Edmund Hillary, mountaineer (1919); Diana Rigg, actress (1938); Natalie Wood, actress (1938)

Margaret of Antioch (dates unknown): Patron saint of pregnant women and women in childbirth.
Jerome Emiliani (16th century): Founded the Somaschi clerks regular.

21 July

Ernest Hemingway, author (1899); Robin Williams, actor (1952)

Victor (3rd century): May have been a Roman soldier martyred for his faith.
Laurence of Brindisi (16th century): A Franciscan friar who worked mainly among Jews and Lutherans. He is one of the doctors of the Church.

22 July

Terence Stamp, actor (1939)

Mary Magdalen (1st century): Patron saint of ladies' hairdressers, penitents and repentant prostitutes. One of Christ's disciples and the first person to whom he appeared after the resurrection.

23 July

David Essex, singer (1947)

Cassian (5th century): A priest who founded two monasteries in Marseilles.
Bridget of Sweden (14th century): Patron saint of Sweden.

Neptune, god of the sea, was honoured in Ancient Rome.

24 July

Christina (4th century): A martyr about whom very little is known.
Boris and Gleb (11th century): Murdered by their half-brother, the eldest son of St Vladimir.

25 July

James the Great (1st century): Patron saint of knights, pilgrims, sufferers of rheumatism and soldiers. He was an Apostle and brother to the Apostle St John. He was the first of the Apostles to be martyred and, according to some sources, his accuser repented at the last minute and was beheaded with him.
Christopher (3rd century): Patron saint of travellers. Legend has it that he carried a baby who turned out to be Christ across a river.

26 July

George Bernard Shaw, dramatist (1856); Mick Jagger, singer (1943); Helen Mirren, actress (1946); Susan George, actress (1950)

Joachim and Anne (1st century): The parents of the Blessed Virgin Mary.

27 July

Celestine I (5th century): Elected Pope in 422.
Aurelius and Natalia (9th century): Martyrs beheaded for their faith.
Clement Slovensky (9/10th century): A bishop in Bulgaria.

28 July

Beatrix Potter, author (1866); Jacqueline Kennedy Onassis, wife of John F. Kennedy and Aristotle Onassis (1929)

Samson (6th century): Abbot of a monastery on Caldey Island before moving to Cornwall and then on to Brittany where he established a monastery at Dol.

29 July

Martha (1st century): Patron saint of cooks, hoteliers, homemakers and lay-sisters. The sister of Lazarus and Mary. At her request, Jesus came to her house when her brother died and raised him from the dead.
Olaf (11th century): Patron saint of Norway.

30 July

Emily Brontë, author (1818); Paul Anka, singer (1941); Arnold Schwarzenegger, actor (1947); Kate Bush, singer (1958)

Peter Chrysologus (5th century): A bishop of Ravenna, and one of the doctors of the Church.
Justin de Jacobis (19th century): Worked as a missionary in Ethiopia.

31 July

Wesley Snipes, actor (1962)

Neot (9th century): A monk in Glastonbury before living as a
   hermit in Cornwall.
Ignatius Loyola (16th century): The founder of the Jesuits.

1 August

Jerry Garcia, actor/editor/composer (1942)

Faith, Hope and Charity: Sisters who were supposed to have
   been martyred in Rome under Hadrian.

2 August

Peter O'Toole, actor (1932)

Basil the Blessed (16th century): He used to take goods from
   shops and give them to the poor.

3 August

Tony Bennett, singer (1926); Terry Wogan, presenter (1938);
Martin Sheen, actor (1940)

Peter Eymard (19th century): Founded the Priests of the
   Blessed Sacrament.

4 August

Queen Elizabeth, The Queen Mother (1900); Louis
Armstrong, musician (1901)

Jean-Baptiste Vianney (19th century): Patron saint of parish
   priests. His reputation as a confessor led many to travel
   there and it became a place of pilgrimage.

5 August

Neil Armstrong, astronaut (1930)

Afra (3rd century): Probably a prostitute arrested for her faith during the Diocletian persecution. She was burned to death when she refused to sacrifice to the gods, saying: 'My body has sinned, let it suffer. But I will not corrupt my soul by idolatry." Her mother, who took her daughter's body and gave it a decent burial, was also put to death.

6 August

Alfred, Lord Tennyson, poet (1809); Lucille Ball, comedienne (1911); Robert Mitchum, actor (1917); Frank Finlay, actor (1926); Andy Warhol, artist (1928); Geri Halliwell, singer (1972)

7 August

Cajetan (16th century): Founded the Theatines, the first congregation of clerks regular.

Sixtus II (3rd century): Elected Pope in 257 and martyred within the year on the orders of Emperor Valerian.

8 August

Dustin Hoffman, actor (1937); Keith Carradine, actor (1949)

Dominic (12th century): Patron saint of astronomers.

The festival of Venus, the goddess of fertility, celebrated in Ancient Rome.

9 August

John Dryden, poet (1631); Philip Larkin, poet (1922); Melanie Griffith, actress (1957); Whitney Houston, singer/actress (1963)

Oswald of Northumbria (7th century): Converted to Christianity while in exile and brought missionaries from Iona, led by St Aidan, to Northumbria when he finally secured his kingdom. After only eight years on his throne, however, he was killed in battle fighting the pagan Penda of Mercia. According to the story, as he died he prayed for the souls of those who fell with him.

10 August

Eddie Fisher, singer (1928); Rosanna Arquette, actress (1959); Antonio Banderas, actor (1960)

Laurence (3rd century): Patron saint of cooks, deacons and firefighters. He was ordered to hand over the valuables of the city of Rome and so gathered together the poor and the sick and presented them. According to tradition, he was put to death by being roasted on a grid but it is more likely that he was beheaded.

11 August

Enid Blyton, author (1897)

Susanna (3rd century): Supposed to be the beautiful niece of the Bishop of Rome who was beheaded for rejecting marriage to one of Diocletian's partners.
Clare (13th century): Patron saint of television. The founder of the Poor Clare Order of nuns.

12 August

George Hamilton, actor (1939); Mark Knopfler, musician (1949)

13 August

John Logie Baird, inventor of the television (1888); Alfred Hitchcock, director (1899)

Maximus the Confessor (7th century): A theologian who was flogged and lost his hand and tongue for his defiance of Emperor Constans II.

14 August

Steve Martin, actor (1945)

Maximilian Kolbe (20th century): A Franciscan whose community at Teresin sheltered many refugees, mostly Jews, after German troops invaded Poland. He was sent to Auschwitz in 1941 where he put himself forward in place of a man with a family who had been chosen to die in retaliation for an escape.

15 August

Napoleon Bonaparte (1769); Sir Walter Scott, novelist (1771)

The Assumption of the Blessed Virgin Mary (1st century): Patron saint of mothers, nuns and virgins.
Tarsicius (3rd century): Patron saint of altar servers.

The festival of Vesta, goddess of the hearth, celebrated in Ancient Rome.

16 August

Ted Hughes, poet (1930); Madonna, singer/actress (1958)

Stephen of Hungary (11th century): The first King of Hungary, he worked tirelessly to convert his people to Christianity.
Roch (14th century): Patron saint of invalids and prisoners.

17 August

Mae West, actress (1892); George Melly, singer (1926); Robert de Niro, actor (1943); Belinda Carlisle, singer (1958); Sean Penn, actor (1960)

Hyacinth of Cracow (13th century): A Domincan friar who worked in Cracow.

The festival of Diana, goddess of the moon and hunting, was celebrated in Ancient Rome.

18 August

Robert Redford, actor (1937); Patrick Swayze, actor (1954)

Florus and Laurus (dates unknown): Twin brothers, both
stonemasons. They were building a heathen temple when
they were converted to Christianity and so handed the
building over to Christians instead. For this, they were
killed by being drowned in a well.
Helena (3rd century): The mother of Constantine the Great.
She was converted to Christianity and worked to spread the
word for the rest of her life.

19 August

Gabrielle 'Coco' Chanel (1883); Bill Clinton, US President
(1945)

John Eudes (17th century): Founded the Eudists priests and the
Sisters of Our Lady of Charity and Refuge.

20 August

Robert Plant, singer (1948)

Bernard of Clairvaux (12th century): Patron saint of beekeepers
and the founder of the Cistercian Order.

21 August

Princess Margaret (1930); Kenny Rogers, singer (1938)

Abraham of Smolensk (13th century): Became abbot of a
monastery in Smolensk.
Pius X (19th century): Elected Pope in 1903.

22 August

Joseph Strauss, composer (1827); Honor Blackman, actress
(1926); Tori Amos, singer (1963)

23 August

Gene Kelly, actor (1912); Keith Moon, musician (1947); Shelley Long, actress (1949); River Phoenix, actor (1970)

Philip Benizi (13th century): Head of the Servite friars.
Rose of Lima (16th century): Patron saint of florists and South America.

24 August

Bartholomew (1st century): Patron saint of shoemakers and tanners. As one of the Apostles he was martyred by being flayed alive and beheaded.
Emily de Vialar (19th century): Founded the Sisters of St Joseph of the Apparition.
Joan Thouret (19th century): Founded the Sisters of Charity.

25 August

Leonard Bernstein, composer (1918); Sean Connery, actor (1930); Frederick Forsyth, author (1938); Elvis Costello, singer (1954)

Genesius of Arles (3rd century): Patron saint of actors and secretaries.
Gregory of Utrecht (8th century): A missionary and friend of St Boniface of Crediton.
Louis IX of France (13th century): Patron saint of France and kings.
Joseph Calasanz (17th century): Founded the Clerks Regular of the Religious Schools and set up free schools in Italy, Bohemia and Poland.

26 August

Macaulay Culkin, actor (1980)

Elizabeth Bichier des Ages (19th century): Founded the Daughters of the Cross, a community dedicated to the teaching of girls and caring for the sick.

27 August

Mother Teresa of Calcutta (1910); Barbara Bach, actress (1947)

Monica (4th century): The mother of St Augustine of Hippo (28 August).

28 August

David Soul, actor/singer (1944); Emma Samms, actress (1960)

Augustine of Hippo (5th century): One of the four Latin doctors of the Church.
Julian of Brioude (3rd century): One of the early Christians martyred for their faith.

29 August

Ingrid Bergman, actress (1915); Richard Attenborough, actor/director (1923); Elliott Gould, actor (1938); Lenny Henry, comedian/actor (1959); Michael Jackson, singer (1958)

Sebbi (7th century): Uncle of King Sighere of the East Saxons and martyred for his faith.

30 August

Felix and Adauctus (3rd century): Martyred for their faith in Rome.

31 August

James Coburn, actor (1928); Van Morrison, singer (1945); Richard Gere, actor (1949)

Aidan (7th century): Known as the Apostle of Northumberland, he founded the monastery at Lindisfarne.
Raymund Nonnatus (13th century): Said to have volunteered himself as a slave in Algiers to save others.

1 September

Barry Gibb, singer (1946); Gloria Estefan, singer (1957)

Giles (7th century): Patron saint of mothers, the crippled, hermits, lepers and horses.

2 September

Keanu Reeves, actor (1964)

3 September

Pauline Collins, actress (1940); Charlie Sheen, actor (1965)

Gregory the Great (6th century): Patron saint of musicians, popes and singers. Elected Pope in 590.

4 September

Henry Ford II, automobile maker (1917); Tom Watson, golfer (1949); Ione Skye, actress (1970)

5 September

Raquel Welch, actress (1940); Freddie Mercury, singer (1946)

Laurence Giustiniani (15th century): A bishop of Castello before becoming patriarch of Venice.

6 September

Britt Ekland, actress (1942)

Bee (7th century): Very little is known about her except that she was probably an Irish nun after whom the village of Saint Bees in Cumbria is named.

7 September

Anthony Quayle, actor (1913); Buddy Holly, singer (1936); Chrissie Hynde, singer (1952)

Cloud (6th century): A Frankish prince who, as an adult, turned his back on the throne and was instead ordained a priest.

8 September

Harry Secombe, comedian (1921); Peter Sellers, actor/comedian (1925); Patsy Cline, singer (1932)

Adrian (3rd century): An imperial officer who converted to Christianity after watching the persecution of Christians. After his execution, Adrian's body was thrown on to a fire but a rain-storm put it out before the bodies burned. His wife Natalia saved one of his hands and kept it with her until her death.

The Birthday of the Blessed Virgin Mary.

9 September

Otis Redding, singer/songwriter (1941); Hugh Grant, actor (1960)

Isaac the Great (5th century): The head of the Armenian church.
Joseph of Volokolamsk (15/16th century): Abbot of Borovsk before he founded a new community near Volokolamsk.
Peter Claver (17th century): Patron saint of people of African origin and race relations.

10 September

Arnold Palmer, golfer (1929); Amy Irving, actress (1953)

Finnian of Moville (6th century): Founded a community at Moville in Ireland, which became a famous school.
Nicholas of Tolentino (13th century): A friar in Tolentino to whom several miracles were attributed.

11 September

Protus and Hyacinth (dates unknown): Both were martyred for their faith, and it is possible that they were brothers.

12 September

Maurice Chevalier, actor (1888); Barry White, singer (1944)

Guy of Anderlecht (10/11th century): Having lost both his money and his job, he spent several years visiting shrines far and wide.

13 September

Roald Dahl, author (1916); Jacqueline Bisset, actress (1944)

John Chrysostom (4th century): Patron saint of preachers. Also known as 'John of the Golden Mouth'.

14 September

Sam Neill, actor (1947)

15 September

Agatha Christie, author (1890); Margaret Lockwood, actress (1916); Tommy Lee Jones, actor (1946); Prince Henry, 'Harry' (1984)

Catherine of Genoa (15th century): Having converted to Christianity, she worked among the sick, becoming matron of the Pammatone hospital in Genoa where she cared for those affected by the plague.

16 September

Lauren Bacall, actress (1924); Peter Falk, actor (1927)

Cornelius (3rd century): Ordained Pope in 251 and forced into exile due to conflicts within the Church itself.

Cyprian (3rd century): Refused to sacrifice to the Roman gods and was beheaded in Carthage.

Edith (10th century): Spent most of her life at a nunnery near Salisbury.

Ludmilla (10th century): Grandmother to St (Good King) Wenceslas. A Christian, she was murdered by Wenceslas's mother, who resented the influence she had over her grandson.

17 September

Anne Bancroft, actress (1931)

Lambert (7th century): Patron saint of children and Liege, Belgium.

Columba of Cordoba (9th century): Living as a nun when her community was dispersed by the Moors. She was beheaded after she denounced Muhammad as a false prophet.

Robert Bellamarmine (16th century): A theologian who eventually became Archbishop of Capua and one of the doctors of the Church.

18 September

Samuel Johnson, writer (1709); Greta Garbo, actress (1905)

Joseph of Copertino (17th century): Patron saint of astronauts, air passengers and aviators.

19 September

Derek Nimmo, comedian/actor (1932); Zandra Rhodes, fashion designer (1940); Jeremy Irons, actor (1948)

Theodore of Canterbury (7th century): As Archbishop of Canterbury, he organised the first council of the English Church in 672 and is credited with establishing the organisation of the Church of England.

Emily de Rodat (19th century): A foundress, who was described by a contemporary as 'a saint, but a headstrong saint'.

20 September

John Dankworth, musician (1927); Sophia Loren, actress (1934)

Eustace (dates unknown): Patron saint of hunters.

21 September

Larry Hagman, actor (1931); Shirley Conran, author (1932); Stephen King, author (1947)

Matthew (1st century): Patron saint of accountants, bankers, book-keepers and tax-collectors. A tax-collector before becoming one of the Apostles.

22 September

Thomas of Villanova (15th century): An Augustinian friar who became prior of Salamanca before accepting the post of archbishop.

23 September

Mickey Rooney, actor (1920); Ray Charles, singer (1930); Julio Iglesias, singer (1943); Bruce Springsteen, singer (1949)

Thecla of Iconium (1st century): Said to have been converted by St Paul, she survived various attempts to kill her before moving to live in a cave.

24 September

Jim Henson, creator of the Muppets (1936); Linda McCartney, photographer/singer (1941)

Gerard Sagredo (11th century): The first Bishop of Csanad.

25 September

Michael Douglas, actor (1944); Christopher Reeve, actor (1952); Heather Locklear, actress (1961); Will Smith, actor/singer (1968)

Finbar (6th century): Patron saint of Cork, Ireland, and Barra, Outer Hebrides.

Vincent Strambi (18th century): Very little is known about him except that he was a bishop in Italy.

Francis of Camporosso (19th century): A laybrother with the Capuchin Franciscans.

26 September

George Gershwin, composer (1898); Bryan Ferry, singer (1945); Olivia Newton-John, singer/actress (1948)

Cosmas and Damian (dates unknown): Patron saints of doctors, barbers and surgeons. According to legend, they were twin brothers who practised medicine without charging. They were martyred during a persecution of Christians.

Colman of Lann Elo (6/7th century): Founded a monastery at Lann Elo in Meath. It is said that he was so pleased with his intellect that he suffered the punishment of temporary memory loss.

27 September

Alvin Stardust, singer (1942); Meatloaf, singer (1947); Barbara Dickson, singer (1948)

Vincent de Paul (17th century): Patron saint of charities, who founded the Congregation of the Mission, a society of missionary priests.

28 September

Peter Finch, actor (1916); Brigitte Bardot, actress (1934); Gwyneth Paltrow, actress (1973)

Wenceslas (10th century): Patron saint of Czechoslovakia. He tried to promote Christianity within his country and was murdered by his brother in 929.

29 September

Horatio Nelson, admiral (1758); Elizabeth Gaskell, author (1810); Trevor Howard, actor (1916); Jerry Lee Lewis, singer (1935)

Michael, Gabriel and Raphael: Archangels.

30 September

Deborah Kerr, actress (1921); Truman Capote, author (1924); Angie Dickinson, actress (1931); Johnny Mathis, singer (1935)

Sophia (dates unknown): The mother of St Faith (1 August) who was probably martyred for her faith.
Jerome (4th century): Patron saint of archaeologists, librarians and scholars.

1 October

Walter Matthau, actor (1920); George Peppard, actor (1928); Richard Harris, actor (1932); Julie Andrews, actress/singer (1935)

Gregory the Enlightener (4th century): Brought Christianity to Armenia.
Theresa of Lisieux (19th century): Patron saint of missionaries. She lived as a Carmelite nun before dying of tuberculosis, aged 24. Before she died, she wrote *Story of a Soul*, the famous story about her life.

2 October

Groucho Marx, comedian/actor (1890); Bud Abbott, comedian/actor (1896); Graham Greene, author (1904); Don McLean, singer (1945); Sting, singer (1951)

Guardian angels

3 October

Michael Horden, actor (1911); James Herriott, vet/author (1916); Eddie Cochran, singer (1938)

Garard of Brogne (10th century): Abbot of a monastery which he had built in Brogne. He then went on to reform many other Benedictine monasteries.

Thomas of Hereford (13th century): Chancellor of Oxford University and England before being elected Bishop of Hereford. After his death, several miracles were reported at his tomb.

4 October

Buster Keaton, comedian/actor (1895); Charlton Heston, actor (1924); Susan Sarandon, actress (1946)

Francis of Assisi (12th century): Patron saint of animals, birds and ecologists. Founded the Friars Minor and suffered the marks of the stigmata not long before his death.

Ceres, Roman goddess of the harvest, was honoured in Ancient Rome.

5 October

Donald Pleasance, actor (1919); Bob Geldof, singer (1954); Kate Winslet, actress (1975)

Placid (6th century): A monk at the monastery at Subiaco, who was reportedly miraculously saved from drowning by St Maurus.

6 October

Carole Lombard, actress (1909)

Faith (3rd century): Very little is known about her except that she was probably martyred for her faith in Aquitaine.

Bruno (11th century): Founded the Carthusian monks.

7 October

Desmond Tutu, South African archbishop (1931); Clive James, presenter/author (1939)

Osyth (7th century): Wife to the king of the East Saxons who founded a nunnery at Chich.

8 October

Paul Hogan, actor (1939); Chevy Chase, actor (1943); Sigourney Weaver, actress (1949); Matt Damon, actor (1970)

Keyne (6th century): Patron saint of St Keyne, Cornwall.

9 October

Alastair Sim, actor (1900); Donald Sinden, actor (1923); Brian Blessed, actor/author (1937); John Lennon, singer and ex-Beatle (1940)

Denis (3rd century): Patron saint of France.
Luis Bertran (16th century): Patron saint of Columbia.
John Leonardi (16th century): Founded the Order of the Mother of God.

10 October

Harold Pinter, playwright (1930); Charles Dance, actor (1946)

Gereon (3rd century): Patron saint of headache sufferers.
Daniel and companions (13th century): Franciscan friars martyred for their faith in Morocco.
Francis Borgia (16th century): A member of the notorious Borgia family who became a Jesuit priest, working in Spain and Portugal. His reputation spread, and he was eventually made head of the order.

11 October

Eleanor Roosevelt, US President's wife (1884); Daryl Hall, singer (1949)

Canice (6th century): Worked to spread the word in Scotland before returning to his native Ireland and founding a monastery in Ossory and possibly Kilkenny.
Alexander Sauli (16th century): A bishop in Corsica and Italy.

12 October

Magnus Magnusson, quizmaster (1929); Luciano Pavarotti, opera singer (1935)

Wilfred (7th century): A bishop who worked tirelessly to convert the South Saxons during a period of exile from the north.

13 October

Lillie Langtry, actress (1852); Paul Simon, singer (1941); Marie Osmond, singer (1959)

Gerald of Aurillac (9th century): A deeply religious count of Aurillac who founded a monastery there.
Edward the Confessor (10th century): A deeply religious and peaceful king of England.

14 October

Bud Flanagan, comedian (1896); Roger Moore, actor (1927); Cliff Richard, singer (1940); Justin Hayward, singer (1946)

Callistus (3rd century): Became Pope in 217 and was eventually killed, probably by a mob.

15 October

Tecla (8th century): An abbess of Kitzingen.

Teresa of Avila (16th century): A Carmelite nun, recognised as one of the doctors of the Church. She founded St Joseph's convent at Avila, the first of seventeen in Spain.

16 October

Oscar Wilde, author (1854); Max Bygraves, singer (1922); Angela Lansbury, actress (1925); Simon Ward, actor (1940)

Garard Majella (18th century): Patron saint of laybrothers. He was supposed to be able to read minds and was said to be seen in two places at the same time.
Margaret Mary Alacoque (17th century): A nun who experienced several visions of Christ.
Margaret d'Youville (18th century): The first native Canadian to be canonised.

17 October

Rita Hayworth, actress (1918); Montgomery Clift, actor (1920)

Ignatius of Antioch (1st century): The second Bishop of Antioch after St Peter, he was sentenced to be thrown to the wild beasts in Rome.

18 October

Chuck Berry, singer (1926); George C. Scott, actor (1927)

Luke (1st century): Patron saint of artists, doctors and surgeons. He wrote the Gospel of St Luke and the Acts of the Apostles.

19 October

Michael Gambon, actor (1940); Evander Holyfield, boxer (1962)

John of Rila (10th century): Founded the monastery of Rila.
Peter of Alcantara (16th century): A reforming Franciscan friar.

Jean de Brebeuf and Isaac Jogues (17th century): Among the first Jesuits sent to Canada to teach the faith to the pagans. They were separately captured by Indians and subjected to some of the worst torture. Isaac Jogues died in October 1647, his head cut off and his body thrown into the Mohawk river. John de Brebeuf died in March 1648.

Paul of the Cross (18th century): Founded the Passionist missioners.

20 October

Christopher Wren, architect (1632); Anna Neagle, actress (1904)

Andrew of Crete (8th century): Martyred in Constantinople.

21 October

Manfred Mann, musician (1940); Carrie Fisher, actress (1956)

Ursula (4th century): Patron saint of schoolgirls. She was martyred for her faith with ten companions, although their legend grew until it was said that she died with eleven thousand!

John of Bridlington (14th century): Prior of the Austin canons.

22 October

Joan Fontaine, actress (1917); Doris Lessing, author (1919); Derek Jacobi, actor (1938); Catherine Deneuve, actress (1943); Jeff Goldblum, actor (1952)

Philip of Heraclea (3rd century): Bishop of Heraclea at the time of Diocletian's persecution. He was arrested and, when he refused to renounce his faith, was dragged to jail by his feet. After seven months, he was interrogated again and beaten before being sentenced to death. He was so badly wounded that he had to be carried to the stake.

23 October

Diana Dors, actress (1931)

John of Capistrano (15th century): Patron saint of jurists.

24 October

Bill Wyman, musician (1936); Kevin Kline, actor (1948)

Felix of Thibiuca (3rd century): Martyred for his faith at
  Carthage.
Antony Claret (19th century): Founded the Claretian
  Missionaries and became chaplain to Queen Isabella of
  Spain. He went into exile with her in 1868 and never
  returned.

25 October

Pablo Picasso, artist (1881)

Chrysanthus and Daria (dates unknown): Martyred by being
  buried alive in a sandpit outside Rome.
Crispin and Crispinian (3rd century): Patron saints of leather
  workers and shoemakers.
John of Beverley (8th century): Bishop of Hexham and York and
  founded a religious house at Beverley.

26 October

Bob Hoskins, actor (1942); Jaclyn Smith, actress (1947)

27 October

Dylan Thomas, poet (1914); Sylvia Plath, poet (1932); John
Cleese, comedian (1939); Simon Le Bon, singer (1958)

28 October

Evelyn Waugh, author (1903); Francis Bacon, artist (1909);
Cleo Laine, singer (1927); Joan Plowright, actress (1929);

Hank Marvin, musician (1942); Bill Gates, entrepreneur (1955); Julia Roberts, actress (1967)

Simon (1st century): Patron saint of fishermen. The Apostle known as the 'Zealot'.
Jude (1st century): Patron saint of hopeless causes. An Apostle.

29 October

Robert Hardy, actor (1925); Richard Dreyfuss, actor (1947); Kate Jackson, actress (1948); Winona Ryder, actress (1971)

Colman of Kilmacduagh (7th century): An abbot-bishop of Kilmacduagh.

30 October

Ezra Pound, poet (1885); Henry Winkler, actor (1945)

Marcellus the Centurion (3rd century): Martyred for his faith at Tangiers.

31 October

John Keats, poet (1795); Michael Landon, actor (1937)

Foillan (7th century): Founded a monastery at Fosses in France and was murdered by robbers.

1 November

All Saints' Day.

The feast of Pomona, goddess of fruit, celebrated in Ancient Rome.

2 November

Burt Lancaster, actor (1913); Stefanie Powers, actress (1942)

All Souls' Day.

3 November

Charles Bronson, actor (1922); Lulu, singer (1948); Roseanne Barr, actress (1952); Adam Ant, singer (1954); Dolph Lundgren, actor (1959)

Hubert (8th century): Bishop of Tongres-Maestricht.
Malachy (12th century): Founded the first Cistercian house in Ireland.
Martin de Porres (17th century): Patron saint of the poor, and of work for inter-racial harmony.

4 November

Loretta Swit, actress (1937); Lena Zavaroni, singer (1963)

Charles Borromeo (16th century): Patron saint of bishops.

5 November

Vivien Leigh, actress (1913); Art Garfunkel, singer (1941); Bryan Adams, singer (1959); Tatum O'Neal, actress (1963)

Zachary and Elizabeth (1st century): The parents of John the Baptist.

6 November

Sally Field, actress (1946)

Leonard (6th century): Patron saint of prisoners. Probably a hermit and founder of a monastery near Limoges.

7 November

Marie Curie, scientist (1867); Joan Sutherland, actress (1926); Jean Shrimpton, model (1942)

Engelbert (13th century): Archbishop of Cologne.

8 November

Margaret Mitchell, author (1900); Christiaan Barnard, surgeon (1922)

Cybi (6th century): A missionary monk.
Geoffrey of Amiens (11/12th century): A reforming Bishop of Amiens.

9 November

Katharine Hepburn, actress (1909)

Theodore (4th century): Probably a Roman soldier martyred for his faith by being thrown into a furnace.

10 November

Martin Luther, Protestant reformer (1483); William Hogarth, artist (1697); Richard Burton, actor (1925); Roy Scheider, actor (1932)

Leo the Great (5th century): Elected Pope in 440 and one of the doctors of the Church.
Andrew Avellino (16th century): A priest with the Theatine clerks regular in Naples who established a further Theatine house in Milan.

11 November

June Whitfield, actress (1925); Demi Moore, actress (1962); Leonardo DiCaprio, actor (1974)

Martin of Tours (4th century): Patron saint of beggars. He is regarded as the father of French monasticism.
Theodore the Studite (8th century): Abbot of the famous Studite monastery in Constantinople.
Bartholomew of Grottaferrata (11th century): Abbot of the Greek monastery at Grottaferrata.

12 November

Grace Kelly, actress (1929); Neil Young, singer (1945)

Josaphat (17th century): Patron saint of ecumenics.

Jupiter, god of the sky, Minerva, goddess of household arts, and Juno, goddess of women and marriage, were all honoured in Ancient Rome.

13 November

Robert Louis Stevenson, author (1850); Whoopi Goldberg, actress (1949)

Brice (5th century): A bishop of Tours.
Nicholas I (9th century): Elected Pope in 858.
Homobonus (12th century): Patron saint of clothworkers, merchants and tailors.
Frances Cabrini (19/20th century): Patron saint of emigrants. The first citizen of the United States to be canonised.

14 November

Claude Monet, artist (1840); Charles, Prince of Wales (1948)

Laurence O'Toole (12th century): An archbishop of Dublin.
Gregory Palamas (14th century): A theologian and, after a period of excommunication for his beliefs, archbishop of Salonika.

15 November

Aneurin Bevan, statesman (1897); Petula Clark, singer (1932)

Leopold of Austria (11/12th century): A deeply religious ruler of Austria.
Albert the Great (13th century): Patron saint of medical technicians and scientists.

16 November

Griff Rhys Jones, comedian (1953); Frank Bruno, boxer (1961)

Margaret of Scotland (11th century): The deeply religious wife of King Malcolm III and mother of St David.
Edmund of Abingdon (13th century): An archbishop of Canterbury.

17 November

Rock Hudson, actor (1925); Peter Cook, comedian (1937); Lauren Hutton, actress (1942); Danny DeVito, actor (1944)

Gregory the Wonderworker (3rd century): A bishop of Neocaesarea who, it is said, was the first person to whom a vision of the Virgin Mary appeared.
Gregory of Tours (6th century): A historian and bishop of Tours.
Hilda (7th century): Abbess of a convent in Hartlepool and founder of a double monastery, for men and women, at Whitby.
Elizabeth of Hungary (13th century): Patron saint of charitable societies and nurses.

18 November

Linda Evans, actress (1942); Kim Wilde, singer (1960)

Mawes (5th century): Patron saint of Mawes, Cornwall.
Odo of Cluny (10th century): The second abbot of Cluny.

19 November

Meg Ryan, actress (1961); Jodie Foster, actress (1962)

John de Castillo (17th century): Martyred for his faith in Paraguay.

20 November

Bo Derek, actress (1956)

Edmund (9th century): King of the East Angles killed defending his realm from the heathen Danes. According to one story he was tied to a tree and shot with arrows.

21 November

Goldie Hawn, actress (1945); Mariel Hemingway, actress (1961)

22 November

Mary Ann Evans (George Eliot), author (1819); Benjamin Britten, composer (1913); Robert Vaughn, actor (1932); Terry Gilliam, comedian/film director (1940); Tom Conti, actor (1941); Jamie Lee Curtis, actress (1958)

Cecilia (3rd century): Patron saint of musicians and singers. According to legend, she told her pagan husband on their wedding day that she had given her virginity to God. He and his brother were converted to Christianity only to be arrested and put to death for their faith. Cecilia, too, was arrested and sentenced to be stifled to death in her bathroom. When this didn't work, a soldier tried to behead her but failed in his task and she died three days later.

23 November

William H. Bonney, 'Billy the Kid', outlaw (1859); Harpo Marx, comedy actor (1888)

Felicity (dates unknown): Little reliable information is known about her, although she may have been martyred for her faith, possibly after her seven sons had been killed.
Clement (1st century): Patron saint of lighthouse-keepers. The third Pope after St Peter to head the Church.

Alexander Nevski (13th century): A Russian grand prince who upheld Christianity in his lands.

24 November

Scott Joplin, musician (1868); Billy Connolly, comedian/actor (1942)

Colman of Cloyne (6th century): Founded the church of Cloyne.
Flora and Mary (9th century): Lived during the persecution in Spain. Flora was denounced as a Christian by her brother, arrested, whipped and returned to his keeping. She escaped and, with Mary, gave herself up. They were beheaded together.

25 November

Catherine of Alexandria (4th century): Patron saint of young women, philosophers and students. The famous Catherine of the 'catherine wheel'! When she refused to marry the Emperor of Alexandria and denounce her faith, she was tortured. This included being put on a spiked wheel, but this broke into pieces. She was eventually beheaded.

26 November

Tina Turner, singer (1939)

Peter of Alexandria (3/4th century): A bishop of Alexandria martyred for his faith.
John Berchmans (17th century): A Jesuit.
Leonard of Port Maurice (18th century): Patron saint of missionaries.

27 November

Ernie Wise, comedian (1925); Bruce Lee, actor (1940); John Alderton, actor (1940); Jimi Hendrix, musician (1942)

Gregory of Sinai (14th century): Founded a monastery on Mount Paroria on the Black Sea.

28 November

William Blake, poet/artist (1757); Nancy Mitford, author (1904)

Stephen the Younger (8th century): Martyred for his faith by being battered to death.

James of the Marches (15th century): A mission preacher who worked closely with St John of Capistrano (23 October).

Catherine Laboure (19th century): A Sister of Charity of St Vincent de Paul. She had several visions of the Virgin Mary.

29 November

Louisa May Alcott, author (1832); Busby Berkeley, film director (1895)

30 November

Samuel Langhorne Clemens (Mark Twain), author (1835); Winston Churchill, statesman (1874); Billy Idol, singer (1955)

Andrew (1st century): Patron saint of fishermen, Scotland and Russia. One of the Apostles. Originally a disciple of John the Baptist, he became a follower of Christ.

1 December

Matt Monro, singer (1930); Woody Allen, actor/director (1935); Richard Pryor, actor (1940); Bette Midler, singer/actress (1945)

2 December

Maria Callas, singer (1923)

Viviana of Rome (4th century): A martyr about whom very little is known.

3 December

Andy Williams, singer (1930); Ozzy Osbourne, singer (1948); Mel Smith, comedian (1952)

Francis Xavier (16th century): Patron saint of missionaries.

Rhea and Cybele were honoured in Ancient Greece.

4 December

Deanna Durbin, actress (1921); Ronnie Corbett, comedian (1930); Jeff Bridges, actor (1949); Pamela Stephenson, comedienne/psychologist (1950)

Barbara (dates unknown): Patron saint of architects, gunners, miners and the dying.
John Damascene (8th century): A theologian and monk. He was declared a doctor of the Church in 1890.
Osmund (11th century): Patron saint of the paralysed and toothache sufferers.

5 December

Walt Disney, film producer (1901); Little Richard, singer (1935)

Crispina of Tagora (3rd century): Martyred for her faith.

Poseidon, god of the sea, was honoured in Ancient Greece.

6 December

Nicholas (4th century): Patron saint of children, apothecaries, fishermen, merchants, pawnbrokers, perfumiers and sailors. The origin of 'Father Christmas'.
Abraham of Kratia (6th century): An abbot and later Bishop of Kratia.

7 December

Ambrose (4th century): Patron saint of beekeepers and
  bishops. One of the four Latin doctors of the Church.

8 December

Sammy Davis Jr, actor/singer (1925); David Carradine, actor
(1936); James Galway, musician (1939); Jim Morrison, singer
(1943); Kim Basinger, actress (1953); Sinead O'Connor, singer
(1966)

Budoc (6th century): Patron saint of Budock and Budoc Vean,
  Cornwall, and St Budeaux, Devon.

The Immaculate Conception of the Blessed Virgin Mary.

9 December

Kirk Douglas, actor (1916); Judi Dench, actress (1934); Beau
Bridges, actor (1941); Joan Armatrading, singer (1950); John
Malkovich, actor (1953); Donny Osmond, singer (1957)

Peter Fourier (16/17th century): Founded the Augustinian
  Canonesses of Our Lady, an order of nuns dedicated to
  teaching.

10 December

Emily Dickinson, poet (1830); Dorothy Lamour, actress
(1914); Kenneth Branagh, actor/director (1960)

Eulalia of Merida (3rd century): A martyr about whom little is
  known.

11 December

Christina Onassis, heiress (1950); Jermaine Jackson, singer
(1954)

Daniel the Stylite (5th century): After the death of Simeon the
Stylite (5 January), he decided to follow his path.
Accordingly, he lived for 33 years at the top of two pillars.

12 December

Frank Sinatra, singer (1915); Dionne Warwick, singer (1941)

Finnian of Clonard (6th century): Abbot of the monastery he
established in Meath and particularly influential in
developing stricter monasticism in Ireland.

Jane Frances de Chantal (17th century): Established many
houses of the Order of Visitation. Described by St Vincent
de Paul as 'one of the holiest people I have ever met on this
earth'.

13 December

Dick van Dyke, actor (1925); Christopher Plummer, actor
(1927); Jim Davidson, comedian (1954)

Lucy (3rd century): Patron saint of the visually impaired.

14 December

Lee Remick, actress (1935)

John of the Cross (16th century): Patron saint of mystics and
poets.

15 December

Don Johnson, actor (1949)

Mary de Rosa (19th century): Founded the Handmaids of
Charity of Brescia.

16 December

Jane Austen, author (1775); Noël Coward, playwright (1899)

Adelaide (10th century): The second wife of Otto the Great. St Odilo described her as 'a marvel of beauty and goodness'.

17 December

Tommy Steele, singer/actor (1936)

Olympias (4th century): A deaconess in Constantinople.

Saturn was honoured in Ancient Rome.

18 December

Betty Grable, actress (1916); Keith Richards, musician (1943); Steven Spielberg, director (1947); Brad Pitt, actor (1964)

Winebald (8th century): The first abbot of the adjoining monasteries at Heidenheim.

19 December

Ralph Richardson, actor (1902); Edith Piaf, singer (1915); Gordon Jackson, actor (1923)

Sabine was honoured in Ancient Rome.

20 December

Uri Geller, psychic (1946); Jenny Agutter, actress (1952)

21 December

Jane Fonda, actress (1937); Frank Zappa, musician (1940); Kiefer Sutherland, actor (1967)

Peter Canisius (16th century): A Jesuit missioner working particularly in southern Germany, Austria and Bohemia.

22 December

Peggy Ashcroft, actress (1907); Noel Edmonds, presenter (1948); Maurice and Robin Gibb, singers (1949); Ralph Fiennes, actor (1962)

23 December

John of Kenty (15th century): Patron saint of university
lecturers.

24 December

Howard Hughes, film producer/aviator (1905); Ava Gardner,
actress (1922)

25 December

Isaac Newton, scientist (1642); Kenny Everett, comedian
(1944); Sissy Spacek, actress (1949); Annie Lennox, singer
(1954)

Eugenia (dates unknown): Supposed to have dressed as a man
and become abbot of a monastery in Egypt. Accused of
some serious misconduct, she finally admitted her true sex
and was cleared. She was eventually beheaded in Rome for
her faith.
Anastasia (3rd century): A martyr about whom little is known.

26 December

Stephen (1st century): Patron saint of bricklayers, deacons and
headache sufferers.

27 December

Marlene Dietrich, actress (1901); Gérard Depardieu, actor
(1948)

John the Evangelist (1st century): Patron saint of publishers,
theologians and writers.

28 December

Maggie Smith, actress (1934); Denzel Washington, actor
(1954); Nigel Kennedy, violinist (1956)

Day of the Holy Innocents (1st century).

29 December

Mary Tyler Moore, comedienne/TV producer (1937); Jon Voight, actor (1938); Marianne Faithfull, singer (1946); Ted Danson, actor (1947)

Thomas of Canterbury (12th century): Famously fell out with King Henry II after being appointed Archbishop of Canterbury and was murdered by four of the king's knights in the cathedral.

30 December

Rudyard Kipling, author (1865); Davy Jones, singer (1945); Tracey Ullman, comedienne (1959)

Egwin (8th century): A bishop of Worcester and founder of a monastery at Evesham. He is said to have had a vision of the Virgin Mary near the Avon.

31 December

John Denver, singer (1943); Ben Kingsley, actor (1943); Barbara Carrera, actress (1945); Patti Smith, singer (1946); Donna Summer, singer (1948); Val Kilmer, actor (1959)

Sylvester (4th century): Elected Pope in 313.
Melania the Younger (4/5th century): Granddaughter of St Melania the Elder (8 June). After the death of her husband, she founded a community on the Mount of Olives.

3. A TO Z OF GIRLS' NAMES

A

Aamor: A Breton name, derived from the Greek for 'sun', and so meaning 'sunbeam'.

Abigail: From the Hebrew meaning 'my father rejoices'. In the Bible, Abigail is the beautiful, intelligent and loyal second wife of King David. It became the normal name for the character of a maid in Elizabethan plays and in fact was once a nickname for a lady's maid. Despite this, Abigail remains a firm favourite. Its short forms, **Abbie** or **Abby**, are also popular.

Ada: From the German name Adelheid, which also gave Adelaide and Adela, meaning 'noble'. Others have linked it to the name Adah, which is the name of the second woman mentioned in the Bible, and derives from the Hebrew meaning 'ornament'. In a far more modern context, Ada is the name of a computer-programming language which was named after the Christian name of the nineteenth-century Lady Lovelace, daughter of the poet Byron and assistant to the man who invented the calculator.

Adela: A popular medieval European name from the German name Adelheid meaning 'noble'. It was the name given to one of William the Conqueror's daughters, the mother of King Stephen.

Adelaide: The French form of the Old German name, Adelheid, meaning 'noble'. It was borne by the tenth-century wife of Otto the Great, Holy Roman Emperor, and by the nineteenth-century wife of William IV of England. It was the latter Queen Adelaide who requested that the Australian city be given her name. (*16 December*)

Adele: French form of the name Adela.

Adelina: Italian form of the name Adela.

Adeline: French pet form of Adele.

Adriana: The feminine form of Adrian, used by Shakespeare for one of his characters in *A Comedy of Errors*, c. 1594. Similar forms of the name are **Adrienne** and **Adrianna**.

Aelita: A name invented by Alexei Tolstoy for the princess of Mars in his novel of the same name, published in 1922. Tolstoy based the name on the Greek words meaning 'air' and 'stone'.

Aemilia: A form of Amelia that appears in Shakespeare's *A Comedy of Errors*.

Aerona: Also used in the form **Aeronwen**, this name is based on the Welsh meaning 'berries'.

Africa: Most usually taken from the continent. However, it is possible that there was a twelfth-century Queen Africa of the Isle of Man.

Aiofe: An increasingly popular name in Ireland, Aiofe means 'beautiful'. It was the name of a legendary warrior queen.

Agatha: From the Greek meaning 'good'. It was first popularised by the third-century St Agatha, and more recently by the best-selling author, Agatha Christie, creator of the popular conceited Belgian detective Hercule Poirot. (*5 February*)

Agnes: From the Greek meaning 'pure' or 'chaste' although it has also been associated with the Latin meaning 'lamb'. The fourth-century martyr, St Agnes, is often pictured carrying a lamb. (*21 January, 20 April*)

Aida: Probably from the Arabic meaning 'reward', although it has been linked to the French meaning 'to save' and the Greek meaning 'modesty'. Whatever the origin, the name is famous as that of the Ethiopian princess sold into slavery in Verdi's nineteenth-century opera of the same name.

Aileen: The Scottish form of Eileen, itself a form of Helen. A variant spelling is **Ailene**.

Ailsa: A Scottish name taken from Ailsa Craig, an island in the Clyde estuary. The island's name may mean 'eagle rock'.

Aine: From an old Irish name meaning 'brightness', or from the Gaelic meaning 'delight'. There may have been a fertility goddess of the same name. An alternative form is **Annie**, which is not connected to the name Anne, both this form and Aine being pronounced 'awnya' with the first element rhyming with 'torn'.

Ainsley: Originally a Scottish surname meaning 'one meadow'. Today it is a popular first name that can also be spelled **Ainslie** and **Ainslee**.

Aisling: From the Gaelic meaning 'dream'. Other forms of the name include **Aislin** and **Ashling**.

Alana: Either the feminine form of Alan, or the Gaelic meaning 'child' or 'darling'. **Alanna** and **Alannah** are alternative forms of the name.

Alberta: The feminine form of Albert and one of the names given to one of Queen Victoria's daughters in honour of her father, Prince Albert. The Canadian province of Alberta was named after her.

Alcina: A sister of Morgan Le Fay, half-sister to King Arthur.

Alcyone: From the Greek words meaning 'sea' and 'I am pregnant'. The name is famous from the character in Greek mythology, the daughter of Aeolus, King of Thessaly, and wife of Ceyx. Her husband left in search of an oracle only to drown in the sea. When Alcyone found her husband's body on the shore, she too threw herself into the waves. The gods turned them both into kingfishers, which traditionally breed during the winter. It is at this time that Aeolus, commander of the winds, sends calm weather to allow the kingfishers to hatch their eggs and it is this story that has led to the term 'halcyon days' for calm and peaceful times. A slightly less romantic version of the story has Ceyx being turned into a gannet and Alcyone into a kingfisher as punishment for displeasing the gods. Alcyone is also the brightest star in the Pleiades.

Aldan: In some sources, Aldan is the mother of Merlin, King Arthur's magician and counsellor.

Alethea: From the Greek meaning 'truth'. This is a different name from Althea, of which it is often seen as an elaborate form.

Alexa: Either a short form of Alexandra, or a variant of Alexis.

Alexandra: The feminine form of Alexander, which has been in use in England since the thirteenth century. It really came into its own in the nineteenth century when it came to be associated with Queen Alexandra, the Danish wife of Edward VII. London's famous Alexandra Palace, which opened in 1863, the year she arrived in England, was named in her honour. In 1913, the now widowed Queen inaugurated the annual Alexandra Rose Day, a flag day to raise money for sick and disabled causes, to commemorate what she described as 'the fiftieth anniversary of my coming to this beloved country'. Alexandra Rose Day continues to raise money today and is held on 26 June each year. Another famous and regal bearer of the name was the tragic Empress Alexandra of Russia. A granddaughter of Queen Victoria, she married Nicholas II, the last emperor and tsar of Russia. While he was ineffective, she drew increasing resentment towards the royal family for her dependence on the disliked monk, Rasputin. Revolution broke out in Russia in 1917 and Alexandra, her husband and four children were murdered in July 1918. The name continues in our royal family today with Princess Alexandra, Lady Ogilvy. The form **Alexandria** is also sometimes used after the Egyptian port founded in the fourth century BC by Alexander the Great. Most recently, it was this form of the name that was chosen by David Bowie and Iman as the name for their daughter. The name has developed many short forms, some of which are now used as names in their own right. These include **Alex**, **Alexa**, **Sandra**, **Sandy**, **Alexis** and **Alix**.

Alexis: A form of Alexander and, therefore, based on the Greek word meaning 'to defend'. It was originally a male name and was that of both a fifth-century saint and the only son of Tsar Nicholas II and Alexandra, who was shot alongside his parents and sisters during the Russian Revolution. Today, it is more usually used as a female name and is more likely to be associated with the character played by Joan Collins in the hugely successful American soap, *Dynasty*. (*17 February, 17 July*)

Alice: The French form of the Old German name Adelheid, meaning 'noble'. It was introduced to England by the Normans after the Conquest and the early form of the name, **Alys**, still continues today both with this spelling and as **Alyce**. In Arthurian legend, Alice was the 'Beautiful Pilgrim' who helped Alisander to escape from King Arthur's half-sister, Morgan Le Fay. The name was made particularly popular in the nineteenth century when Lewis Carroll published his classic children's story, *Alice's Adventures in Wonderland*. This was written for Alice Liddell, daughter of the Dean of Christ Church, Oxford. The Central Australian town, Alice Springs, which was originally a watering hole and a telegraph station, was named after Lady Alice Todd, wife of the Postmaster General of South Australia.

Alicia: A modern form of Alice, which can also be spelled **Alissa** or **Alyssa**.

Alina: Either a form of Aline or, possibly, based on an Arabic word meaning 'noble'.

Alinda: A Germanic name, a form of Adelinde, which is made up of words meaning 'noble' and 'soft'.

Aline: A contracted form of Adeline used in the Middle Ages. Its use in Ireland and Scotland could also be influenced by the Gaelic word meaning 'lovely'.

Alison: Originally a French pet form of Alice that has become a name in its own right. The form **Allison** is also used.

Alizabeth: A fanciful alternative spelling of Elizabeth.

Allegra: From the Italian word meaning 'jaunty' or 'cheerful'. It was probably first used as a given name in 1817 when it was given to the poet Lord Byron's illegitimate daughter, who died at the age of just five years.

Alma: As a forename, Alma is based on the Latin word meaning 'kind'. A virginal beauty called Alma appears in Sir Edmund Spenser's sixteenth-century romance *The Faerie Queene*. Its popularity, however, increased in the mid-nineteenth century after the Battle of Alma at which English and French armies defeated the Russians during the Crimean War. The battle was fought at the River Alma, which was named after the Turkish word meaning 'apple'.

Aloise: The feminine form of Aloysius.

Altair: The brightest star in the constellation Aquila. From an Arabic word meaning 'bird'.

Althea: From the Greek meaning 'to heal'. In Greek mythology, Althea is the mother of the hunter Meleager. At his birth, the Fates told her that when a log burning in the fire had completely burned out, he would die. She immediately took it from the fire, smothered and kept it. When, as a young man, Meleager killed his two uncles, Althea's brothers, she retrieved the log, put it back on a fire and, as the Fates had predicted, he died.

Amanda: From the Latin meaning 'fit to be loved', the same origin as Amandus, the male name borne by several medieval saints. However, this feminine version was probably first used in the seventeenth century after a character in the play *Love's Last Shift*, by Colley Cibber. The name is often shortened to **Mandy**.

Amaryllis: Probably from the Greek meaning 'I sparkle'. Virgil used the name generally to represent a country girl and, more recently, it was used by George Bernard Shaw in *Back to Methuselah*, published in 1920. Today, it is just as likely to be given after the dramatic, fast-growing flower.

Amber: From the name of the gemstone. As with most names taken from jewels, flowers and so on, it was first used as a girl's name in the nineteenth century.

Amelia: Although this name is sometimes linked with the old Roman family name, Aemilius, it is actually based on an Old

German word meaning 'hard working'. It achieved increased popularity in the late eighteenth century after it was given to the youngest daughter of King George III.

Amena: A Celtic name based on the word meaning 'pure'. Alternative spellings are **Amine** and **Amina**.

Amene: According to legend, Amene was a queen at the time of King Arthur. When her kingdom was under attack by the knight Roaz, Arthur sent help and saved her throne.

Amy: From the Old French meaning 'beloved', which makes it a popular choice among parents. Its form **Aimee** is also used and has become a popular name in Northern Ireland.

Anaïs: A name of uncertain origin that has recently found fame as that chosen by Noel Gallagher and Meg Mathews for their daughter. In their case, the name was chosen in honour of Anaïs Nin, the French twentieth-century writer and leading figure of new feminism.

Ananda: From the Sanskrit meaning 'joy'. According to Buddhist history, Ananda was Buddha's first cousin.

Anastasia: From the Greek meaning 'awakening' or 'resurrection'. Because of this, it was popular among early Christians for their daughters. It is almost completely associated with the tragic story of the youngest daughter of Tsar Nicholas II and Empress Alexandra who, it is believed, was shot along with her parents, two sisters and brother during the Russian Revolution in 1918. For years, stories surrounded Princess Anastasia with many believing that she had survived the massacre. There was certainly one fairly credible woman who claimed to be the princess but it is unlikely that any of the stories were anything more than wishful thinking. (*25 December*)

Andrea: Probably the feminine form of Andreas, the Greek version of Andrew. However, it was first used in the seventeenth century and was not in use in medieval times, so it is possible that the origins are different.

Andromache: From the Greek meaning 'she who fights against men'! In Greek mythology, Andromache is a Trojan princess married to Hector. She had a tragic life: her father, brothers and husband were all killed by the warrior Achilles. In a particularly unpleasant episode, her baby son was thrown to his death from the walls of Troy after the city had fallen. Hardly surprising, then, that she fought!

Andromeda: From the Greek words meaning 'men' and 'ruler', so someone 'fit to rule over men'. In Greek mythology, she was left to drown as sacrifice to a monster. She was found and saved by Perseus who then married her, but not before he had turned another suitor and his men into stone.

Angel: From the Greek meaning 'messenger', this was originally a male name. In Thomas Hardy's classic *Tess of the D'Urbervilles*, published in 1891, he appears as a self-centred idealist. Today, however, it would be far more appropriate as a female name.

Angela: The feminine form of Angel, which itself is now used as a female name. Like it, Angela is based on the Greek meaning 'messenger'. (*27 January*)

Angelica: An Italian name based on the Latin meaning 'angelic'. In Arthurian legend, Angelica was the mother of King Arthur's illegitimate son, Tom a'Lincoln.

Angelina: An elaborate form of Angela.

Angharad: A Welsh name based on words meaning either 'much loved' or 'without reproach'. In Arthurian legend, Angharad was the lover of Percival, one of the Knights of the Round Table. It was a fairly popular name in the Middle Ages and has recently seen a marked revival, although primarily used in Welsh families or those conscious of their Welsh roots.

Anita: A Spanish pet form of Anna.

Ann(e): The English form of Hannah that, like it, means 'favoured' or 'grace'. The spelling 'Anne' is influenced by the French. The name is popular throughout Europe, mainly because of its association with St Anne, the mother of the Virgin Mary. Indeed, the two are often linked together in names such as Anne-Marie. (*26 July*)

Anna: The Italian form of Anne that is now used generally. It is often linked with the sister of the Queen of Carthage in Virgil's *Aeneid*. Others, however, have linked the name to the Latin meaning 'year'. In Arthurian legend, Anna is sometimes named as the sister of King Arthur.

Annabel: Probably from the Latin meaning 'lovable'. The final element 'bel' has also been linked to the French meaning 'beautiful', so overall it could represent 'beautiful and lovable'. Quite a name to live up to! One of the most famous bearers of the name was the fourteenth-century Annabella Drummond, mother of James I of Scotland. A similar variation is **Annabelle**.

Annelies: The German form of Anne.

Annette: The French pet form of Anne.

Antares: The name of the brightest star in the constellation Scorpius.

Anthea: The feminine form of the Greek word meaning 'flowery'. In Greek mythology, it is used as a byname of the goddess Hera, wife of Zeus. Its popularity increased markedly in the seventeenth century but it has only fairly recently become widely used.

Antigone: From the Greek meaning 'contrary birth'. In Greek mythology, she is Oedipus's daughter by his own mother, Jocasta. Despite this 'contrary birth', she was loyal to Oedipus and stayed with him until he died. She then defied her uncle Creon, who had refused her brother a burial, by organising a funeral and was punished by being imprisoned in his tomb. A tragic story but Antigone's characteristics of loyalty and determination might make what is a lovely name appeal to some.

Antoinette: The French feminine form of Anthony. It is most readily associated with the eighteenth-century Queen Marie Antoinette who was guillotined in 1793 during the French Revolution.

Antonia: The feminine form of Anthony which has been used since medieval times and was a popular Roman family name. Only became popular with English speakers from the twentieth century, but was in continental European use much earlier.

Aphrodite: The goddess of love in Greek mythology who wore a magic girdle around her waist, which made her irresistible! It obviously worked because she had several children by several gods and mortals.

Apollonia: Feminine form of Apollo, the god of song and music in Greek mythology. (*9 February*)

April: Probably from the Latin meaning 'to open', which is very relevant for the month of the year when flowers begin to open and trees start to bud. Some see its origins in Aphrodite, the goddess of love and beauty in Greek mythology. Either way, it makes a very attractive name for any girl, although it is usually given to those born in this month.

Arabella: Of uncertain origin but possibly based on the Latin meaning 'someone who can be entreated'. It became popular in the early eighteenth century after Alexander Pope dedicated his famous poem, 'The Rape of the Lock', to Arabella Fermor. A character of the name also appears in Charles Dickens's *Pickwick Papers*, published in 1837.

Ariadne: From the Greek words meaning either 'very pure' or 'to delight'. In Greek mythology, Ariadne is the daughter of King Minos of Crete, who fell in love with Theseus and helped him in his quest to kill the Minotaur by giving him a ball of thread with which to find his way out of the creature's labyrinth. Theseus and Ariadne never married though, and her eventual husband was the god of wine, Dionysus, who, when they married, gave her a crown made up of seven stars. Other forms of the name include **Arianne** and **Arianna**.

Ariel: From the place name based on the Hebrew meaning either 'lion of God' or 'hearth of the altar'. In the Bible, it is the name of one of the male companions of Ezra. Shakespeare also features it in *The Tempest*, written in 1611, where it is used as a male name for the character who is a spirit of the air. Today it is almost exclusively used as a female name and is most commonly associated with the leading character in Disney's extremely successful film, *The Little Mermaid*. Other forms include **Arielle** and **Ariella**.

Arlene: A relatively modern name of uncertain origin. It may simply be a name created under the influence of Charlene.

Arlette: Of uncertain origin, although it has been linked with the Old German meaning 'eagle'. It is an ancient name, in use from medieval times when it was that of William the Conqueror's mother, mistress of the Duke of Normandy.

Artemis: The virgin goddess of the hunt and protector of animals and children in Greek mythology.

Ashley: Although originally a boys' name (see boys' names listing), Ashley is increasingly chosen by parents for their daughters and is a particularly popular girls' name in the United States.

Astrid: From the Old Norse words meaning 'god' and 'fair', so 'divinely beautiful.' It was in use in Norway in medieval times, when it was the name of the eleventh-century wife of the King of Norway, and has remained a popular royal name in Europe.

Atalanta: From the Greek meaning either 'equal in weight' or 'joyful'. In Greek mythology, Atalanta is a great huntress who claimed she would only marry the man who could beat her in a race. Even the man who eventually succeeded had to distract her with three golden apples!

Athene: From the Greek meaning either 'immortal' or 'not nursed'. Either version would be relevant to the Athene (or **Athena**) of Greek mythology. She was the daughter of Zeus who had been told that the child would be a boy who would kill him, a threat which made him swallow the mother! Athene was born only after his head had been cut open (so 'not nursed'). She was the goddess of wisdom, arts and crafts who 'won' the city of Athens through the gift of an olive and became its patron.

Aude: Possibly from the Celtic meaning 'blessed'. It is best known as the name of Aude the Fair in *The Song of Roland*. She loved Roland and died rather than marry another – even if the 'other' was Charlemagne's son.

Audrey: From the Old English meaning 'noble strength', a descendant of the ancient name Etheldreda. Through the seventh-century St Audrey, it has an unfortunate association with the word 'tawdry', meaning cheap and nasty. St Audrey was the Queen of Northumbria whose early love of necklaces gave her a fatal neck tumour. In the Middle Ages, fairs were held in her honour and the word tawdry developed from her name to describe the goods sold at these! More recently, though, the name became more popular because of its association with the beautiful actress Audrey Hepburn.

Augusta: The feminine form of Augustus or Augustine. It was given to the wives of Roman emperors who assumed the title 'Augustus'. It was briefly a royal name, being that of the eighteenth-century Princess Augusta, mother of George III, after whom the American town in Georgia is named. George III then used the name for two of his own daughters. The second American city of this name, in Maine, was named after the daughter of a local hero of the American Revolution.

Aurelia: The feminine form of the Latin meaning 'golden'.

Auriel: A form of Aurelia.

Aurora: The goddess of the dawn in Roman mythology, whose name is taken from the Latin meaning 'dawn'.

Ava: Possibly from the Latin meaning 'bird', but more likely a variation on Eva. It became more prominent as a name thanks to the film star Ava Gardner.

Avalon: Probably from the Celtic word meaning 'apple'. Avalon is a name steeped in romantic history, being the name of the island paradise where King Arthur was taken to die having been mortally wounded on Salisbury Plain fighting Mordred's rebellion. According to legend, Arthur did not die there but will return again when justice and chivalry are restored.

Aveline: Introduced to Britain and Ireland by the Normans, this is probably based on the words meaning 'longed-for child'.

Avril: The French form of April.

Ayesha: From the Arabic meaning 'flourishing'. Its most famous bearer was the favourite wife of Muhammad. **Aisha** is an alternative spelling of the name.

Azalea: From the Greek meaning 'dry', which was given to the flower that grows best in dry soil. Alternative forms are **Azalia** and **Azelia**.

Azania: From the Hebrew meaning 'heard of God'. Originally a male name.

Azaria: From the Hebrew meaning 'helped by God'. Originally a male name.

B

Barbara: From the Greek meaning 'foreign woman'. One of the most famous bearers of the name is the third-century St Barbara. The variation **Barbra** is increasingly used, after the singer and film star Barbra Streisand. (*4 December*)

Beatrice: From the Latin meaning 'she who brings joy', although some have linked it to the Latin word meaning 'voyager', as though 'through life'. The name was used by Dante for the woman he loves and who guides him through paradise in his classic, *The Divine Comedy*. In Arthurian legend, Beatrice was a woman turned into an animal by a wizard. She was saved when the knight Carduino killed the wizard and kissed her. Beatrice and Carduino then married. The alternative spelling, **Beatrix**, is also used, as with the famous children's author Beatrix Potter, whose animal stories are still favourites with children today. The name was given to the eldest daughter of the Duke and Duchess of York.

Belinda: Of uncertain origin although it has been linked with the French and Spanish words meaning 'pretty'. It has been popular since the seventeenth century and was used by Alexander Pope as the name of his heroine in his poem, 'The Rape of the Lock'.

Bella: A short form of Isabella, from the Italian meaning 'beautiful'.

Belle: The French form of Bella and, like it, means 'beautiful'.

Bellona: The goddess of war in Roman mythology.

Beltane: The Celtic name for May Day, 1 May, which marks the beginning of summer. An attractive name for a child born on this day.

Berenice: From the Greek meaning 'victory bringer'. The shorter form, **Bernice**, is often used. In the Bible, she is the sister of Herod Agrippa II, before whom St Paul was brought to explain his faith.

Bernadette: The feminine form of Bernard. It is usually associated with the nineteenth-century St Bernadette Soubirous whose visions of the Virgin Mary ultimately led to the founding of Lourdes as a place of pilgrimage for the sick. (*16 April*)

Berry: From the vocabulary word.

Bertha: From the Old German meaning 'famous'. It is an ancient name that lost some of its popularity after 'Big Bertha', the nickname given to the German howitzers in the First World War.

Beryl: From the name of the precious pale-green stone of which the emerald is also a variety. The jewel takes its name from the Sanskrit meaning 'precious stones'. In the Bible, the jewels are among those seen by St John decorating the city walls in his vision of the New Jerusalem.

Beth: A short form of Elizabeth now sometimes used in its own right.

Bethan: Either the Welsh pet form of Beth, a form of Bethany, or from the Gaelic word meaning 'life'.

Bethany: From the Hebrew meaning 'house of figs'. In the Bible, this was a place name for a village near Jerusalem where Lazarus lived with his sisters, Mary and Martha. Jesus stayed with the family and it was here, too, that he raised Lazarus from the dead.

Bette: A pet form of Elizabeth. It was made particularly famous by the great actress Bette Davis, whose own second name was Elizabeth.

Beverley: Originally a place name based on the Old English meaning 'beaver stream'. It is used for both boys and girls, although the more usual female spelling is **Beverly**.

Bianca: From the Italian meaning 'white'. The name was used by Shakespeare for characters in both *The Taming of the Shrew* and *Othello*, although a more recent association is with Bianca Jagger, first wife of the Rolling Stone, Mick.

Billie: Form of Billy, used mostly for girls.

Blanche: From the Old German meaning 'white', this name was introduced to England by the Normans following the Conquest in 1066.

Blasine: According to Arthurian legend, Blasine was a sister of King Arthur.

Blodwen: From the Welsh meaning 'white flower'.

Blossom: From the word for flowers on a fruit tree.

Bonita: From Spanish meaning 'pretty'.

Bonnie: Meaning 'pretty'. The name was used as a nickname for Rhett and Scarlett's daughter in Margaret Mitchell's *Gone with the Wind*. The massive success of the film helped to increase the popularity of the name, despite its association with the outlaw Bonnie Parker, who was made infamous by the similarly successful 1967 film *Bonnie and Clyde*.

Brenda: A name that has long been popular in Scotland and may be a feminine form of Brendan, so meaning 'royal'. It may also be from a Scandinavian word meaning 'flaming sword'. It has come to be used widely outside Scotland since the beginning of the twentieth century.

Briana: The female version of Brian, so probably meaning 'high'.

Briar: From the name given to the thorny bush of wild roses or brambles.

Brice: Possibly from the Welsh meaning 'speckled'. The name is also used in the form **Bryce**. (*13 November*)

Bridget: From the Irish meaning 'strength' or 'virtue'. In Ireland, it has many forms including **Brid**, **Bride**, **Brighid** and **Birgitta**. Brid was the name of a Celtic goddess of healing but it is the association with the sixth-century St Bridget, also known as St Bride, who is a patron saint of Ireland, that has ensured its popularity through the years. (*1 February, 23 July*)

Brigitte: The French form of Bridget.

Britt: The Swedish form of Bridget.

Bronwen: From the Welsh meaning 'white breast'. The spelling **Bronwyn** is also popular. In Welsh legend, Bronwen was the wife of an Irish king. She was so unhappy that she trained a bird to take a message to her brother. Her plan worked and he launched a fleet to cross the Irish Sea to save her.

Bryony: From the name of a climbing plant. **Briony** is an alternative spelling.

Bunty: From a pet name for a lamb.

C

Caelia: Meaning 'heavenly', the name of the mother of Faith, Hope and Charity in Sir Edmund Spenser's sixteenth-century epic, *The Faerie Queene*. In some versions of the Arthurian legend, Caelia is also the lover of King Arthur's illegitimate son, Tom a'Lincoln.

Caitlin: The Irish form of Katherine. It has several variations, including **Cathleen**, **Katelin** and **Kaytlin**. Today it is markedly more popular than Katherine.

Cale: Based on the word meaning 'beautiful', Cale is one of the Graces mentioned by Homer, another being Pasithea. It is possible that these two were actually based on one goddess, whose collective name would mean 'the goddess who is beautiful to all'.

Camilla: The feminine form of the Roman family name Camillus, which is of uncertain origin. More recently, it has been associated with the name of the plant, camellia, but this was named after Georg Josef Kamel, who introduced the flower into Europe during the eighteenth century. In the *Aeneid*, Virgil uses the name for a female warrior who fought in the army of Aeneas. (*14 July Camillus*)

Camille: According to legend, Camille was a sorceress in love with King Arthur. She captured him only for him to be rescued by Sir Lancelot.

Candace: An hereditary title of several queens of Ethiopia. In the Bible, a queen of this name is mentioned in the story of the conversion by Philip of her treasurer as he was travelling from Jerusalem to Ethiopia. The form **Candice** is more commonly used.

Candida: From the Latin meaning 'white' or 'shining', the name therefore implies 'purity' and 'beauty'.

Cara: From the Irish meaning 'friend' or the Italian meaning 'beloved'.

Carey: Usually taken as a feminine form of Cary, so probably based on the Celtic word meaning 'well loved'.

Carina: A relatively recent name, probably influenced by Cara.

Carla: The feminine form of Carl, so based on Charles, meaning 'free man'.

Carly: A form of Carla.

Carmel: From the Hebrew meaning 'fertile field'. A range of hills in Israel, it is mentioned in the Bible as both the home of Abigail before she married David and where Elijah called on Israel to choose between God and the prophets of Baal. It is from this area that the Carmelite orders of friars and nuns take their name.

Carmen: The Spanish form of Carmel, which was influenced by the Latin word 'carmen', meaning 'song'. Carmen is the name of the tragic heroine of Bizet's famous opera written in 1875, which no doubt increased its popularity.

Carol: This name is either a short form of Caroline, itself the feminine form of Charles, or taken from a Welsh name meaning 'courageous in war'. Its French form, **Carole**, is also popular.

Carolina: From the Italian form of Charles. The two American states, North and South Carolina, were originally named Caroline in honour of Charles IX of France, but were renamed Carolina in 1663 when King Charles II of England regranted the region.

Caroline: The French form of Carolina.

Carolyn: A form of Caroline.

Carrie: A pet form of Caroline, now sometimes used as a name in its own right. It came to prominence after the young girl with supernatural powers in Stephen King's thriller, *Carrie*, published in 1974 and subsequently made into a popular film starring Sissy Spacek.

Carys: A popular Welsh name that is either a form of Carol, as with a similar name **Caryl**, or influenced by the word meaning 'love'.

Cassandra: From the Greek words meaning 'entangler of men'! In Greek mythology, Cassandra is the daughter of King Priam of Troy to whom Apollo gave the gift of prophecy. However, she angered him and, as a result, he ensured that no one would ever believe her. This had tragic consequences when her warnings about the Trojan horse were ignored and Troy was lost. Cassandra herself was captured by Agamemnon and later became his mistress, only for them both to be murdered by his wife.

Catherine: Possibly from the Greek word *katharos*, meaning 'pure', and it is this association that has influenced the spellings **Katherine** and **Katharine**. Its most famous early bearer was the third-century St Catherine, who was tortured on a spiked wheel for her Christian faith (hence the name of the popular firework the Catherine Wheel) before being beheaded. The name in this spelling has many short forms including **Cathy**, **Cath**, **Catrina** and **Catriona**. The latter form was used by Robert Louis Stevenson for the title of his sequel to *Kidnapped*, 1893. (*13 February, 9 March, 24 March, 29 April, 15 September, 25 November, 28 November*)

Cecilia; From the Latin meaning 'blind'. Its popularity certainly owes a certain amount to the third-century martyr St Cecilia, who is the patron saint of music, and maybe even more to the song of the same name by Simon and Garfunkel. (*22 November*)

Cecily: A form of Cecilia.

Ceinlys: A Welsh name based on the words meaning 'jewels' and 'sweet'.

Celeste: A French name based on the Latin meaning 'heavenly', which made it particularly popular amongst early Christians. (*27 July Celestine*)

Celia: From a Roman family name that is of uncertain origin but may be related to the Latin word meaning 'sky' or 'heaven'. It became popular after a character of the same name was used by Shakespeare in *As You Like It*.

Ceres: An ancient goddess of corn and the harvest in Roman mythology.

Ceridwen: A legendary Welsh name from the words meaning 'poetry' and 'fair'. In Welsh mythology, she is the goddess of poetry and mother of the great Celtic poet Taliesin.

Cerise: A relatively modern name that is either based on the French meaning 'cherry' or from the light red colour.

Cerwyn: A Welsh name meaning 'fair love', that could be used for a boy or girl.

Chantal: Originally a French surname meaning 'stone'. It was first used as a given name in honour of the seventeenth-century St Jeanne-Françoise Fremiot, wife of the Baron de Chantal, who founded an order of nuns. **Chantel** and **Chantelle** are variations in the spelling.

Charis: From the Greek meaning 'grace'. It was first used as a given name in the seventeenth century. Charis is one of the Graces or Charities named by Homer in his epic poem *The Iliad*.

Charissa: A form of Charis.

Charity: From the word 'charity' which today denotes both the giving to and the work of organisations that help those in need. In the Bible, however, the word was used for the early Christians' love for one another based on God's unconditional love for them. (*1 August*)

Charlotte: The French feminine form of Charles, which became popular in England in 1761 after the wife of George III. Charlotte, the largest city in North Carolina, was named in her honour, as was Charlottetown, the capital of Canada's Prince Edward Island. The authoress Charlotte Brontë ensured the name remained popular in the nineteenth century and it remains so today.

Charmaine: First used in the 1920s, this is probably based on the word 'charm', itself based on the Latin meaning 'song'.

Charmian: From the Greek meaning 'delight', although it is sometimes used as an alternative to Charmaine.

Chelsea: From the Old English meaning 'chalk landing place', which was given to the area on the Thames in London where, not surprisingly, chalk was unloaded. It was an area which became synonymous with the 'Swinging 60s' which may have encouraged its use as a first name.

Cherie: From the French meaning 'darling'.

Cherry: From the name of the fruit, although it is also used as a pet form of Charity. In his 1844 book, *Martin Chuzzlewit*, Charles Dickens gives his characters, Charity and Mercy, the nicknames Cherry and Merry.

Cheryl: A relatively modern name that was first used in the 1920s. Its original source is uncertain but was probably influenced by the names Cherry and Beryl.

Chloe: From the Greek meaning 'young green shoot'. In early Greek romances, she is a young girl loved by Daphnis. The name is also mentioned in the Bible as that of a woman who warned St Paul of problems with a church at Corinth. It is this mention that made the name popular among the seventeenth-century Puritans and it remains so today.

Christa: A short form of Christine and Christina.

Christabel: A development of Christine that was probably invented by the nineteenth-century poet Samuel Taylor Coleridge for his poem of that name.

Christelle: The French version of Christine. Its use in some cases is probably influenced by its association with crystal.

Christiana: The feminine form of Christian that is probably also influenced by the names Christine and Anna. The name was used by John Bunyan in his novel *The Pilgrim's Progress*, written in 1678.

Christina: A short form of Christiana, which has been popular since the eighteenth century. (*24 July*)

Christine: The French form of Christina.

Ciara: From the Celtic word meaning 'dark'. The name has many variations in spelling including **Ciarra**, **Kiera**, **Keera** and **Kyara**.

Cilla: The short form of Priscilla. In Greek mythology, Cilla is the sister of King Priam of Troy whose son died in place of her brother's child, Paris.

Claire: The French form of Clara, which was introduced to England after the Norman Conquest. In the Arthurian romances, Claire is the sister of Sagremor, one of the Knights of the Round Table. However, the name did not become popularly used until the nineteenth century when it was taken as an alternative form of Clare.

Clara: From the Latin meaning 'famous' or 'bright'.

Clare: A development of Clara. The form **Clarette** is sometimes used. (*11 August*)

Clarice: The Old English form of the Latin name Claritia, which is probably based on the word meaning 'famous'. An alternative form is **Clarissa**. In Arthurian legend, **Clarisse** is a sister of Sir Gawain, one of King Arthur's most prominent knights.

Clarinda: An elaborate form of Clara that was first used in Sir Edmund Spenser's sixteenth-century *The Faerie Queene*. It was also used by the famed Scottish poet, Robert Burns, in his series of poems *To Clarinda*.

Clarine: According to some versions of the Arthurian legend, Clarine is the mother of Sir Lancelot.

Clarisse: In Arthurian legend, Clarisse is a sister of Sir Gawain, one of King Arthur's most prominent knights.

Claudette: An elaborate form of Claudia.

Claudia: The feminine form of Claud. In the Bible, Claudia is a friend of St Paul. He wrote a letter addressed to her and Timothy shortly before he was martyred for his faith.

Clematis: From the flower name that, rather uninspiringly, is named after the Greek meaning 'climbing plant'.

Clemence: The medieval French and English form of the Latin meaning 'merciful'. As such, it is the feminine form of Clement.

Clemency: A form of Clemence, meaning 'merciful', used as a descriptive name like Faith and Hope. It was particularly popular with the seventeenth-century Puritans. (*27 July, 23 November*)

Clementine: A female form of Clement that was first used in the nineteenth century and is probably most readily associated with the nursery rhyme 'Oh my darling Clementine'. All the same, it is not widely used. An alternative form is Clementina.

Clio: The Muse of history and a daughter of Zeus in Greek mythology. Her name is based on the Greek meaning 'fame', so she proclaimed famous events.

Clover: From the plant name.

Colleen: A well-known Irish name based on the Irish meaning 'girl'. It is sometimes used as a feminine form of Colin.

Columbine: From the plant name, which itself is based on the Italian meaning 'dove'. The plant is so called because its petals look like a cluster of five doves. With the dove representing peace, this makes a lovely name for a girl and has been in use since the nineteenth century. A similar name, **Columba**, is used in Ireland for both boys and girls after a fourth-century saint. (*9 June Columbia, 17 September Columba*)

Constance: From the French meaning 'steadfast'. The name of one of William the Conqueror's daughters, it was introduced to England after 1066. In some sources of the Arthurian legend, Constance was the mother of Sir Lancelot.

Cora: From the Greek meaning 'maiden'. Its use in Ireland is sometimes influenced by the male name Corey. It was possibly first used as a name by James Fenimore Cooper for a character in *The Last of the Mohicans*, published in 1826.

Coral: A name first used in the nineteenth century, taken from the pink, white or red coral found on the sea bed.

Cordelia: A name with several possible interpretations, each as good as the other! It was used by Shakespeare for the name of the one faithful daughter of King Lear. It could be based on the Latin *cor* meaning 'heart' with the 'delia' acting as an anagram of 'ideal'. Alternatively, it could be based on the Latin *cor de illa*, meaning 'from her heart'. In some early versions of the Lear story, the name is, in fact, spelled Cordeilla, which would make this interpretation likely. Others have seen some link with 'Coeur de Lion', the nickname of the twelfth-century King Richard I who will be forever associated with the romance of medieval England through Robin Hood, Maid Marian, the Crusades and bad King John. Last, but not least, the name could be based on the Celtic word meaning 'harmony'.

Corinna: Probably from the Greek meaning 'maiden', so it is similar to Cora. The form **Corinne** is also sometimes used.

Cornelia: The feminine form of Cornelius.

Cosima: The feminine form of Cosmo that was perhaps most famously borne by Cosima Wagner, wife of the composer Richard, and daughter of Franz Liszt.

Courtney: From the place Courtenay in France, meaning 'domain of Curtius', which became an aristocratic surname. It was also given as a nickname to someone with a short nose (*court nez*)!

Cressida: From either the Greek word meaning 'stronger' or that meaning 'golden'. Shakespeare made the name famous through his play *Troilus and Cressida*, written in 1601, in which she is the daughter of a Trojan priest who becomes the unfaithful lover of Troilus.

Crystal: From the Greek meaning 'ice', this name became popular in the nineteenth century when it was taken from the high-quality glass. In the Bible, St John describes the water of life, which flows from the throne of God in his vision of heaven, as 'clear as crystal'. In Ireland, the use of the surname McCrystal is common. The forms **Krystle**, **Kristell** and **Chrystal** are also used.

Cyane: From the Greek meaning 'blue'. In Greek mythology, it is the name of a Sicilian nymph who gave her name to a fountain. 'Cyan' is still used today in printing for a light blue colour produced by mixing blue and green.

Cynthia: In Greek mythology, Cynthia is another name given to Artemis, goddess of hunting. She and Apollo were both believed to have been born on Mount Cynthus in Delos and were thus called Cynthia and Cynthus. The origin of the name of the mountain is uncertain.

D

Daffodil: A rarely-used flower name. The flower itself was named in the fourteenth century after the Dutch *de affodil* meaning 'the asphodel' (lily).

Dahlia: From the flower, which was named after the eighteenth-century botanist Anders Dahl.

Daisy: From the familiar flower, which was itself called after 'day's eye' because it reveals its sun-like yellow centre in the morning and covers it again with its petals in the evening. The name is often associated with Daisy Buchanan, the tragic, but weak, object of Jay Gatsby's affection in F. Scott Fitzgerald's classic novel *The Great Gatsby*, published in 1925. The novel was made into a famous film in which the character of Daisy was played by Mia Farrow.

Dale: From the surname given to someone who, surprisingly enough, lived in a dale or valley.

Dalia: Usually used as a simplified form of Dahlia. Sometimes, though, its use is influenced by the modern Hebrew meaning 'flowering branch'.

Dana: One of the oldest Celtic names based on that of an ancient mother god, itself of uncertain origin. Its use in Ireland is probably influenced by either the Gaelic word meaning 'poem' or that meaning 'brave'.

Daniela: A feminine form of Daniel.

Danielle: The French feminine form of Daniel, which is now used generally.

Daphne: From the Greek meaning 'laurel', a fact which made it popular during the nineteenth-century craze for flower names. In Greek mythology, Daphne is a nymph, the daughter of the river god Penelus. The unhappy recipient of Apollo's attentions, she fled through the woods and, on the verge of capture at the banks of the river, called to her father to save her. He then, rather drastically, turned her into a laurel tree. It was said that the disappointed Apollo then made himself a laurel wreath, which became the prize at the games held in his honour.

Dara: Either from the Gaelic meaning 'oak grove' or the Hebrew meaning 'pearl of wisdom'.

Darcy: Ultimately from a French surname based on the word meaning 'fortress'. It was introduced to England after the Norman Conquest. In Ireland, the use of the name is certainly influenced by the Gaelic meaning 'dark haired'.

Daria: The feminine form of Darius. (*25 October*)

Darryl: From the French place name Airelle. It was brought to England by the Normans after the Norman Conquest. Alternative spellings are **Daryl** and **Darrell**.

Davina: The feminine form of David, which is also sometimes used in the form **Davinia**.

Dawn: From the word for 'daybreak', the name was first used in the 1920s.

Deborah: From the Hebrew meaning 'bee', so implying both 'sweetness' and 'diligence'. In the Bible, Deborah was the only woman ever to become a Judge, or ruler, of Israel. She went with Barak to fight the Canaanites and famously thanked God for their victory in the 'Song of Deborah'. It was a popular name among the seventeenth-century Puritans.

Dee: Either a short form of any name beginning with the letter 'D', or taken from the River Dee, itself of Celtic origin from the word meaning 'goddess'.

Deirdre: A great romantic name of uncertain origin. It has been linked to several Celtic words meaning 'end', 'angry' or, most appropriately, 'brokenhearted'. The name is that of a tragic Celtic heroine often referred to as Deidre of the Sorrows. Legend has it that she was promised to the King of Ulster but ran away to Scotland instead with her real love, Naoise. He was killed by the King after the couple were tricked into returning to Ireland and Deidre died brokenhearted.

Delia: A name taken from the Greek island of Delos. It became an alternative name for Artemis, the goddess of hunting in Greek mythology, who was supposed to have been born on the island.

Delicia: A fairly modern name taken from the Latin meaning 'delight'.

Delilah: Probably from the Hebrew meaning 'delight' although it has been linked to another Hebrew word meaning 'night' and even to the Arabic meaning 'to flirt'! Delilah is most famously known as the woman who tricked Samson into telling her the secret of his tremendous strength and then betrayed him to the Philistines. More recently, it is the title of one of singer Tom Jones's most famous songs, recorded in 1968.

Della: Of uncertain origin but it may be a form of Delia, Delilah or Adela.

Delphine: From the Latin meaning 'woman from Delphi' although it is sometimes used because of its association with the blue delphinium plant.

Demelza: From a Cornish place name. It is a relatively recent name that came to be used in the 1970s after the heroine of the popular television series, *Poldark*.

Demeter: The name of the goddess of the fertility of the earth in Greek mythology, which is based on the Greek words meaning 'earth' and 'mother'. She was the mother of Persephone who was kidnapped by Hades and taken to the Underworld. Demeter forbade the earth to bear fruit, so threatening a famine, until Zeus agreed that her daughter should be brought back on condition that she had not eaten anything. Persephone, however, had eaten a pomegranate and was therefore condemned to spending four months of each year back in the Underworld. This time corresponds to the winter months.

Dena: A modern name that is possibly taken as a feminine form of Dean.

Denise: The French feminine form of Denis, which is now in general use.

Desdemona: Probably from the Greek meaning 'ill fated'. If so, it is a good choice for Shakespeare's tragic heroine of the play *Othello*. She is Othello's loyal wife who is murdered by him in a jealous rage after he has been wrongly convinced of her adultery.

Desiree: From the French meaning 'desired'.

Dia: A byname of Hera, wife of Zeus and queen of heaven in Greek mythology. It is taken from the Greek meaning 'godlike one'.

Diamond: From the gemstone.

Diana: Of uncertain origin although it is likely to contain some element of the Greek meaning 'divine'. In Roman mythology, Diana is the beautiful goddess of the moon and of hunting. It is said in the Bible that St Paul had much opposition from the worshippers of Diana. As such, it was not a popular name among early Christians. More recently, it achieved increased popularity because of its association with Princess Diana, although her tragic death in 1997 and the subsequent saintlike portrayal of her the world over may, again, prevent parents from giving this name to their child. It would be a lot to live up to.

Diane: The French form of Diana. The alternative forms of **Diahann** and **Dianne** are also used.

Dido: Probably from the Phoenician meaning 'bold'. In Roman mythology, Dido was a princess of Tyre who fled with others to Libya after the murder of her husband and subsequently founded Carthage. According to Virgil, she fell deeply in love with Aeneas but killed herself on a funeral pyre when he abandoned her.

Dilys: A Welsh name, probably from the word meaning 'genuine'.

Dinah: From the Hebrew meaning 'revenged', an appropriate name for the Dinah whose awful story is told in the Bible. In this, Dinah was raped by the son of the ruler of Shechem who then begged for her hand in marriage. Dinah's brothers finally agreed to the marriage but only on condition that all the men of Shechem were circumcised! The marriage must have been an important one because all the men agreed but, as they 'recovered', Dinah's brothers killed them all.

Dione: From the Latin meaning 'Zeus'. In Greek mythology, Dione was an earth goddess, the daughter of Atlas, who was a consort of Zeus and, with him, the mother of Aphrodite. The form **Dionne** is more recent and only seems to have been used since the 1950s.

Dolly: An early pet form of Dorothy.

Dolores: A Spanish name which is based on the title of the Virgin Mary, *Maria de los Dolores*, 'Mary of the Sorrows'.

Dominique: The feminine form of Dominic. The form **Dominica** is also used.

Donna: The Italian meaning 'lady' which is now used generally.

Dora: The short form of names such as Theodora or Dorothy, which is now sometimes used as a name in its own right.

Dorcas: From the Greek meaning 'doe' or 'gazelle'. In the Bible, it is used as a translation of the name Tabitha.

Doreen: A form of Dora with the addition of the Irish 'een'.

Dorian: A name probably invented by Oscar Wilde for the beautiful young man who was the main character in *The Portrait of Dorian Gray*, published in 1891. It is likely that he took the name from the Dorian race of Greek-speaking people. Today, it is often used as a girl's name.

Dorinda: An elaborate form of Dora, which was first used in the eighteenth century.

Doris: From the Greek meaning 'Dorian woman', from the race of Greek-speaking people. In Greek mythology, Doris was a goddess of the sea who married her brother and bore him 50 daughters! Some have linked the name to the Greek word for 'gift'.

Dorothy: From the Greek meaning 'gift of God'. The present form is a development of the earlier name, Dorothea, which uses the same two elements as the name Theodora, just the other way round. Perhaps one of the best known Dorothys was the heroine of L. Frank Baum's classic novel *The Wizard of Oz*, published in 1900 and made into a hugely popular film starring Judy Garland. (*6 February*)

Drusilla: The feminine form of the Roman family name, which was itself probably based on the Greek meaning 'soft eyed'. The Roman name was first used by one Livius, who killed a Gaul bearing this name and, by custom, took it himself. In the Bible, Drusilla was the wife of Felix, the governor of Jerusalem, who was converted by St Paul.

Dulcie: From the Latin meaning 'sweet'.

Dusty: A pet form of Dustin that is sometimes used as a female name, probably influenced by the singer Dusty Springfield.

Dwynwen: Dwynwen, or *Dwyn*, is the Welsh patron saint of lovers whose name is probably based on the words meaning 'holy' and 'fair'. According to legend, she turned a suitor into a block of ice.

E

Ebony: From the name of the black wood.

Echo: In Greek mythology, Echo is a nymph who kept the goddess Hera distracted by her incessant talking while Hera's husband, Zeus, was with other nymphs. Hera was furious and condemned Echo only to be able to speak when spoken to and then only to repeat the endings of the words she heard. She fell in love with Narcissus but pined away to nothing, leaving only her voice, when he rejected her. Narcissus, though, got his just desserts when Artemis condemned him to love only his own reflection, a punishment so terrible that he killed himself and was turned into a flower.

Edith: From the Old English words meaning 'prosperity' and 'battle', so implying someone who would be a successful fighter. It is therefore similar to the name Edgar and was in fact given to the tenth-century daughter of King Edgar. The Anglo-Saxon custom was to give children a name using the same element as their father. (*15 July, 16 September*)

Edna: From the Hebrew meaning 'rejuvenation', although it has become associated with the Garden of Eden, in which case it means 'perfect happiness'. In Ireland, the name represents the anglicised form of Eithne, meaning 'kernel'. Edna was extremely popular in the 1920s but has become much less frequently used in recent years.

Edwina: The feminine form of Edwin or Edward that was first used in the nineteenth century. Perhaps its most famous bearer was the beautiful Edwina, Countess Mountbatten, leader of 'society' in the 1920s and wife to Lord Louis Mountbatten, who spent the post-war years dedicating herself to the relief of suffering until her death in 1960.

Eileen: A name closely associated with Ireland, Eileen is a form of Helen.

Eileithyia: The goddess of childbirth in Greek mythology. Although it would be a mouthful today, it could provide the basis for an unusual name taken from it.

Eilwen: A Welsh name meaning 'fair brow', so 'beautiful'.

Eirwen: A Welsh name meaning 'white snow'.

Elaine: A form of Helen. There are several Elaines in Arthurian legend. One of the most prominent is the Elaine who falls in love with Lancelot and deceives him into sleeping with her, a liaison that produced Sir Galahad. Another is Elaine the White, the original Lady of Shalott, who loved Sir Lancelot. In fact, he wore her colours during a joust. However, her love for him led her to die and her body was brought in a boat up the Thames to King Arthur's court.

Eleanor: Although associated by many with the name Helen, this is probably of Germanic origin from a word meaning 'foreign'. It was introduced to England in the twelfth century by Eleanor of Aquitaine, the French wife of Henry II and mother to King Richard I and King John.

Electra: From the Greek meaning 'amber', so 'radiant'. In Greek mythology, Electra was the daughter of Agamemnon and Clytemnestra who persuaded her brother to avenge their father's death by killing Clytemnestra and her lover. Sigmund Freud used the name for his theory of the 'Electra complex' where a girl has an extreme father fixation. Others have linked the name to the words meaning 'not bedded'.

Eliabella: In Arthurian legend, Eliabella is a cousin of King Arthur who marries his rival, King Meliodas of Liones, to bring peace.

Elise: The French short form of Elisabeth.

Elissa: A name used by Sir Edmund Spenser in his sixteenth-century romance, *The Faerie Queene*, for the jealous sister of Perissa and Medina. In Greek mythology, it was the original name of Dido.

Eliza: A short form of Elizabeth that is sometimes used as a name in its own right. This is perhaps influenced by the character of Eliza Doolittle in George Bernard Shaw's *Pygmalion*, published in 1913. In this, she is the flower girl transformed into a lady by Professor Henry Higgins, and a character memorably played by Audrey Hepburn in the film *My Fair Lady*.

Elizabeth: From the Hebrew meaning 'my God gave the oath'. In the Bible, Elizabeth is the mother of John the Baptist. Both she and her husband Zechariah were quite old when an angel told Zechariah that they would have a son. His disbelief led to his being struck dumb until the baby was indeed born. It was to Elizabeth that the Virgin Mary went when she, too, was told she would bear a child. The name has become associated with the royal family, with both the present Queen and Queen Mother having the name – not forgetting the great Elizabeth I in the sixteenth century. It has given rise to a massive number of short or pet forms, including **Bessie**, **Betty**, **Lisa**, **Liz**, **Bette**, **Elisa** and **Elise**, to name just a few. The name is also spelled **Elisabeth**. (*4 January, 18 June, 4 July, 26 August, 5 November, 17 November*)

Ella: From the German meaning 'foreign'. It was introduced to England by the Normans following the Conquest of 1066 and is still used today. In some cases, it is regarded as a pet form of Ellen. Interestingly, two celebrity couples – John Travolta and Kelly Preston, and Warren Beatty and Annette Bening – have chosen the name for their daughters. Perhaps this is why, at the beginning of the 21st century, Ella ranked among the top 50 names given to girls.

Ellen: A form of Helen that was very popular at the turn of the nineteenth century. In Wales, the form **Elen** is used after a legendary woman who was famed for her beauty. In Arthurian legend, Ellen is one of King Arthur's daughters.

Ellie: A short form of names such as Eleanor and Ellen that is now used as a given name in its own right.

Elsa: One of the many short forms of Elizabeth. It is perhaps best associated with the lioness in Joy Adamson's classic

Born Free. In Arthurian legend, Elsa is the daughter of the Duke of Brabant whose husband told her never to ask his name. After bearing two of his children, she finally asked the question, at which point he left her.

Elsie: A Scottish form of Elspeth.

Elspeth: The Scottish form of Elizabeth.

Eluned: A Welsh name that probably means 'object of adoration'.

Elvira: A Spanish name of uncertain origins. It was used by Noël Coward as the taunting spirit of Charles's first wife in the popular *Blithe Spirit*, written in 1941. Mozart also used the name for Don Juan's wife in his opera *Don Giovanni*, written in 1789, as did Lord Byron in his poem 'Don Juan'.

Elyzabel: According to Arthurian legend, Elyzabel was a cousin of Queen Guinevere whose imprisonment by Claudas led King Arthur to declare war.

Emerald: From the green gemstone that has become immediately associated with Ireland, the 'Emerald Isle'. In the Bible, the emerald is found among other precious stones in the foundations of St John's vision of the New Jerusalem.

Emily: From a Roman family name probably meaning 'rival' although some interpret its meaning as 'eager'. It is now one of the most popular names across the English-speaking world.

Emma: Originated as a short form of Germanic names such as Ermintrude, where 'ermen' means 'entire'. It is probably most readily associated with the matchmaking heroine of Jane Austen's novel of that name, published in 1816, and the subject of several film and television adaptations. Perhaps this has contributed to the fact that Emma remains one of the most popular names across the English-speaking world.

Emmeline: An Old French name of Germanic origin that is possibly a form of Emma. In Arthurian legend, she is the blind daughter of a duke of Cornwall who was abducted by Oswald, King of Kent. Merlin restored her sight and she was rescued by King Arthur.

Ena: An anglicised form of the Irish name Eithne, meaning 'little fire'.

Enid: Probably from the Welsh meaning 'soul'. In the Arthurian romances, Enid is the wife of Geraint. He insisted she accompany him to battle because he wrongly thought she had a lover.

Enya: An Irish name meaning either 'nut kernel' or 'flame'.

Enyo: A goddess of battle in Greek mythology.

Eos: The goddess of the dawn in Greek mythology, the equivalent to the Roman Aurora. She is the mother of the stars and most of the winds.

Epona: A Celtic goddess, also honoured by the Romans, whose name is possibly based on the Welsh meaning 'breed'. According to legend, she carried soldiers who had died in battle straight to paradise.

Erica: The feminine form of Eric.

Erin: From the name of one of the ancient goddesses of Ireland, after whom Ireland got its name. Its expanded form, **Erina**, therefore means 'Irish girl'.

Eris: The goddess of discord in Greek mythology. According to legend, it was Eris who, during a wedding, threw an apple inscribed 'for the fairest'. Zeus suggested that the three goddesses, Hera, Athena and Aphrodite, should ask Paris to decide the winner. Aphrodite won and this was one of the causes of the Trojan War.

Ersa: From the Greek meaning 'dew', so perhaps a good name for a child born at dawn. In Greek mythology, Ersa is the daughter of Zeus and Selene.

Esmeralda: The Spanish for 'emerald'. The name was used by Victor Hugo for the gypsy dancer in *The Hunchback of Notre Dame*, published in 1831.

Estella: An Old French name meaning 'star'. She is perhaps most readily associated with the woman brought up by Miss Haversham to hate all men in Charles Dickens's classic novel *Great Expectations*, published in 1861. The form **Estelle** is also used.

Esther: From the Hebrew meaning 'myrtle'. In the Bible, Esther is the beautiful second wife of King Xerxes of Persia. As a Jewess, when she heard of a plot to kill all Jews in the country, she sought permission from the king for the Jews to defend themselves and the massacre was averted. Others have linked the name with that of the Babylonian goddess of love, whose name probably means 'star'.

Ethel: From the Old German meaning 'noble' which was originally used in names such as Ethelberta.

Eugenia: The feminine form of Eugene. (*25 December*)

Eugenie: The French form of Eugenia, which came to prominence after it was chosen by the Duke and Duchess of York for their daughter.

Eunice: From the Greek meaning 'good victory'. In the Bible, Eunice is the mother of Timothy whose teaching of the Scriptures to her son was praised by St Paul.

Europa: Of uncertain origin but possibly meaning 'wide eyed' or 'broad browed'. In Greek mythology, she is the daughter of the Phoenician King Agenor and the granddaughter of Poseidon who rode a white bull to Crete only to find it was Zeus in disguise! Europa and Zeus then had three sons together before she married the King of Crete. Legend has it that Zeus gave her a necklace that made the wearer irresistibly beautiful. The name for Europe came from Europa so it's perhaps a good name for those in favour of Britain's active participation there.

Eurwen: A Welsh name meaning 'golden girl'.

Evadne: Possibly from the Greek meaning 'fair flowering'. In Greek mythology, Evadne is the daughter of Poseidon and the nymph Pitane.

Evangeline: From the Latin meaning 'gospel'.

Eve: From the Hebrew meaning 'life'. In the Bible, she is, of course, the first woman, created by God. It says that Adam first named every living creature and then 'called his wife's name Eve; because she was the mother of all living'. Despite taking the blame for her and Adam's sin, she was told by

God that one of her descendants would save the world from it.

Evelina: A form of Evelyn.

Evelyn: Although originally a boy's name, this is now used more for girls. It is taken from a Norman personal name, Aveline, and was introduced by them to England after the Conquest. The meaning is uncertain but has been linked by some to the Old German meaning 'hazelnut'. The alternative forms of Evelina and **Eveline** are also used. Perhaps the original Aveline will come back into fashion.

F

Fabia: From the old Roman family name, Fabius, which was probably based on the word meaning 'bean'.

Fabiola: Like Fabia, from the old Roman family name, Fabius, so probably based on a word meaning 'bean'. (*27 December*)

Faith: From the word meaning 'trusting in God'. Along with the similar names of Hope and Charity, it was popular among seventeenth-century Puritans. (*1 August, 6 October*)

Fatima: From the Arabic meaning 'weaner', given to someone who either weans a baby or abstains from forbidden things. It is a popular Muslim name and is perhaps best known as that of Muhammad's favourite daughter who died in AD 632. The village of Fatima in central Portugal was named after her. Today it is a Roman Catholic centre of pilgrimage after the Virgin Mary is said to have appeared to three children there in 1917.

Fauna: From the Latin meaning 'she who favours'. It is now used as a collective name for animals; 'flora' denotes plants.

Fay: Either from the French meaning 'faith', and so now regarded as a short form of the name, or from the word meaning 'fairy'. It was popular in the nineteenth century, possibly influenced by its association with Morgan Le Fay, half-sister to King Arthur in the Arthurian romances. The versions **Fae** and **Faye** are also used.

Felicia: The feminine form of Felix.

Felicity: From the word meaning 'lucky' or 'opportune' and so related to the male name, Felix. (*7 March, 23 November*)

Fenella: A form of the Irish name Fionnuala, meaning 'white shouldered'. In Celtic legend, she and her three brothers were supposed to be killed by a sorcerer hired by their stepmother who was jealous of her husband's love for his children. The sorcerer could not see through the murder because they were so pure; instead he turned them into swans. Other forms of the name are **Fionola** and **Finola**, although Fenella is the most usual form outside Ireland.

Fern: From the plant.

Ffion: The Welsh form of Fiona.

Fflur: A Welsh name meaning 'flower'. According to legend, Fflur was incredibly beautiful and possible suitors were sent far and wide on quests in the hope of winning her.

Fiona: From the Gaelic meaning 'white' or 'fair'.

Flavia: From the old Roman family name meaning 'yellow' or 'fair haired'.

Fleur: From the French meaning 'flower'.

Floella: A fairly recent name which seems to be simply a blend of Flo and Ella.

Flora: The goddess of flowers and the spring in Roman mythology whose breath was said to spread flowers over fields. Her festival, held in April each year, was supposedly a particularly drunken affair. (*24 November*)

Florence: From the Latin meaning 'blossoming' or 'flowering'. In Arthurian legend, Florence was the name of a son of Gawain. He was one of the knights who discovered Queen Guinevere and Sir Lancelot together. As Lancelot escaped, he killed several of the knights, including Florence. Perhaps the most famous bearer of the name was the nineteenth-century heroine, Florence Nightingale, the Lady with the Lamp, who nursed the soldiers in the Crimean War and founded a school of nursing in London. She, however, was so named because she was born in Florence in Italy.

Fortuna A goddess believed to bring good luck in Roman mythology.

Frances: The feminine form of Francis. (*9 March, 13 November*)

Francesca: The Italian form of Frances that is now generally used.

Freda: A feminine form of Frederick.

Frederica: Like Freda, a feminine form of Frederick.

Freya: From an Old Norse word meaning 'noble'. In Scandinavian mythology, Freya was the goddess of love, fertility and beauty.

G

Gabriella: The feminine form of Gabriel, which is sometimes shortened to **Gaby**.

Gabrielle: The French feminine form of Gabriel.

Gaia: The goddess of earth in Greek mythology. Her name is based on the Greek word meaning 'earth'. This was the name chosen by Emma Thompson and Greg Wise for their daughter.

Gail: The short form of Abigail, which has come to be used as a given name in its own right.

Gaynor: Probably an anglicised form of the medieval name Guinevere, who was the unfaithful wife of King Arthur. Like it, Gaynor means 'fair and beautiful'.

Gemma: From the Italian meaning 'jewel', although it is also used as a variation of Emma. (*11 April*)

Genevieve: From the Old German words meaning 'race' and 'woman', so probably meaning 'kinswoman'. The name is particularly associated with France after the fourth-century St Genevieve, who is the patron saint of Paris. (*3 January*)

Georgette: The French feminine form of George.

Georgia: The feminine form of George, which is also elaborated to **Georgiana** or **Georgina**.

Geraldine: The feminine form of Gerald that was invented in the sixteenth century by the poet Henry Howard, Earl of

Surrey, for the subject of his sonnet, 'The Fair Geraldine'. The actual 'Geraldine' is believed to have been Lady Elizabeth Fitzgerald, daughter of the ninth Earl of Kildare.

Germaine: The feminine form of the unusual male name Germain, which itself was based on the Latin meaning 'brother'. (*15 June*)

Gertrude: From the Old German words meaning 'spear' and 'strength', so implying an 'able warrior'. It was a popular name in the Middle Ages but is little used today.

Ghislain: A fairly recent name that is probably based on Giselle.

Gigi: The French pet form of Giselle.

Gillian: A form of Julian, which itself was originally a girl's name.

Ginger: Used either as a nickname for someone with red hair or as a pet form of Virginia. Probably its most famous bearer was the actress Ginger Rogers, famous for her series of 'song and dance' films with Fred Astaire. Her actual name was Virginia.

Giselle: From the Old German meaning 'pledge', which probably arose from the medieval practice of leaving children as pledges for an alliance.

Gladys: From the Welsh name Gwladys, which probably means 'delicate flower'.

Glen: Originally a surname based on the Gaelic word meaning 'valley'. The form **Glenn** is used both as a male and female name, as in the actress Glenn Close. Another form, **Glyn**, has recently come into use as a first name.

Glenda: From the Welsh meaning 'clean' and 'good', although it may be based on the word meaning 'valley' and so imply a 'girl from the valley'.

Gloria: From the Latin meaning 'glory'. The name first came into popular use in the twentieth century.

Gloriana: Queen of the Faeries in Spenser's romance, *The Faerie Queene*. This poetic work was Spenser's representation of the England of his time, and Gloriana was Elizabeth I.

Glynis: Probably from the Welsh word meaning 'pure' or that meaning 'valley'. The form **Glenys** is also used.

Grace: From the word 'grace', which today is used to describe elegance and beauty. In the Bible, however, it denotes God's love for man. The name was first used by the seventeenth-century Puritans and has been in fairly constant use since.

Gracia: According to one of the sources of the Arthurian legends, Gracia was the name of one of King Arthur's nieces.

Greta: A short form of Margareta.

Griselda: Possibly from the Old German meaning 'grey' and 'battle'.

Gudrun: From the Old Norse words meaning 'god' and 'secret'. In Norse mythology, she is the wife of Sigurd.

Guinevere: From the Welsh meaning 'fair and beautiful'. The name is most readily associated with the beautiful wife of King Arthur whose affair with Sir Lancelot marked the beginning of the end for Arthur and his Round Table. When Queen Guinevere and Sir Lancelot were discovered together by some of Arthur's knights, Lancelot fled and Guinevere was sentenced to death. Lancelot returned to save her and the pair fled, leading Arthur to declare war on Lancelot. It was while Arthur was away on this battle that Mordred rebelled against him, forcing Arthur to return and fight what was to be his final battle. The Cornish form of the name, **Jenniver**, led to the more familiar Jennifer.

Gwen: From the Welsh meaning 'white' or 'pure'. In some sources of the Arthurian legend, Gwen is King Arthur's grandmother. There are several variations of the name, including **Gwynn**, Winifred and **Wynne**.

Gwendolen: With its other forms, **Gwendolina** and **Gwendolyn**, this is based on the Welsh words meaning 'white' and 'ring'. Gwendolina was the wife of Merlin in the Arthurian romances.

Gwenllian: From the Welsh meaning 'flaxen', so 'blond'.

Gwyneth: Either from the Welsh word meaning 'luck' or that meaning 'bliss'.

H

Hafwen: From the Welsh meaning 'fair summer', which would make a lovely name for a child born in the summer months.

Hannah: From the Hebrew meaning 'favoured'. In the Bible, she is the barren wife of Elkanah who prays to God for a son, promising that she would give him to the service of the Lord. God answered her prayers and she became the mother of the great prophet Samuel.

Harriet: The English form of the French name Henriette, itself a pet feminine form of Henri (Henry).

Hayley: Originally a surname from the Old English meaning 'hay clearing', although some have linked it to the Gaelic word meaning 'escape'. It has only been popularly used since the 1960s and is particularly associated with the actress Hayley Mills.

Hazel: From the name of the tree and the light-brown colour. It would be a good name for someone with 'hazel' eyes.

Heather: From the plant. It was first used in the late nineteenth century and has remained popular ever since.

Hebe: From the Greek meaning 'young'. In Greek mythology, Hebe is a daughter of Zeus and the personification of youth.

Heidi: The Swiss pet form of the name Adelheid, itself a form of Adelaide. It was certainly made popular by Johanna Spyri's classic 1881 children's book of the same name.

Helen: From the Greek meaning 'bright'. In Greek mythology, Helen is the beautiful daughter of Zeus and Leda. Her elopement with the Trojan prince, Paris, sparked the Trojan War.

Helena: A form of Helen. (*18 August*)

Henrietta: The Italian form of Henriette.

Hera: From the Greek meaning 'lady', which also gave the word 'hero'. In Greek mythology, she is the 'Queen of

Heaven'. The sister and wife of Zeus and goddess of marriage, she renewed her virginity every year by bathing in a magical spring.

Hermione: The daughter of Helen and Orestes in Greek mythology.

Hester: A form of Esther that is now regarded as a name in its own right.

Hestia: The goddess of the hearth and home in Greek mythology who was worshipped by every family. She was the sister of Zeus and swore to him that she would always remain a virgin.

Heulwen: From the Welsh meaning 'sunshine'.

Hilary: From the Latin meaning 'joyful' and directly linked to the modern English word 'hilarious'. It was originally used as a boy's name, and still is occasionally, but is now generally regarded as a name for girls. (*13 January, 5 May*)

Hilda: From the Old German meaning 'battle'. It was originally part of longer names such as Hildegard. (*17 November*)

Holly: From the evergreen plant that has become synonymous with Christmas, so often given to girls born around this time.

Honesty: A relatively modern name used partly because of the quality and partly after the flower.

Honey: From the word meaning the produce of bees, which has an associated meaning of 'sweet' and has been a term of endearment for a long time.

Honour: A form of the medieval name Honoria, it was used by the seventeenth-century Puritans after the quality of integrity. Alternative forms such as **Honor** and **Honora** are also used.

Hope: Originally a surname based on the Old English place name meaning 'small valley', which can still be found in places such as Stanford le Hope. However, it was first used as a given name by the seventeenth-century Puritans as one of the three Christian virtues of Faith, Hope and Charity. (*1 August*)

Horatia: The feminine form of the Roman family name, Horatius, which gave Horace. Horatio Nelson gave the name to his daughter.

Hortense: From the old Roman family name, Hortensius, which is of uncertain origin but possibly based on the Latin meaning 'garden'.

Hyacinth: From the name of the flower. In Greek mythology, Hyacinthus was a beautiful boy loved by Apollo. Apollo accidentally killed him with a discus and a flower sprung up where his blood fell. The origin of his name is uncertain. It was originally used as a boy's name but has come to be regarded as exclusively female. (*17 August, 11 September*)

I

Ida: From the Old German meaning 'work'. However, it is more usually associated with Mount Ida, where, according to Greek mythology, Zeus was brought up in a cave. In Ireland, it is sometimes used as a form of **Ide**, meaning 'thirst for knowledge'.

Ilia: The mother of Romulus and Remus in Roman mythology who was also called Rhea Silvia.

Iliona: Possibly from the Greek meaning 'Lady of Troy', as Ilion was another name for Troy. In Greek mythology, Iliona is the daughter of Priam, King of Troy.

Ilona: The Hungarian form of Helen.

Imogen: The name was first used by Shakespeare for the daughter of Cymbeline in his play of that name. Although it suggests a link to the word 'image', it is more likely to have been a development of the Celtic name **Innogen**, which probably means 'daughter'. Whether the altered spelling was intentional or simply a mistake will never be known.

India: From the name of the country, which itself is taken from the river Indus, now mostly flowing through Pakistan.

Ingrid: Based on the Old Norse god of fertility, Ing, and the word meaning 'fair' or 'beautiful'.

Inira: A Welsh name meaning 'honour'.

Inogen: In some sources of Arthurian legend, Inogen is one of Merlin's daughters.

Iole: From the Greek meaning 'violet'. In Greek mythology, she was the daughter of the King of Oechalia and was won by Heracles in an archery contest. When her father refused to give her up, Heracles invaded Oechalia and defeated him. However, Heracles's jealous wife, Deianeira, gave him a shirt dipped in blood, which was supposed to make him love her forever. Instead it burned off pieces of his body and he was left in so much pain that he ordered his son both to build him a funeral pyre and to marry Iole himself!

Iona: In use as a given name since the mid-nineteenth century, this is taken from the island in the Hebrides where St Columba founded a monastery in AD 563. An alternative spelling is **Ione**.

Irene: From the Greek meaning 'peace'. In Greek mythology, she is the daughter of Zeus and the goddess of peace. (3 *April*)

Iris: Either given after the flower or after the messenger of the gods in Greek mythology. Her name came from the Greek meaning 'rainbow' because the rainbow was seen as the means of communication between the gods and man. It was the name chosen by Jude Law and Sadie Frost for their daughter.

Irma: From the Old German meaning 'whole', this used to be the first part of several other names. It was introduced to England in the nineteenth century.

Isabel: The Spanish form of Elizabeth, with an ending suggesting 'beautiful'. Along with the Italian version, **Isabella**, and the French, **Isabelle**, it has been a popular name since medieval times. It was the name of three royal wives, those of King John, King Edward II and King Richard II. In Spain, it is used as a generic name for any member of the British royal family. The Queen, for example, is known as Isabel II de Gran Bretana. The spelling **Isobel** is also used.

Iseult: From the Welsh meaning 'beautiful one'. It is the name of the beautiful Irish princess tragically in love with Tristan in the Arthurian romances. Here Iseult, the daughter of the King of Ireland, mistakenly drank a love potion and fell hopelessly in love with Tristan. The couple separated but, when Tristan was badly wounded, he sent for her saying that the ship should have white sails if she were aboard and black if she were not. Tristan's resentful wife falsely told him the sails were black and he died. Iseult herself died of a broken heart when she learned of his death.

Isidora: The feminine form of Isidore. An alternative spelling is **Isadora**.

Isla: A recent name, fairly popular in Scotland, which is taken from the island and pronounced in the same way.

Ivy: From the plant.

J

Jacqueline: The feminine form of the French male name Jacques, which corresponds to the English James and Jacob. This name has many variations, including **Jacqui**, **Jakelyn** and **Jacolyn**.

Jade: From the precious stone, which was known in Spain as the 'stone of the bowels' because it was thought to protect against bowel disorders! It is probably most readily associated with Jade Jagger, daughter of the Rolling Stones' Mick.

Jan: A short form of either John for men, or names such as Janet and Janice in women.

Jancis: A relatively modern name that appears to be a mixture of Jan and Frances. It was first used by Mary Webb in her novel *Precious Bane*, published in 1924.

Jane: From the Old French name Jehanne, itself a feminine form of John. As an historical royal name it has unfortunate associations. In the sixteenth century, Jane Seymour, the third wife of King Henry VIII, died shortly after giving birth to the future Edward VI. Even sadder was the case of Lady Jane Grey, made queen by the Protestants after the death of Edward VI, who lasted just a few days before being overpowered by Queen Mary I and executed for treason. She was only sixteen when she died. The spelling **Jayne** is also used. (*12 December*)

Janelle: A modern elaborate form of Jane, which is also sometimes spelled **Janella**.

Janet: Originally a Scottish form of Jane but now used as a given name in its own right.

Janice: A form of Jane that was probably first used by Paul Leicester Ford in his novel *Janice Meredith*, published in 1899. The name has also developed the spelling **Janis**.

Janine: A simplified form of Jeannine, the French feminine form of John.

Jasmine: From the name of the sweet-smelling plant.

Jean: The medieval spelling of the Old French name Jehanne, so the same as Jane and Joan. It is popularly associated with the inspiring and sometimes harsh Edinburgh schoolteacher in Muriel Spark's novel *The Prime of Miss Jean Brodie*, published in 1961. The name has developed many variations, including **Jeane**, **Jeanette** and **Jeannie**.

Jemima: From the Hebrew meaning 'dove'. In the Bible, Jemima was the beautiful daughter of Job, the eldest of ten children – three girls and seven boys. Today, though, it is a name that is more likely to be associated with Beatrix Potter's *Jemima Puddleduck*.

Jennifer: The Cornish form of Guinevere, so meaning 'fair and beautiful'. It is only relatively recently that the name has been in general use outside Cornwall.

Jenny: Although this is generally used as a pet form of Jennifer, it started as a medieval form of Jean.

Jessica: Probably invented by Shakespeare for the daughter of Shylock in his play *The Merchant of Venice*, written in 1596. He may have based it on the biblical name Iscah, Lot's sister, but this is uncertain.

J

Jewel: From the Old French meaning 'plaything', this has only recently been used as a given name rather than solely for precious stones.

Jezebel: From the Hebrew meaning 'domination'! In the Bible, she is the wife of King Ahab who persecuted those who believed in the true God. In more recent times, it has come to be used to describe a shameless woman.

Jill: A short form of Gillian that has been in use since medieval times. In fact, it was then taken as a generic word for 'girl', where 'Jack' meant 'boy'; hence the use of both names in the nursery rhyme.

Joan: From the Old French name Johanne, so the same as Jane and Jean. Perhaps the most famous bearer of the name was the fifteenth-century French heroine, Joan of Arc. (*2 February, 4 February, 30 May, 24 August*)

Joanna: From the Greek name Iaonna, the male equivalent of which became John. There are many variations of the name, including **Joanne** and **Johanna**. In the Bible, Joanna is wife of the manager of King Herod's household. She was healed by Jesus and was with him at the end of his life.

Jocasta: Possibly from the Greek meaning 'woe adorned'. In Greek mythology, Jocasta was the famous tragic mother of Oedipus who became, through several misunderstandings, his wife and the mother of his children. When she learned the truth, she hanged herself.

Jocelyn: From a surname that was based on an Old French male name derived from the name of the Gauts, a Germanic tribe. It was introduced to England following the Norman Conquest and has since been used as both a male and female name. Another spelling would be **Josceline**.

Jody: Along with **Jodie**, this is a fairly modern name of uncertain origin, although it may be a form of Judy.

Joelle: The feminine form of Joel.

Jolene: A relatively recent name that seems to have originated in the USA in the 1940s. The Jolene of the title of the famous country and western song was obviously beautiful since she was entreated not to take a man 'just because you can'!

Jonquil: From the name of the flower, which is based on the Latin meaning 'reed'.

Josephine: The feminine form of Joseph made famous by the Empress Josephine, to whom Napoleon is popularly supposed to have said, 'Not tonight, Josephine'. Even in her case, though, it was a pet form as her actual name was Marie Josephe.

Josette: A modern French pet form of Josephine.

Joy: From the vocabulary word. It was popular among the seventeenth-century Puritans who gave it to their children to represent their 'joy in the Lord'.

Joyce: Not connected to the words 'joy' and 'rejoice' as is commonly believed, but actually from a Norman male name meaning 'Lord'. The name became a fairly common surname, particularly in Ireland, before becoming an exclusively female given name.

Judith: From the Hebrew meaning 'woman of Judea', although it has also been linked to the Hebrew meaning 'praise'. In the Bible, Judith is the wife of Esau, whose parents had opposed the wedding because she came from a heathen tribe. In the Book of Judith, she saved her people from the Assyrians by gaining the confidence of their leader, Holofernes, and cutting off his head as he slept.

Judy: A pet form of Judith that is sometimes used as a name in its own right.

Julia: The feminine form of Julian. It is sometimes elaborated to **Juliana** and **Julianne**. The French form, **Julie**, is also used. (*19 June Juliana*)

Juliet: The anglicised form of both the Italian Giulietta and the French **Juliette**, both ultimately forms of Julia. The name will always be associated with one of the star-crossed lovers in Shakespeare's play *Romeo and Juliet*. In this, she was specifically named after the month of July – itself named after Julius Caesar – which was when she was born.

June: A name given after the month of the year. The month is supposed to have been named after Juno, the goddess of womanhood and childbirth in Roman mythology.

Juniper: From the name of the plant with which gin is flavoured. The plant name itself is of uncertain origin.

Juno From the name of the Roman goddess of womanhood and childbirth, who was the wife of Jupiter.

Justina: The feminine form of Justin. (*7 October*)

Justine: The French feminine form of Justin.

Juventas: The goddess of youth in Roman mythology and, more recently in the form **Juventus**, the name of a famous football team.

K

Karen: The Danish form of Katherine, which was introduced to the USA by Scandinavian immigrants in the early twentieth century.

Karin: A Swedish form of Katherine which, like another Swedish version, Katarina, is occasionally used.

Kate: A short form of Katherine that has been used since medieval times. Shakespeare used the name in both *Henry V*, where she is the daughter of the King of France, and *The Taming of the Shrew*. It is in this latter play that the famous line 'Kiss me Kate' appears, which was adopted as the title of a popular Broadway musical in 1948.

Katelyn: Used either as an elaborate form of Kate or as a form of the Irish **Caitlin**, itself a form of Catherine.

Katharine: A slightly altered version of Katherine. The spelling is popular in the USA and is, for example, the form used by the actress Katharine Hepburn.

Katherine: See Catherine.

Kathleen: The anglicised form of the Irish Caitlin. As with the original name Catherine, this can also be spelled **Cathleen**.

Katie: A short form of Katherine that has become particularly popular as a name in its own right.

Katya: The Russian pet form of Yekaterina, itself a form of Katherine.

Kay: A name with several possible origins, so take your pick. It could be related to the Old English meaning 'key' and so would have been given to a key-maker; it might have developed from a name given to someone who lived near a quay or even to someone who had the features of a jackdaw, which was known as a kay (from its call).

Kayla: A recent name that appears to be a form of Kayley/Kayleigh.

Kayley: A recent name that is either a mixture of Kay and Kelly or taken from the Irish surname, which is ultimately based on a word meaning 'slender'. An alternative spelling is **Kayleigh**.

Kelly: A name used for both boys and girls, which is probably based on an Irish surname that ultimately comes from the word meaning 'church'.

Kendall: From the surname that derived from either Kendal in Cumbria, which was so named because it is in the valley of the river Kent, or from Kendale, which got its name from the Old Norse word meaning 'spring'.

Keren: A short form of the biblical name, Keren-happuch, of one of Job's daughters. It is taken from the Hebrew meaning 'horn of eye-paint'.

Kerry: A fairly recent name that is probably taken from the Irish county. The name of the county ultimately means 'country of the dark children'.

Kestrel: Sometimes used as a girl's name, this is taken from the name of the bird, which is ultimately from the Old French meaning 'rattle'.

Kimberley: From the South African city founded in 1871 after diamonds were found there. It was named after John Woodhouse, first Earl of Kimberley, who was British Secretary of State for the Colonies at the time. The short form, **Kim**, is now used as a girl's name in its own right.

Kirsten: The Danish and Norwegian form of Christine that, like its variant **Kirstin**, is now generally used.

Kirstie: Originally a Scottish pet form of **Kirstine**, itself a form of Christine, but now generally used. An alternative spelling is **Kirsty**.

Kit: Either a pet form of Christopher or, if female, of Katherine.

Kristen: The Danish form of Christian.

Kristene: An elaborate form of Christine.

Kristie: A form of Christie.

Kristina: The Swedish and Czech form of Christina.

Kyla: A relatively recent name which appears to be a feminine form of Kyle.

Kylie: A particularly Australian name that is probably a blend of Kyle and Kelly. It is most readily associated with the actress and singer, Kylie Minogue.

L

Lamia: From the Greek meaning 'throat'. In Greek mythology, Lamia is one of the daughters of Hecate, who were able to turn themselves into cows or young girls. As girls, they slept with men before sucking their blood when they slept. An ancient 'black widow spider', so to speak.

Lara: The Russian short form of Larissa. In Roman mythology, Lara is a talkative nymph who has her tongue cut out to keep her quiet. The name appears to have been invented by the poet Ovid to mean 'chatterer'. In a rather more romantic association, Lara is one of the main characters in Boris Pasternak's classic novel, *Dr Zhivago*.

Larissa: A name of uncertain origin but possibly from the ancient town of Larissa, in Greek mythology thought to be the birthplace of Achilles.

Lark: From the name of the bird that traditionally sings at dawn.

Laura: The feminine form of the Latin name meaning 'laurel'.

Laurel: From the name of the tree. In Arthurian legend, Laurel is the wife of Sir Gawain's brother Agravain.

Lauren: Of uncertain origin but possibly a feminine form of Laurence. It may have been first used by the actress Lauren Bacall.

Lauretta: The Italian form of Laura.

Lavender: From the name of the sweet-smelling plant.

Laverna: The goddess of thieves in Roman mythology.

Lavinia: In Roman mythology, she is the wife of Aeneas and so the mother of the Roman people. She is supposed to have given her name to the Latin town of Lavinium but it was probably the other way round and she was invented to explain the place name.

Lea: A form of Leah.

Leah: From the Hebrew meaning 'gazelle', although it has also been linked to the word meaning 'to be weary'. In the Bible, Leah is the first wife of Jacob. He had worked for her father for seven years to get permission to marry her sister Rachel. It was only after the wedding that he found out he had married the wrong sister and had to work another seven years before marrying Rachel as well.

Leanne: A modern name that combines Lee and Anne.

Leda: Probably from the Lycian word meaning 'woman'. In Greek mythology, she is the Queen of Sparta. She was seduced by Zeus, who was, surprisingly, disguised as a swan, and laid two eggs. From these hatched two sets of twins.

Lee: From the Old English surname meaning 'clearing in a wood', so it would have been given to someone who lived there. Alternatively, it may derive from the Gaelic meaning 'poem'.

Leigh: A form of Lee.

Leila: From the Arabic meaning 'night', used to describe a dark-haired or dark-skinned woman. It has several forms including **Laila** and **Layla**.

Lena: Either a shortened form of Helena or taken from the very long river in Siberia.

Lenora: A short form of Leonora.

Leona: A feminine form of Leo.

Leonie: The French feminine form of Leo.

Leonora: The short form of Eleonora, itself the Italian form of Eleanor.

Leslie: From a Scottish surname, itself from a place name of uncertain origin. As a girl's name, the spelling is usually **Lesley**.

Letitia: From the Latin meaning 'joy'. Its original form was Lettice.

Lia: An Italian name that is probably a short form of Rosalia.

Libby: A short form of Elizabeth, which is now used as a given name in its own right.

Lilac: From the name of the plant. The plant name comes from the Persian word meaning 'bluish'.

Lilian: This may well have developed as a pet form of Elizabeth, although it is now popularly associated with the lily flower.

Lilith: From the Hebrew meaning 'night'. In Babylonian mythology, she is the goddess of the night said, by some, to stalk menacingly on dark nights.

Lily: From the name of the flower, which is often used as a symbol of purity. As such, it was a lovely name for Johnny Depp and Vanessa Paradis to choose for their daughter, Lily-Rose.

Linda: A name of uncertain origin that may have developed from the Spanish meaning 'pretty' or the Italian meaning 'neat'. Others have associated it with the Old German meaning 'serpent', a creature that was highly respected for its supposed wisdom and grace.

Lindsay: From a Scottish surname, although this was based on the place Lindsey in Lincolnshire, which has the meaning 'the wetland belonging to Lincoln'. It is now used for both boys and girls, with various forms including **Lindsey**, **Linsy** and **Lynsey**.

Lisa: One of the many pet forms of Elizabeth that has come to be used as a given name in its own right.

Lisette: The French form of Lise, itself a short form of Elizabeth.

Livia: Either used as a short form of Olivia or from an old Roman family name, Livius. This is of uncertain origin but is possibly from the Latin meaning 'bluish'.

Lois: Of uncertain origin but possibly from the Hebrew meaning either 'good' or 'desirable'. In the Bible, Lois was grandmother of St Timothy, converted by St Paul with her daughter Eunice. Together they brought Timothy up as a Christian and St Paul later took him with him on his travels.

Lola: The Spanish pet form of Dolores.

Lora: The German form of Laura.

Loretta: A pet form of Laura, which is also spelled **Lauretta**.

Lorna: Invented by R. D. Blackmore for the name of the heroine of his famous novel *Lorna Doone*, published in 1869. It is possible that he based it on a word such as 'forlorn', which would make sense given that the young Lorna was kidnapped by Exmoor outlaws. However, he may also have based the name on the place in Scotland, Lorn, as the story reveals her to be of noble Scottish birth.

Lorraine: From the Latin meaning 'kingdom of Lothair', which was the origin of the region in eastern France. In the ninth century, the kingdom itself was given to Lothar II, great-grandson of Charlemagne, by his father.

Lotta: Of uncertain origin. In Arthurian legend, Lotta is a Queen of Ireland and mother to the tragic Iseult.

Lottie: A pet form of Charlotte, which is now sometimes used as a name in its own right.

Louisa: Feminine form of the French name Louis. The actual French form, **Louise**, is now generally used. (*15 March*)

Lourdes: From the famous centre of pilgrimage in France where the Virgin Mary appeared to St Bernadette in 1858. The most famous current bearer of the name is the young daughter of the singer Madonna.

Luana: A relatively recent name, having been first used in the 1932 King Vidor film, *The Bird of Paradise*.

Lucia: The feminine form of an old Roman given name, Lucius, which is probably based on the Latin meaning 'light'.

Lucilla: An early pet form of Lucia, which is also used in the form **Lucille**.

Lucinda: An elaborate form of Lucia.

Lucretia: The feminine form of the Roman family name, Lucretius, which may be based on the Latin meaning 'gain'. Certainly its most infamous bearer was Lucretia Borgia who, in the fifteenth century, is said to have committed incest with both her father, himself a Pope, and her brother. In Greek mythology, Lucretia, the wife of Tarquinius Collatinus, was raped by Sextus and killed herself. She was the inspiration for Shakespeare's poem, 'The Rape of Lucrece'. For all that, it is a lovely name that deserves to come back into fashion.

Lucy: As with Lucia, this is probably based on the Latin meaning 'light'. (*13 December*)

Ludmila: A Russian and Czech name from the words meaning 'people' and 'grace'. In the tenth century, St Ludmila was the grandmother of St Wenceslas, hero of the popular Christmas song. St Ludmila was murdered by her mother-in-law and regarded as a martyr. The form **Ludmilla** is also used. Short or pet forms include **Mattie**, **Matty** and **Matya**. (*16 September*)

Lulu: A pet form of Louise.

Luna: The goddess of the moon in Roman mythology.

Lydia: From the Greek meaning 'woman of Lydia', where Lydia is an ancient region in Asia Minor. In the Bible, Lydia is a woman who plied her trade of selling purple cloth in Philippi. Here she met St Paul and was baptised by him. Centuries on, Lydia remains one of the most popular names given to girls.

Lynette: A Celtic name, also spelled **Linet**, which is possibly based on the word meaning 'waterfall'. According to legend, Linet had the power to rescue imprisoned knights.

Lynn: Probably a pet form of Linda.

M

Mabel: From the Old French meaning 'lovely'. The form
   Mabelle has developed from the French meaning 'my
   beautiful one'. A popular name until the 1940s, it has since
   dropped completely out of fashion, which is a pity.
Madeleine: The French form of the second word of the name
   Mary Magdalene. This was based on the place Magdala, a
   biblical town in the modern Israel. In a very different vein,
   Madeline is the name of the little schoolgirl, heroine of the
   book by Ludwig Bemelmans published in 1952. The story is
   having a second lease of life, having recently been serialised
   on television and made into a film, so the name may
   become more popular.
Madge: A pet form of Margaret.
Madison: A popular name in Canada, Madison was the
   surname of James Madison, the fourth president of the
   United States. The origins are uncertain but it could mean
   good or mighty.
Madonna: From the Italian title of the Virgin Mary, meaning
   'my lady'.
Mae: A form of May.
Maeve: The anglicised form of the Irish Madhbh, which may
   be based on a word meaning 'bringing joy' or 'intoxicating'.
   It is the name of a legendary Queen of Connacht who
   argued with her second husband over a herd of cows and
   went to war with Ulster in an attempt to capture a bull.
Maggie: One of the many pet forms of Margaret that is
   sometimes used as a name in its own right.
Maia: From the Greek meaning 'mother' or 'nurse'. In Greek
   mythology, Maia is the eldest and most beautiful of the
   seven daughters of Atlas, known as the Pleiades, who were
   turned into doves by Zeus. She is the mother of Hermes by
   Zeus. She was adopted by the Romans, who identified her

with another goddess of nature and the spring and named the month of May after her.

Maidie: Originally a pet name for a maid that became a nickname before being used as a given name.

Maisie: A pet form of Margaret that developed from the Scottish version, Mairead. It has become quite popular, perhaps influenced by the little mouse of the children's books by Aileen Paterson.

Malvina: A name invented by the eighteenth-century Scottish poet, James Macpherson, for his alleged translation of an ancient Gaelic bard called Ossian. From where he got the name is uncertain, although it has been linked to words meaning 'smooth brow' or 'follower of Mena'.

Mandy: A short form of Amanda, now sometimes used as a given name in its own right.

Mara: From the Hebrew meaning 'bitter'. In the Bible, it is the name that Naomi asks to be called after the death of her husband and two sons.

Marcella: The feminine form of Marcel. (*31 January*)

Marcia: A feminine form of Marcus. The version **Marsha** is also used.

Margaret: From the Greek meaning 'pearl'. This has been a favourite royal name for centuries, from the eleventh-century St Margaret of Scotland, wife of King Malcolm, to the current Princess Margaret. The name has many forms including **Margery**, **Marjorie**, **Meg** and **Peggy**. (*18 January, 22 February, 20 July, 16 October, 16 November*)

Margot: The French pet form of Marguerite.

Marguerite: The French form of Margaret, which is now used in this country mainly because of its association with the large daisy.

Maria: A form of Mary.

Marianne: A combination of Mary and Anne that has become a popular name, particularly since it represents the names of the Virgin Mary and her mother, St Anne. At a very different level, the name became symbolic in the eighteenth-century French Revolution. This may have been after the Spanish historian Juan de Mariana, who had advocated the assassination of tyrant monarchs, although this is uncertain.

Marie: A form of Mary.

Marigold: From the flower. The Old English name of the flower was 'golde'. At some point before the fourteenth century, though, the flower became associated with the Virgin Mary and the name was extended.

Marilyn: A relatively recent combination of Mary and 'lyn' that was made particularly popular by the beautiful actress Marilyn Monroe, whose stage name was markedly more attractive than her given name of Norma Jean. There are several variations in the spelling including **Marilynn**, **Marylyn** and **Marilene**.

Marina: Although frequently used as a form of Mary, this name is actually from the Latin Marinus, which is either based on Mars, the Roman god of war, or from the word meaning 'of the sea'. (*12 February*)

Marion: A form of Marie that has been used since the Middle Ages. Its best-known early bearer was Maid **Marian**, who plays a key role in the legend of Robin Hood. In Arthurian legend, **Marrion** was the name of one of Morgan Le Fay's sisters. (*30 April*)

Marisa: A fairly modern elaborate form of Maria. The spelling **Marissa** is also used.

Marjorie: A development of the name Margery, itself a medieval form of Margaret.

Marlene: A short form of the name Maria Magdalene. It was probably first used by the actress Marlene Dietrich, whose actual name was Maria Magdalena.

Martha: From the Aramaic meaning 'lady' or 'mistress'. In the Bible, Martha is the sister of Lazarus and Mary of Bethany. All three were friends of Jesus, and it was Lazarus whom Jesus later raised from the dead. Martha's name came to be associated with domestic chores after the biblical Martha was 'cumbered with much serving' when Jesus visited the family while her sister sat down and listened to him. (*19 January, 29 July*)

Marti: A short form of Martina or Martine. The forms **Martie** and **Marty** are also used.

Martina: The feminine form of Martin that has been in use since medieval times. The form **Martine** is also used. (*30 January*)

Mary: A form of the earlier name Miriam. Although this has been linked to the Hebrew meaning 'bitter' or 'rebelliousness', the actual origin is more likely to be in the Egyptian suggesting 'strong' or 'fertile'. The latter of these is obviously appropriate for the woman chosen to bear God's son. Mary has been an extremely popular name for many centuries, particularly given in honour of the Virgin Mary. In the Bible's New Testament, though, she is one of several Marys featured, the other prominent bearers of the name being Mary Magdalene, Mary the sister of Martha, Mary the mother of James and Joseph, and Mary the mother of Mark. It has also been a favourite royal name. In this sense it is probably best associated with Mary I, known as Bloody Mary, the sister to Elizabeth I and an ardent Catholic, and Mary, Queen of Scots, who claimed the English throne and was beheaded for her treason by Elizabeth I in 1587. There are a great many variations of the name including **Maria**, **Mariah**, **Mari**, **Maire** and **Marie**. (*25 March, 2 April, 14 May Maria, 25 May, 31 May, 2 July, 6 July Maria, 16 July, 22 July, 15 August, 8 September, 24 November, 8 December, 15 December*)

Matilda: From the Old German meaning 'mighty in battle'. It is apt, therefore, that this was the name of the wife of William the Conqueror. More recently, it has become associated, to a certain extent, with the precocious child in Roald Dahl's children's book of the same name, published in 1988. The form **Mathilda** is also used. Short or pet forms include **Mattie**, **Matty**, **Matya**, **Tilda** and **Tilly**. (*14 March*)

Matuta: A goddess of the dawn in Roman mythology.

Maud: A development of the name Matilda that has been in use since medieval times. The spelling **Maude** is also used.

Maura: An Irish form of Mary.

Maureen: The anglicised form of the Irish name Maire, itself equivalent to Mary.

Mavis: A relatively modern name that probably developed from the alternative name for the song thrush.

May: Originally a pet form of Margaret and Mary but now used as a name in its own right. It has come to be associated with the month, which itself was named after Maia, goddess of the spring in Roman mythology.

Medea: Probably from the Greek meaning 'thought', a word that also gave the English 'meditate'. In Greek mythology, Medea was the daughter of Aetes of Cochis. She loved Jason and helped him steal the Golden Fleece from her father but, after Jason left, she killed his new love and her own children before escaping to Athens on a chariot drawn by winged serpents . . . and that's only half the story!

Megan: A Welsh form of Margaret based on the pet form, Meg..

Melanie: From the Greek meaning 'black' or 'dark', so suitable for someone with dark hair or eyes. (*8 June Melania, 31 December Melania*)

Melinda: A modern name probably combining the pet name 'Mel' with Linda.

Melissa: From the Greek meaning 'bee'. In Greek mythology, Melissa is the daughter of Melissus, King of Crete. She was supposed to be the first person to have discovered how to collect honey from bees, which she used to feed the infant Zeus.

Melody: A modern name based on the Greek meaning 'singer of songs'.

Melora: Of uncertain origin. In some versions of the Arthurian romances, Melora is King Arthur's daughter. When Orlando, the man she loved, was imprisoned on the instructions of Merlin, Melora dressed as a knight and completed several seemingly impossible tasks (including getting the carbuncle of the daughter of the King of Narsinga) in order to free him.

Mena: An Irish name that is either a short form of Philomena, which is based on the Latin meaning 'daughter of light', or based on the Greek meaning 'nightingale'.

Mercedes: From *Maria de las Mercedes* (Mary of the Mercies), which is the Spanish title for the Virgin Mary. Today, of course, it is particularly associated with the make of car, which was itself named after the daughter of racing driver Emil Jellinek.

Mercy: From the Latin meaning 'reward', this was a popular name among the seventeenth-century Puritans and was given by them as a reference to God's forgiveness of sins. Some use the name as an anglicised form of Mercedes.

Meredith: A Welsh name taken from the surname meaning 'great lord'. It was originally used as a boy's name but is now used exclusively for girls.

Merle: Either used as a short form of Muriel or taken from the Old French meaning 'blackbird'.

Merry: A short form of names such as Mercy and Meredith that is sometimes used as a given name in its own right.

Meryl: A recent name made popular by the actress Meryl Streep, whose actual name is Mary.

Mia: The Danish and Swedish pet form of Maria that is now used generally, possibly influenced by the actress Mia Farrow. Kate Winslet and Jim Threapleton chose this name for their daughter.

Michaela: A feminine form of Michael.

Michelle: The French feminine form of Michael that is now used generally, particularly after the success of the Beatles song of the same name.

Mildred: From the Old English meaning 'gentle giant'. It probably came about after the Old English custom of repeating certain elements in the names of all members of a family, regardless of the meaning. For example, in the seventh century, St Mildred, who probably gave the original name, had a sister called Mildburh, which means 'gentle dwelling place'.

Millicent: From the Old German meaning 'strong worker'. The name was brought to England by the Normans following the Conquest of 1066. The short forms of **Milly** and **Millie** are also used.

Mimi: The Italian pet form of Maria. It is perhaps best known as the nickname of the heroine of Puccini's opera *La Bohème*, written in 1896.

Minerva: A goddess of household arts in Roman mythology.

Minnie: A pet form of the name Wilhelmina, Minnie has come to be immediately associated with Walt Disney's Minnie Mouse.

Mirabelle: From the Latin meaning 'lovely'. Along with the Italian form, **Mirabella**, this was a popular name in the Middle Ages.

Miranda: A name invented by Shakespeare for Prospero's daughter in *The Tempest*, written in 1612. It represents the Latin meaning 'fit to be wondered at'.

Miriam: From the Hebrew meaning 'strong' or 'fertile', it is the earlier form of Mary. In the Bible, Miriam is the sister of Moses and Aaron. When their mother hid the baby Moses in the bulrushes, it was Miriam who was given the task of watching over him, and who then suggested her mother as a nurse to the child when Moses was discovered by an Egyptian princess.

Moira: The anglicised form of the Irish name Maire, itself the equivalent of Mary.

Molly: A pet form of Mary. To a certain extent, the name is associated with the character Moll Flanders, who gets through life exploiting her appeal to men in Daniel Defoe's novel of the same name, published in 1722.

Mona: A traditionally Irish name of uncertain origin. It may be from the Gaelic meaning 'noble' or a short form of names

such as Monica or Madonna. Some have linked it to the
Greek meaning 'only' and others have seen a similarity with
the Norman name, Monique, based on the Latin meaning
'giver of advice'.

Moneta: A goddess of money in Roman mythology.

Monica: Of uncertain origin, although it may be based on the
Latin meaning 'giver of advice' or the Greek meaning
'only'. (*27 August*)

Morag: A typically Scottish name from the Gaelic meaning
'great young one'.

Morgan: Both an Irish and Welsh name that is given to both
boys and girls. It derives either from words meaning 'great
queen' or 'bright sea'. It is a fairly common surname that has
been transferred to a first name. In Arthurian legend,
Morgan Le Fay is the half-sister of King Arthur.

Muriel: Probably from the Celtic meaning 'sea bright'.

Myfanwy: A Welsh name meaning 'my lovely little one'.

Myra: A name invented by the seventeenth-century poet,
Fulke Greville, who might have created it as a form of Mary
or from 'myrrh'.

Myrtle: From the name of the evergreen plant.

N

Nadia: From the Russian name meaning 'hope'.

Nadine: The French form of Nadia.

Nana: A name occasionally used in Ireland, either from the
word meaning 'nine' or after the ancient goddess of flowers.

Nancy: Originally used as a pet form of Ann, this has now
come to be used as a given name in its own right. Today,
however, it could be associated with the slang 'nancy boy',
used to describe an effeminate man.

Nanette: A elaborate form of Nan, itself a pet form of Ann.

Naomi: From the Hebrew meaning 'my delight'. In the Bible,
Naomi is the mother-in-law of Ruth. When her husband
and two sons died in Moab, she travelled back to Judah

with Ruth and eventually married Boaz. It was a popular name among the seventeenth-century Puritans.

Natalie: The French form of the Russian name Natalya, based on the Latin meaning 'birthday'. It is often given to girls born around Christmas, which, of course, is Christ's birthday. The forms **Natalya** and **Natalia** are also used while the Russian pet form **Natasha** has become a very popular choice among parents. (*27 July Natalia*)

Nell: A short form of names such as Eleanor, Ellen or Helen. The spelling comes about after a pet way of using the names by which 'mine' was added. Ellen, for example, became 'mine Ellen', which then was naturally shortened to Nell. Simple, really.

Nerissa: From the Greek meaning 'Nereid'. In Greek mythology, the Nereids were 50 beautiful sea nymphs, daughters of the sea-god Nereus.

Nerys: A Welsh name that is based on the feminine form of the word meaning 'lord', thus meaning 'lady'.

Niamh: From the Gaelic meaning 'beauty' or 'radiance'. The mythical Niamh the daughter of the god of the sea, famed for taking her lover to a timeless land.

Nicola: A feminine form of Nicholas.

Nicole: The feminine form of Nicholas that has become a popular choice among parents.

Nigella: The feminine form of Nigel that is also an alternative name for the flower known as 'love-in-a-mist'.

Nike: The goddess of victory in Greek mythology. Today, though, the name is more likely to be associated with the make of sportswear.

Nina: Originally a pet form of names such as Antonina, the Russian feminine form of Anthony. The form **Nena** is also used.

Nona: From the Latin meaning 'ninth', so it's appropriate for a child born in the ninth month, September, or at nine o'clock.

Nora: Originally a short form of names such as Eleonora or Leonora.

Norma: Possibly a feminine form of Norman. It was probably first used by Felice Romani in his libretto for Bellini's opera of the same name, first performed in 1832.

Nyx: A goddess of the night in Greek mythology.

O

Octavia: From the Latin meaning 'eight', it was used for an eighth child in Victorian families but, given the generally smaller families of today, would be more appropriate for a child born in the eighth month, August, or at eight o'clock. In Roman history, Octavia is famous as the wife of Mark Antony who had to put up with his love for Cleopatra.

Odette: The French feminine form of the old male name, Oda, meaning 'prosperity'.

Odile: A French name from the same root as Odette so, like it, meaning 'prosperity'. (*13 December Odilia*)

Olga: The Russian form of a Scandinavian name meaning 'healthy' or 'holy'. The name was brought to Russia in the ninth century by Scandinavian settlers and became popular there after St Olga of Kiev, who converted to Christianity after the murder of her husband, Prince Igor. (*11 July*)

Olive: From the name of the plant, an ancient symbol of peace and friendship.

Olivia: A name first used by Shakespeare for the wealthy countess who is a character in *Twelfth Night*. It is certainly based on the name Olive and so relates to the plant.

Olwen: A Welsh name meaning 'white footprints'. In Welsh legend there is a woman who, wherever she walked, white flowers sprang up.

Opal: From the name of the gemstone.

Ophelia: From the Greek meaning 'help'. It was first used by the fifteenth–sixteenth-century Italian poet Jacopo Sannazzaro, and it was probably from here that Shakespeare got the name for the beautiful, tragic daughter of Polonius in *Hamlet*.

Ophrah: From the Hebrew meaning 'fawn'. In the Bible, it is used as a male name but is now more usually used as a female name. The forms **Oprah**, **Ophra** and **Ofra** are also used.

Ops: The goddess of plenty in Roman mythology.

Oriana: From the Latin meaning 'to rise'. The name is famous as that of the beloved of Amadis in the medieval romance *Amadis of Gaul*. Perhaps a good name for a child born at sunrise.

Oriel: Probably a form of Auriel, meaning 'golden'.

P

Page: From the Greek meaning 'child', it was originally an occupational name for a young servant. The form **Paige** has become increasingly popular.

Pamela: A name invented by Elizabethan pastoral poet Sir Philip Sidney for a character in his famous romance, *Arcadia*, written in 1581. He probably took it from the Greek words meaning 'all' and 'honey', so implying 'very sweet'.

Pandia: From the Greek meaning 'all divine'. In Greek mythology, Pandia is the daughter of Zeus and Selene, goddess of the moon.

Pandora: From the Greek words meaning 'all gifts'. In Greek mythology, Pandora was given a box and told not to open it. Her curiosity got the better of her and, on opening it, she released all the troubles of the world. Only hope remained.

Pansy: From the name of the flower, which is based on the Old French meaning 'thought'. Today, though, the name is more readily associated with the slang for an effeminate man.

Patience: From the Latin meaning 'to suffer'. As one of the Christian virtues, it was a favourite among the seventeenth-century Puritans.

Patrice: The medieval French form of Patrick or Patricia. In modern France it is a male name, but elsewhere it can be used as a female name.

Patricia: The feminine form of Patrick.

Patsy: A pet form of Patricia or Patrick. However, it should be carefully used because it is the slang word for a homosexual in Australia.

Paula: A feminine form of Paul.

Pauline: From the French feminine form of the Latin name that gave Paul.

Pax: From the Latin meaning 'peace' and, as such, an appropriate aspirational name for today.

Pearl: From the gemstone found inside an oyster. In St John's vision of the New Jerusalem, the gates of the city are made of pearl.

Peggy: A pet form of Margaret.

Penelope: Probably from the Greek meaning 'thread'. In Greek mythology, Penelope, the wife of Odysseus, was besieged by suitors after her husband went away for a long time (wandering the world, that is, not in jail!). Determined to stay faithful to him, she claimed that she could not remarry until she had finished weaving a shroud for her father-in-law. She wove by day and spent each night unravelling what she had done. It was a ruse that lasted for three years, when Odysseus finally returned and killed the suitors. In another version of the story, Penelope threw herself into the sea when she heard a rumour that her husband was dead. She was saved by some ducks. The penelops is a type of duck.

Perdita: A name invented by Shakespeare for the daughter of Leontes and Hermione in *The Winter's Tale*, written in 1611. He took it from the Latin meaning 'lost'. Today, though, it is more likely to be associated with the mother of the 101 Dalmatians in the book by Dodie Smith, published in 1956, and made into one of the most popular Disney films. Anyone without children will not make this association but,

believe me, when you've watched the Disney movie a
hundred times with your child – and that's if you're lucky –
it will be the only association you do make!

Persephone: From the Greek meaning 'bearer for death'. In
Greek mythology, Persephone is the daughter of Zeus and
Demeter who was abducted by Hades and made his wife
and Queen of the Underworld every autumn and winter. In
the spring, she was allowed to return to her mother and she
thus became the goddess of vegetation. The meaning of the
name, however, stems from the fact that winter comes
whenever she is in the Underworld.

Peta: A modern feminine form of Peter that was first used in
the 1930s.

Petal: From the part of the flower.

Petra: A feminine form of Peter.

Petula: A modern name, probably most readily associated
with the singer Petula Clark. Its origins are uncertain.

Phaedra: From the Greek meaning 'shining bright'. In Greek
mythology, she is the wife of Theseus, and falls in love with
her stepson, killing herself when he rejects her.

Philippa: The feminine form of Philip.

Philomela: From the Greek meaning 'sweet song'. In Greek
mythology, Philomela is the sister of Procne and the one
whom Procne's husband, Tereus, desired. Tereus cut out
Procne's tongue, then told Philomela that Procne was dead
before seducing her. Procne managed to reach her sister and
tell her the truth by sewing it on her dress and both sisters
fled. As Tereus closed in on the sisters they prayed to the
gods for help and Procne was turned into a swallow while
Philomela was turned into the sweet-singing nightingale.

Philomena: Probably from the Greek words meaning 'to love'
and 'strength'. It was the name of an obscure third-century
saint whose bones were discovered in a church in Italy. The
name became popular in the nineteenth century after the
remains of another St Philomena were supposedly found in
1802. This time, however, the name was actually a

misreading of the Latin words on the inscription that meant 'peace be with you beloved'.

Phoebe: From the Greek meaning 'radiant'. In Greek mythology, Phoebe is the daughter of Heaven and Earth. Phoebe is also mentioned in the Bible as a member of the church in Cenchrea who helped St Paul.

Phoenix: A mythological name meaning 'blood red'. It occurs both in Greek legend, where he is the tutor of Achilles, but more famously in Egyptian mythology where the phoenix is a bird that burns on a fire and rises again from the ashes.

Phyllida: From the Greek meaning 'leafy'.

Phyllis: Like Phyllida, this name is based on the Greek meaning 'leafy'. In Greek mythology, Phyllis is a Thracian princess who was married to Demophon. When he sailed away and did not return when he had promised, she hanged herself and was transformed into an almond tree. According to some versions of the legend, the tree originally had no leaves but when Demophon returned, he hugged the tree and it immediately began to flourish.

Pia: An Italian name based on the Latin meaning 'dutiful'. It has come to be used generally in recent years.

Pippa: A short form of Philippa. It was made popular by Robert Browning through his 1847 poem 'Pippa Passes', in which Pippa is a young girl working in a silk mill.

Polly: A form of Mary based on Molly.

Pollyanna: A combination, obviously, of the names Polly and Anna. It came to prominence through the heroine of the popular children's story written by Eleanor H. Porter in 1913.

Polydora: From the Greek meaning 'many gifts'.

Pomona: The goddess of fruit in Roman mythology. She was loved by Vertumnus, the god of changing seasons, who for some reason disguised himself as a harvester, a herdsman and an old woman in his pursuit of her. He only won her when he finally appeared as himself, so he might have saved himself a lot of time and effort.

Poppy: From the name of the flower that has become synonymous with the remembrance of the war dead.

Portia: From the Latin meaning 'pig'. It was based on an old Roman family name and was used by Shakespeare in both *The Merchant of Venice* and *Julius Caesar*. The form **Porsha** is also used.

Posy: Originally a pet form of Josephine, although it is also associated with the word for a small bunch of flowers.

Primrose: From the name of the flower, itself based on the Latin meaning 'first rose'.

Priscilla: Based on an old Roman family name meaning 'ancient'. In the Bible, Priscilla is the wife of Aquila, and both are close friends of St Paul. He lived with them for a while and all three travelled to Syria together. It was a popular name among the seventeenth-century Puritans.

Prudence: From a Roman male name meaning 'circumspect' or 'cautious'. It was taken up by the seventeenth-century Puritans who used it as a female name representing the quality. 'Dear Prudence' was, more recently, the title of a song by The Beatles.

Prunella: From the Latin meaning 'plum'. It was taken as a given name in the nineteenth century when 'flower' names were popular.

Q

Quinta: The feminine form of Quintin.

R

Rachel: From the Hebrew meaning 'ewe'. In the Bible, Rachel was the beautiful second daughter of Jacob's uncle, Laban. When Jacob fell in love with her, he promised Laban that he would work for free for seven years if, at the end of that time, he could marry her. At the marriage ceremony, however, Jacob found that it was Rachel's sister, Leah, he had married. Undaunted, he agreed to work another seven years and they eventually married. The forms **Rachael** and **Rachelle** are also used.

Rainbow: A popular name in the 1960s, this is taken from the Old English words meaning, not surprisingly, 'rain' and 'bow'.

Raine: Of uncertain origin but possibly either from the French meaning 'queen' or from the surname spelled Raine or Rayne, which is based on the Old German meaning 'advice'.

Raquel: The Spanish form of Rachel.

Reanna: A modern name that is possibly based on the Welsh Rhiannon, meaning 'moon goddess' or 'nymph'.

Rebecca: Either from the Hebrew meaning 'to fatten' or, possibly, from the Akkadian meaning 'to be gentle'. In the Bible, Rebecca, or **Rebekah**, is the beautiful wife of Isaac and mother to Esau and Jacob. Although God had said that he would work through Jacob, Esau was the elder son and his father's favourite. Rebecca helped Jacob to deceive his father into blessing him instead, an act that so enraged his brother that Jacob fled. The name is also particularly familiar as that of the first wife of Max de Winter in Daphne du Maurier's famous novel *Rebecca*, published in 1938.

Regan: Probably based on the Irish Gaelic meaning 'queen'. The name was first used by William Shakespeare for one of the three daughters of King Lear.

Regina: From the Latin meaning 'queen'.

Reine: The French form of Regina, so meaning 'queen'.

Rhea: Of uncertain origin. In Greek mythology she is an earth goddess and mother of Zeus.

Rhian: A short form of Rhiannon.

Rhiannon: From the Welsh meaning 'moon goddess' or 'nymph'. In Welsh mythology, Rhiannon is the beautiful daughter of the King of the Underworld.

Rhianwen: From the Welsh meaning 'pure maiden'.

Rhoda: Probably from the Greek meaning 'rose' although it could possibly mean 'woman from Rhodes'. In the Bible,

Rhoda is the maidservant working in a house in Jerusalem where Christians had prayed for the release of the apostle Peter, who had been imprisoned by Herod. When their prayers were answered and Peter came knocking on the door of the house, Rhoda was so surprised to hear his voice that she forgot to open the door and left him standing outside while she went to tell the others.

Rhode: From the Greek meaning 'rose'. In Greek mythology, she is the nymph daughter of Poseidon and Aphrodite who is said to have given her name to Rhodes.

Rhona: Of uncertain origin. The name is often spelled **Rona**, which may derive from the Gaelic meaning 'seal'. According to tradition, beautiful women living in the sea would appear as seals. Once they had taken their seal skin off, if it was found by a man, the woman would have to stay and marry him. If not, she would return to the sea as a seal. There is also a Hebridean island named Rona.

Rhonda: A relatively modern name of uncertain origin, although possibly based on the Welsh meaning 'gift'.

Ria: A short form of Maria now used as a name in its own right.

Richelle: A modern feminine form of Richard.

Rigel: From the Arabic meaning 'foot'. Rigel is the brightest star in the constellation Orion; it was thought to mark the giant's left foot.

Rina: A short form of names such as Katerina.

Rita: Originally a short form of Margarita, the Spanish form of Margaret, although now used as a name in its own right. The name was made famous by the actress Rita Hayworth. More recently, use of the name has probably been influenced by the 1979 film *Educating Rita*, in which the central character's real name is Susan but she prefers Rita because it sounds better. (*22 May*)

River: Another name, like Sky and Rainbow, that became popular in the 1960s.

Roberta: The feminine form of Robert, and often shortened to **Bobbie**.

Robin: A pet form of Robert that is now used as a given name in its own right. Two of the most common associations are with the legendary medieval hero and scourge of bad King John, Robin Hood, and the young sidekick of Batman. In recent years, the name has also been used for girls, probably as an association with the bird, and is often respelled **Robyn**.

Rochelle: Of uncertain origin.

Rosa: A form of Rose.

Rosalie: From the Latin name Rosalia, based on the word meaning 'rose'.

Rosalind: From the Old German meaning 'tender horse', although it is also traced by some to the Latin or Spanish meaning 'lovely rose'. The name was used by William Shakespeare for the heroine of *As You Like It*. The forms **Rosaline** and **Rosalyn** are also used.

Rosamund: From the Old German words meaning 'horse' and 'protection'. However, like Rosalind, it is often associated with the Latin meaning 'rose of the world'. Perhaps its most famous bearer is the twelfth-century legendary beauty known as 'Fair Rosamund'. She was actually called Rosamund Clifford and was said to have been the mistress of King Henry II. She was murdered by Henry's jealous queen, Eleanor of Aquitaine, in 1176.

Rosanna: A relatively modern name that is simply a blend of Rose and Anna. The form **Rosanne** is also used.

Rose: From the Old German meaning either 'horse' or 'fame'. However, it is now associated exclusively with the flower. As such it became particularly popular in the nineteenth century although the name was brought to England at the time of the Norman Conquest. (*23 August*)

Rosemary: From the name of the herb, itself based on the Latin meaning 'sea dew'. The form **Rosemarie** is also used.

Rosetta: The Italian pet form of Rosa.

Rowan: An ancient Irish name based on the Gaelic meaning 'little red one'.

Rowena: Of uncertain origin although it has been linked to the Welsh meaning 'white lance' and the Old German words meaning 'fame' and 'joy'. It was probably first used by Sir Walter Scott for the beautiful Lady Rowena in his novel *Ivanhoe*, published in 1819.

Roxana: From the Persian meaning 'dawn'. Possibly the most famous bearer of the name was Roxanna, wife of Alexander the Great. The forms **Roxane**, **Roxanne** and **Roxanna** are also used.

Ruby: From the Latin meaning 'red'. The given name is taken from the name of the gemstone and was particularly popular in the nineteenth century. In the Bible, the ruby was one of the gemstones on Aaron's breastplate. Aaron was the high priest at the time of Moses and each stone on his breastplate was engraved with the name of one of the twelve tribes of Israel.

Ruth: Of uncertain origin although it has been linked to the Hebrew meaning 'friend'. It was popular among the seventeenth-century Puritans who associated it with the word 'ruth' meaning 'compassion'. In the Bible, Ruth was the daughter-in-law of Naomi who remained devoted to her mother-in-law even though she was widowed. She and Naomi travelled to Bethlehem, where Ruth eventually met and married Boaz. Their son was David.

S

Sabina: From the Latin meaning 'Sabine woman'. The Sabines were an ancient race conquered by the Romans.

Sabrina: From the Roman name for the River Severn. In Welsh legend, Sabrina was the illegitimate daughter of King Locrine. She was drowned in the Severn on the orders of his wife, Gwendolen.

Sadie: A pet form of Sarah that is now used as a name in its own right.

Saffron: From the name of the spice, the most expensive to produce in the world.

Sally: A pet form of Sarah that is now used as a name in its own right. In much the same way, Hal became a pet form of the name Harry.

Salome: From the Hebrew meaning 'peace'. Perhaps the most famous bearer of the name is the stepdaughter of King Herod who demanded the head of John the Baptist when Herod offered her anything she wanted. However, she is not actually named in the Bible. Another biblical bearer, who is named, is one of the followers of Jesus who was present at the crucifixion.

Samantha: A feminine form of the name Samuel.

Sandra: A short form of Alexandra now used as a given name in its own right. The forms **Saundra** and **Zandra** are also used.

Sandy: A pet form of Alexandra as well as a descriptive name for a person with sandy-coloured hair.

Sapphire: From the name of the bright blue gemstone, which is based on a Greek word of uncertain origin.

Sarah: From the Hebrew meaning 'princess'. In the Bible, Sarah was the devoted wife of Abraham and mother of Isaac. Her name was originally Sarai, which probably means 'contentious', but this was changed by God to Sarah.

Sasha: A Russian pet form of Alexander or Alexandra.

Saskia: A Dutch name of uncertain origin that has been in use since the Middle Ages.

Scarlett: Originally an occupational name for someone who dyed or sold brightly coloured cloth. The name became especially popular after Scarlett O'Hara, the Southern belle and heroine of Margaret Mitchell's epic novel *Gone with the Wind*, published in 1936.

Selene: From the Greek meaning 'moon' or, more exactly, 'bright light'. In Greek mythology, Selene is the goddess of the moon and sister to Helios, god of the sun. The forms **Selena** and **Selina** are also used.

Selma: Probably from the Celtic meaning 'beautiful'.

Serena: From the Latin meaning 'calm'.

Shanna: A relatively recent name that, along with **Shannah** and **Shannagh**, is an alternative form of Shannon.

Shannon: From the name of the River Shannon in Ireland, which probably means 'the old one'.

Sharon: From the Hebrew meaning 'flat' or 'a plain'. Popular as a given name in the twentieth century, the original Sharon was a fertile plain, mentioned in the Bible, that ran from Joppa to Caesarea. The famous 'rose of Sharon' is mentioned in the Song of Solomon: 'I am the rose of Sharon and the lily of the valleys'. Sadly, the modern name became synonymous with tarty girls in the 1980s, an association that continues today. Perhaps it is time for its rather better, earlier association to be re-established.

Shauna: The feminine form of Shaun. The form **Shawna** is also used.

Shayna: A relatively modern name that is either from the German meaning 'beautiful' or simply a form of Sheena.

Sheena: The anglicised spelling of Sine, the Gaelic form of Jane.

Sheila: Either a Gaelic form of Cecilia or, possibly, from the Hebrew meaning 'longed for'. In Australia, 'sheila' is used as a general term for a woman.

Shelley: Originally a surname taken from a place name based on the Old English meaning 'wood near a slope'.

Sheridan: Originally a surname meaning either 'descendant of Siridean' or based on the words meaning 'eternal' and 'treasure'.

Shirley: From the surname that was itself taken from a place name meaning 'bright clearing'. As a given name, it was originally used for boys. However, when Charlotte Brontë used the name for the heroine of her novel, published in 1849, it became firmly established as a girl's name. In the novel, Shirley's parents had chosen the name in anticipation of a son but used it anyway when a daughter was born. Shirley became particularly popular in the 1930s, after the successful child actress Shirley Temple. Even more recently, the name has come to be associated with Shirley Valentine, the discontented wife who escapes to Greece in Willy Russell's film of the same name.

Sian: The Welsh form of Jane.

Sibyl: A name taken from the Greek name for various prophetesses. The origin of the Greek word is unknown. The name has many forms including **Sibylla**, **Sibilla** and **Sibella**. The spelling as Sybil became particularly popular after it was used by Benjamin Disraeli for the title of his novel, published in 1845.

Sidony: From the Latin meaning 'woman from Sidon'.

Sigrid: From the Old Norse words meaning 'victory' and 'beautiful'.

Silver: A name taken from the precious metal, so implying 'beauty' and 'value'.

Silvestra: The feminine form of Silvester.

Silvia: Often associated with the Latin meaning 'wood', although it probably had some earlier meaning. In Roman mythology, Rhea Silvia was the niece of the King of Alba Longa, who forced her to become a vestal virgin. Unfortunately, she gave birth to the twins Romulus and Remus, who were later to found the city of Rome. For this, Silvia was imprisoned and her furious uncle threw the babies into the River Tiber. More recently, the usual spelling of the name is **Sylvia**.

Simone: The French feminine form of Simon.

Sine: The Gaelic form of Jane.

Sinead: The Irish form of Janet, made prominent in recent years by the singer Sinead O'Connor.

Siobhan: An Irish form of Joan. The form **Shevaun** is also used.

Sita: From the Sanskrit meaning 'furrow'. In Indian mythology, it is the name of the wife of Rama, who is abducted by the demon Ravana. According to legend, she was born from a furrow in a ploughed field, hence her name. The story does not have a happy ending. Having been found and rescued by Rama, he rejected her after 10,000 years because he thought she had been defiled by the abduction, and she died of a broken heart.

Sky: From the Old Norse meaning 'cloud' but used as one of the 'natural' names in the 1960s. The form **Skye** is also used, which may well be influenced by the Hebridean island.

Sonya: The Russian pet form of Sofia, the equivalent of Sophia. The form **Sonia** is also used.

Sophia: From the Greek meaning 'wisdom'. The forms **Sophie** and **Sofia** are also used, the former being particularly popular. (*30 September*)

Sorcha: From the Celtic meaning 'brightness' or 'light'.

Sorrel: A name taken from the name of the plant, itself probably named from the German meaning 'sour'. The forms **Sorrell**, **Sorell** and **Sorel** are also used.

Stacey: Originally a pet form of Eustace and so a male name. More recently, however, it has developed as a short form of Anastasia and has come to be used as a female given name in its own right.

Star: Another of the 'natural' names based on the word and so could be regarded as a modern version of Stella.

Stella: From the Latin meaning 'star'. It was probably first used in the sixteenth century by Sir Philip Sidney as a pseudonym for the woman he loved in his series of sonnets entitled 'Astrophel and Stella'.

Stephanie: The French feminine form of Stephen.

Sukie: A pet form of Susan that was popular in the eighteenth century.

Summer: From the name of the season.

Susan: The anglicised spelling of Susanna.

Susanna: From the Hebrew meaning 'lily'. In the Bible, Susanna was a follower of Jesus. The forms **Suzanna**, **Susana**, **Suzanne** and **Susannah** are also used. (*11 August*)

T

Tabitha: From the Aramaic meaning 'doe' or 'roe'. In the Bible, Tabitha is a young Christian woman who worked with the poor. When she became ill and died, she was brought back to life by St Peter in an act that converted many to Christianity. The name is also popular among cat lovers after Tabitha Twitchett, the feline central character in the story by Beatrix Potter.

Tacey: From the Latin meaning 'be silent'.

Tacita: From the Old Roman family name based on the word meaning 'silent'. Perhaps a good choice for hopeful parents.

Talitha: From the Aramaic meaning 'little girl'.

Talulla: Probably from the Gaelic meaning 'princess'. However, its variant spelling, **Tallulah**, has been linked to the American Indian meaning 'running water'.

Tamara: Probably a form of the Biblical name Tamar, itself from the Hebrew meaning 'date tree', the name originated in Russia. There are three Tamars in the Bible. The first was Judah's daughter-in-law, the second was the beautiful daughter of King David who was raped by her half-brother, and the third was the beautiful daughter of Absalom.

Tamsin: A short form of the now hardly used name of Thomasina, itself the feminine form of Thomas and so meaning 'female twin'. The forms **Tamasin** and **Tansin** are also used.

Tanya: The Russian pet form of Tatiana. The form **Tania** is also used.

Tara: Taken from the prehistoric fort in Meath, where the High Kings of Ireland were anointed. The meaning is uncertain but is probably based on the word meaning 'hill'. More recently, the name has come to be associated with the name of the home of Scarlett O'Hara in Margaret Mitchell's classic novel *Gone with the Wind*. In Sanskrit, the word 'tara' means 'star'. The form **Tarra** is also used.

Tatiana: A Russian name that may have developed from the Old Roman family name of Tatius, for which the meaning is uncertain. Some, however, have linked the name to the Greek meaning 'I put in order'. In more recent history, Tatiana is probably best associated with one of the daughters of Tsar Nicholas II who was murdered with her family in 1918. (*12 January*)

Tawny: From the word for light-brown hair, itself from the Old French word meaning 'tanned'. Probably a modern name based on the same lines as Ginger and Sandy.

Taylor: From the Old French meaning 'to cut', this was originally an occupational surname for someone who, not surprisingly, worked as a tailor. It is now used for both boys and girls.

Teal: Taken from the name of the small freshwater duck. The form **Teale** is also used.

Tegan: A Welsh name meaning 'beautiful'.

Tegwen: A Welsh name, similar to Tegan, meaning 'beautiful and blessed'.

Terry: Although this is often used as a short form of either Terence or Theresa, it is a medieval name in its own right that originated from the same Old German name that gave Derek.

Tessa: Usually regarded as a pet form of Theresa, although it might be of different origin and is now used as a given name in its own right.

Thalia: From the Greek meaning 'to bloom'. In Greek mythology, Thalia is the Muse of comedy and pastoral poetry. The Muses were the daughters of Zeus and the Titaness Mnemosyne. The forms **Talia** and **Talya** are also used.

Thelma: Probably from the Greek meaning 'wish'. It is likely to have been first used by the popular author Marie Corelli for the heroine of her novel *Thelma, Princess of Norway*, published in 1887.

Themis: In Greek mythology, Themis is the first wife of Zeus. As the one who brought in laws and religious rites, she became the goddess of justice and order.

Theodora: The feminine form of Theodore, so like it means 'gift of God'.

Theodosia: From the Greek words meaning 'God' and 'giving'.

Theresa: Of uncertain origin. Some have linked it to the Greek island of Thera, which is traditionally the birthplace of the fifth-century St Theresa, wife of St Paulinus, the Bishop of Nola. Others see the name deriving from the Greek meaning 'to harvest'. The form **Teresa** is also used and is perhaps best associated with Mother Teresa of Calcutta, whose work among the lepers with her Missionaries of Charity inspired respect throughout the world and won her the Nobel Peace prize in 1979. (*12 April, 17 June, 1 October, 15 October*)

Tiana: A relatively modern name that is probably simply a short version of Christiana.

Tiffany: From the Greek meaning 'appearing of God'. The name represents the medieval English form of the Greek Theophania, 'Epiphany', and, as such, was originally given to daughters born on 6 January. The successful 1961 film *Breakfast at Tiffany's* made the name increasingly popular.

Tilly: The pet form of Matilda that has been used since the Middle Ages. The form **Tillie** is also used.

Tina: A short form of Christina that is now used as a given name in its own right.

Tonia: A short form of Antonia that is now used as a given name in its own right.

Topaz: A relatively modern name taken from the mainly yellow-coloured gemstone.

Tracy: From the surname, itself based on a Norman place name. Even the place name can be traced back to the Roman meaning 'man of Thrace'. The use of Tracy as a first name has been particularly popular since the widely successful 1956 film *High Society*, in which the lead female character, Tracy Lord, was played by Grace Kelly. The forms **Tracey** and **Tracie** are also used.

Troy: Probably from a surname taken from the place name Troyes in France. Many, however, associate it with the ancient city of Troy.

Trudy: Originally a pet form of Gertrude but now used as a given name in its own right.

Tyche: In Greek mythology, Tyche is the goddess of luck and the daughter of Zeus. She is often portrayed juggling a ball, which is symbolic of the uncertainty of fortune.

U

Una: A name that is usually taken to be from the Latin meaning 'one'. However, it has also been seen as a form of the Irish word meaning 'lamb' or another meaning 'banshee'! The forms **Oona** and **Oonagh** are also used.

Unity: A name popular among the seventeenth-century Puritans, this is based on the Latin meaning 'one' and so implies 'unique'.

Ursula: From the Latin meaning 'she-bear'. It was borne by a fourth-century saint said to have been martyred in Cologne. (*21 October*)

V

Valerie: From the Roman name Valeria, itself from the family name Valerius, meaning 'to be strong'.

Valma: From the Celtic meaning 'mayflower'. The name was originally associated with the Virgin Mary, to whom the month of May is dedicated. It has been suggested that the flower in question is the lily of the valley.

Vanessa: A name invented by Jonathan Swift for the heroine of his poem 'Cadenus and Vanessa'. The character's name was created from that of his friend Esther Vanhomrigh by joining the first syllable of the surname with the first name. The forms **Venessa** and **Venesa** are also used.

Velvet: As in Velvet Brown, who rides the winner at the Grand National disguised as a man in Enid Bagnold's *National Velvet*, 1935.

Venetia: Of uncertain origin, but has been in use since the late Middle Ages. Corresponds to the city in Italy.

Venus: Roman goddess of fertility and gardens.

Vera: Russian name meaning 'faith', which was introduced to England at the beginning of the twentieth century.

Verena: Originally a Swiss name, it is now used as an elaborate form of Vera.

Verity: From the word meaning 'truth'. As such, it was a popular name among the Puritans.

Verona: A name that has been in use since the late nineteenth century. It may be a short form of Veronica, or taken from the name of the Italian city.

Veronica: From the Latin expression *vera icon*, meaning 'true image'. The name is actually an anagram of the Latin phrase. It is most commonly associated with St Veronica who gave Jesus a cloth to wipe his face as he made his way to Calvary, and was later said to have found an imprint of his face on it. (*9 July, 12 July*)

Vesta: Roman goddess of victory.

Victoria: From the Latin meaning 'victory', this was also the name of the Roman goddess of victory. The name became known after Queen Victoria (1819–1901), although it did not become particularly popular until the mid-twentieth century.

Viola: From the Latin meaning 'violet', although its use has been influenced more by the name of a type of pansy than by the violet flower itself.

Violet: The name of the flower, itself named after its colour.

Virginia: From the Roman family name, Virginius or Verginius, which may be based on the word meaning 'maiden'. In the sixteenth century, the name was particularly associated with Queen Elizabeth I, the Virgin Queen, and the American state of Virginia which was named for her. The first child born to English parents in America was named Virginia Dare (born 1587).

Vita: A nineteenth-century name that could be from the Latin meaning 'life', or a pet form of Victoria.

Vivian: From the Latin, probably meaning 'alive'. The name is used for both boys and girls, although the 'female' version is usually **Vivien**. (*2 December Viviana*)

Vivienne: A feminine form of Vivian. It is commonly associated with the name of Merlin's mistress in the Arthurian romances. The spelling **Viviane** is also used.

W

Wanda: As in the film *A Fish Called Wanda*! Of uncertain origin.

Wendy: A name invented by J. M. Barrie for the character in his play *Peter Pan* (1904). It was taken from the nickname 'fwendy-wendy', given to him by a young child, Margaret Henley. Sadly, she died very young in 1894.

Whitney: Originally a surname from one of several places in England named as being 'by the white island'. Use of the name increased recently, no doubt after the singer Whitney Houston.

Willow: From the name of the tree.

Wilma: A short form of Wilhelmina, the feminine version of Wilhelm, itself the German form of William.

Winifred: From the Welsh name Gwenfrewi, which is based on the words meaning 'white', 'fair' or 'holy' and 'reconciliation'. However, its use has also been influenced by the Old English words meaning 'joy' and 'peace'.

Wynn: A popular Welsh name meaning 'fair'.

X

Xanthe: From the Greek meaning 'yellow' or 'bright'.
Xaviera: The feminine form of Xavier.
Xenia: From the Greek meaning 'hospitality'.

Y

Yasmin: A form of Jasmine.
Yolande: From the Greek meaning 'violet flower'.
Yseult: The medieval French form of Isolde, so meaning 'fair one'.
Yvette: The French feminine form of Yves, meaning 'yew'.
Yvonne: French feminine pet form of Yves, so like Yvette.

Z

Zara: Of uncertain origin. Some regard it as a form of Sara or Sarah while others have linked it to the Arabic words meaning either 'flower' or 'brightness of the dawn'.
Zelda: A modern name of uncertain origin, although it may be a form of Griselda.
Zena: A form of Xenia.
Zeta: Used either as a form of Zita or based on the sixth letter of the Greek alphabet.
Zina: A short form of the Russian name Zinaida, which itself is based on the Greek Zeus.
Zita: Probably from a medieval Italian word meaning 'girl'. The thirteenth-century St Zita is the patron saint of domestic servants. (*27 April*)
Zoë: From the Greek meaning 'life'. It was a popular name among early Christians who saw it as representing their hope for eternal life. It has been in steady use since then.
Zola: A recent name of uncertain origin. It was the name chosen by Eddie Murphy and Nicole Mitchell for their daughter.

4. A TO Z OF BOYS' NAMES

A

Aaron: From the Hebrew possibly meaning 'mountaineer' or 'high mountain'. In the Bible, it is the name of the brother of Moses and Miriam, appointed by God to be the first High Priest of the Israelites. The Welsh spelling is **Aron**. In the Arthurian romances, Aron is one of the Knights of the Round Table. (*3 July*)

Abel: A name that probably originates from either the Hebrew meaning 'breath', or the Assyrian meaning 'son'. In the Bible, it is given to the second son of Adam and Eve who was killed in a quarrel with his jealous brother, Cain. As a given name, it was made popular by the Puritans in the seventeenth century.

Abner: From the Hebrew meaning 'father of light'. In the Bible, it is the name of the commander of King Saul's army.

Abraham: This name is often explained as meaning 'father of many' from the Old Testament reference: 'Neither shall thy name any more be called Abram, but thy name shall be Abraham; for a father of many nations have I made thee.' However, it is quite possible that Abraham is simply an exaggerated form of the original Abram, which itself means 'father on high'. In the Bible, Abraham is the father of the Hebrew nation and married to Sarah, by whom he had a son Isaac when, we are told, he was 100 years old. The name was popular among the Puritans. (*21 August, 6 December*).

Abraxas: A second-century Gnostic god whose name is made up of seven Greek letters, each of which has a numerical value: alpha (1), beta (2), rho (100), alpha (1), xi (60), alpha (1) and sigma (200). The total, therefore, is 365, the number of days in a year. With seven letters in the name, it also represents the mystical number seven. It is likely that Abraxas gave his name to 'abracadabra', the magic word used by magicians and children the world over.

Adam: From the Hebrew meaning 'red earth', which probably refers to the earth that God used to make Adam, the first man. The New Testament describes Jesus himself as the 'last Adam', meaning that where the original Adam brought sin into the world, so Jesus died on the cross to save people from sin. As such, it is a particularly significant name for Christians.

Adrian: From the Latin name (H)adrianus, used to describe someone 'from the Adriatic'. The name was borne by the second-century Roman emperor, Pubilius Aelius Hadrianus, during whose reign Hadrian's Wall was built across northern England. It was also the name taken by the only Englishman to be made Pope; Nicholas Breakspear (d. 1159) became known as Pope Adrian IV. More recently, the name has come to be associated with Adrian Mole, aged 13¾, whose *Secret Diary* was written by Sue Townsend in 1982. (*9 January, 8 September*)

Agrippa: The name of a first-century BC Roman general, which was probably based on the Latin meaning 'sick' or 'painful'.

Aidan: From the Gaelic name Aedan, itself based on *Aed*, 'fire'. The name was taken by several Irish saints. (*31 August*)

Ainsley: Originally a Scottish surname meaning 'one meadow'. Today it is a popular first name that can also be spelled **Ainslie** and **Ainslee**.

Alan: Probably originally from the Breton meaning 'rock', which was then influenced by the Celtic word for 'harmony'. It was introduced to England by the Normans and has developed many forms since including **Allan** and **Allen**. In France, the spelling **Alain** is most common, while the form **Alun** is almost exclusively used in Wales, where it is often associated with the River Alun.

Alaric: From the Old German name meaning 'ruler of all'. Borne by a Visigoth king in the fifth century, the name enjoyed a revival in the Victorian era.

Alasdair: The Scottish Gaelic form of Alexander. The name has taken on many different spellings including **Alistair**, **Alastair**, **Alaster**, **Alaisdair** and **Alister**.

Alastor: The title of Shelley's poem published in 1816. He borrowed the name from the Greek *alastor*, 'he who does not forget', the name of the Avenging Deity.

Alban: An ancient name based on the Latin word for 'white'. Its most famous bearer was Britain's first martyr, St Alban. (*22 June*)

Albert: Originally a German name, which in Old English became Aethelberht, meaning 'nobly famous'. Its popularity reached a peak in English-speaking countries in the mid-nineteenth century when Queen Victoria married the German Prince Albert of Saxe-Coburg. One of its pet forms, **Bertie**, also became popular after the upper-class twit so dependent on his butler Jeeves in the hugely successful stories by P. G. Wodehouse. Another popular, shortened form is **Bert**. (*15 November*)

Aldous: A name developed from the first part of Old English names such as Ealdwine, where the 'eald' means 'old'. As a name, it was made famous by Aldous Huxley (1894–1963).

Aled: A popular name in Wales, which is based either on the word meaning 'noble brow' or, possibly, on that meaning 'sorrow'.

Alexander: From the Greek meaning 'defender of men'. The name is particularly famous as the alternative name for Paris, son of King Priam in Greek mythology, and of the famous fourth-century BC general, Alexander the Great. It has developed several short forms. **Alex** is now often used as a name in its own right, as is the medieval pet form **Sandy**, while **Alec** is less popular because of its assocation with the phrase 'smart Alec'. The enduring popularity of the name is reflected in the fact that, at the beginning of the 21st century, both Alexander and its short form Alex ranked among the top 50 most popular names given to boys. (*10 July, 11 October, 23 November*)

Alexis: A form of Alexander, so it is based on the Greek word meaning 'to defend'. It was originally a male name and was that of both a fifth-century saint and the only son of Tsar Nicholas II and Alexandra, who was shot alongside his parents and sisters during the Russian Revolution. Today it is now more usually used as a female name and is more likely to be associated with the character played by Joan Collins in the hugely successful American soap, *Dynasty*. (*17 February, 17 July*)

Alfred: From the medieval name Aelfraed, based on two elements meaning 'elf' and 'counsel', so ultimately a 'good adviser'. Alfred the Great, the ninth-century English king, is one of the most famous bearers of the name, along with the nineteenth-century poet, Alfred, Lord Tennyson. The name is often shortened to **Fred**, **Freddie** or **Alf**.

Algernon: A Norman French name based on *als gernons*, 'with whiskers', which, it is thought, was first used in the eleventh century to distinguish between a father and son who were both called Eustace – the son had the whiskers! As a nickname, it was also used in the famous Howard and Percy families who came to adopt it and so gave it the aristocratic association that, to some extent, it still has today. Short forms are **Algy** and **Algie**.

Aloysius: An unusual name today but this was fairly common in Italy in the Middle Ages, although its origins are uncertain. It is probably now best known as the name of Sebastian's beloved teddy bear in *Brideshead Revisited*. (*21 June*)

Altair: The brightest star in the constellation Aquila, named from an Arabic word meaning 'bird'.

Alvin: From the Old English Aelfwine, from the elements meaning 'elf' and 'friend', or Aethelwine, from 'noble' and 'friend'. As a name, it is far more popular in America, although it was brought to prominence in Britain by the singer Alvin Stardust.

Ambrose: From the Greek meaning 'immortal'. Ambrosia was the food of the Greek gods, which gave them immortality. The name is particularly associated with the fourth-century Roman saint, Ambrose, who wrote several hymns as a means both to teach and to praise. (7 *December*)

Amon: The name of the god of life and fertility in classical Theban mythology. It is also spelled **Amen** or **Amun**.

Amos: From the Hebrew meaning 'borne', which can be interpreted either as 'borne by God' or 'bearer of a message from God'. In the Bible, Amos was a wealthy farmer, living in the eighth century BC, who was called on by God to take His message to the people. One of the Old Testament books is named after him.

Andreas: The Greek form of Andrew.

Andred: Of uncertain origin, although it would seem to be linked to Andrew. In Arthurian legend, Andred was a cousin to Tristan who betrayed him and Iseult to King Mark.

Andrew: Originally from the Greek word *andros*, 'man', so meaning 'manly'. In the Bible, Andrew was a fisherman and brother of St Peter who was the first disciple called by Jesus. Andrew is now patron saint of Scotland and Russia. The most popular short forms are **Andy** and **Andie**, while the form **Aindrias** is used in Gaelic-speaking communities. (4 *February, 13 May, 16 May, 4 July, 20 October, 10 November, 30 November*)

Aneurin: A name of uncertain origin, although it has been linked to the Gaelic *nar*, meaning 'noble', and the Latin *Honorius*, meaning 'man of honour'. It was the name of an early seventh-century Welsh poet but is more readily associated with the Welsh labour politician, Aneurin Bevan, who introduced the National Health Service in 1948. He was mostly called by the short form of the name, **Nye**.

Angel: From the Greek meaning 'messenger', this was originally a male name. In Thomas Hardy's classic *Tess of the D'Urbervilles*, published in 1891, he appears as a self-centred idealist. Today, however, it would be far more appropriate as a female name.

Angus: A Celtic name meaning 'unique choice'. This spelling is mostly used in Scotland, while the alternative spellings of **Aengus** and **Aonghus** are more popular in Ireland. The name was originally that of a Celtic god of love and poetry whose trials, endured in his search for a beautiful woman he saw in a dream, were the subject of a poem by Yeats. Another Angus, this one spelled **Aonghus**, was one of three Irish brothers who brought the famous Stone of Scone to Scotland. For hundreds of years, this stone was set under the Coronation Chair in Westminster Abbey, although it was returned to Scotland in the 1990s.

Anthony: From the Roman family name Antonius. One of the most famous members of the family was Mark Antony, the Roman general of the first century BC, who served under Caesar and whose love affair with Cleopatra has been the subject of countless stories and films. Like his, the name can also be spelled **Antony** and shortened to **Tony**. The spelling Antony also appears in Arthurian legend as the name of an Irish bishop who was secretary to Merlin. (*17 January Antony, 10 May Antonio, 13 June, 5 July Antony, 10 July Antony, 24 October Antony*).

Anton: The German and Russian form of Anthony.

Apollo: In Greek mythology, the son of Zeus who was the god both of prophecy and of song and music. He was also leader of the Muses, the daughters of Zeus who watched over the arts and sciences. He has been linked with the god of the sun but it is more likely that they were two different characters.

Archibald: Originally from the Old German name Erkanbald, meaning 'very brave'. It was introduced to England after the Norman Conquest and has been a particularly popular name in Scotland. The most common short form is **Archie**.

Ardan: Of uncertain origin, although it has been linked to the Celtic words meaning 'tall man'. In some sources of the Arthurian legend, Ardan is the uncle of King Arthur.

Arene: Not, as is often assumed, related to the name Irene, but rather based on the Greek meaning 'manly'.

Ares: The god of war in Greek mythology.

Ariel: From the place name and based on the Hebrew meaning either 'lion of God' or 'hearth of the altar'. In the Bible, it is the name of one of the male companions of Ezra. Shakespeare also uses it as a male name for the character who is a spirit of the air in *The Tempest*, written in 1611. Today, however, it is almost exclusively used as a female name and is most commonly associated with the leading character in Disney's extremely successful film, *The Little Mermaid*. Other forms include **Arielle** and **Ariella**.

Arnold: One of many names introduced to England following the Norman Conquest, this is based originally on the Old German name Arnwald, meaning 'eagle rule' or 'eagle power'. It became common as a surname before being reused as a first name in the nineteenth century.

Arthur: A famous name with an uncertain background. It has been linked to the Gaelic word for 'stone' and, more likely, to the Greek for 'keeper of bears'. The Greek word came to be incorporated into the Celtic language and probably developed to mean 'strong as a bear'. The Celts regarded bears as sacred and even had a bear goddess called Artio. Primarily, though, the name will forever be associated with the romantic tales of chivalry that surround the sixth-century King Arthur, who led the Celts against the Saxons. The form **Artur** is also occasionally used.

Asa: From the Hebrew meaning 'doctor' or 'healer'. In the Bible, it is the name of one of the early kings of Judah.

Ashley: From the Old English for 'ash wood', this was originally a surname based on where someone lived. When it started to be used as a first name is uncertain. It might have been used in honour of the nineteenth-century Earl of Shaftesbury, Anthony Ashley Cooper, and was certainly popularised by the character Ashley Wilkes, the mistaken object of Scarlett's affections, in Margaret Mitchell's *Gone with the Wind*, published in 1936.

Aslan: The Turkish word for 'lion'. The name is most commonly associated with the great lion in C.S. Lewis's Narnia books for children.

Atticus: This name, which means 'of Athens', appears in Harper Lee's famous book *To Kill a Mockingbird*, published in 1960. In it, Atticus Finch is the kind and humanitarian lawyer who defies convention to defend a coloured prisoner.

Attila: A name to be reckoned with! It was that of the fifth-century King of the Huns, the 'Scourge of God', who destroyed much of the Roman Empire.

Auberon: A name introduced by the Normans after 1066, although its origins are uncertain. It may be related to the name Aubrey.

Aubrey: The French spelling of the Old German name Alberic. The Old English version was Aelfric, from two elements meaning 'elf' and 'power'.

Augustine: From the Latin name Augustinius, meaning 'great'. The sixth-century St Augustine became the first Archbishop of Canterbury. (*27 May, 28 August*)

Augustus: Like Augustine, this is from the Latin meaning 'great'. As a name, it was popular among Roman emperors, including the adopted son of Julius Caesar, after whom the month of August is named.

Auryn: A Celtic name probably based on the Latin word meaning 'gold', so a good name for either a child with golden hair or one who is especially precious.

Austin: This name is taken from an original surname that developed as a spoken form of Augustine in medieval times. The name is also spelt **Austen**.

Avery: Originally a surname that itself developed from the Norman pronunciation of the Old English name Alfred.

B

Barnabas: From the Aramaic *barnebhu'ah*, which translates literally as 'son of consolation'. In the Bible, Barnabas is a companion of St Paul. His original name was Joseph and the new name seems to have been given as a nickname after he converted to Christianity. The anglicised version of the name is **Barnaby**. (*11 June*)

Barry: There are two origins to this name. The first is from the Celtic word meaning 'spear', which has also led to names such as **Barra**, **Barris** and **Bearach**. In England, Barry can also be a short form of the Celtic name Fionnbarr, meaning 'fair headed'.

Bartholomew: Originally from the Aramaic and meaning 'son of Tolmai'. In the Bible, he is one of the twelve apostles but probably the one about whom the least is known. Other versions of the name include **Bart** and **Tolomey**. (*24 August, 11 November*)

Basil: From the Greek meaning 'royal', a word that also produced basilica, which originally described a royal palace. It was popularised by St Basil the Great, the fourth-century theologian who is regarded as one of the fathers of the Orthodox Church. St Basil's Cathedral is one of the best known in Moscow. In England, the name was originally introduced by the Crusaders. (*2 January, 2 August*)

Beau: From the French word, this was originally a nickname for someone handsome. It also came to be used as the word for a sweetheart, although, unfortunately, not all these are handsome. Its use as an actual name was probably influenced by the novel *Beau Geste* by P. C. Wren, published in 1924.

Beltane: The Celtic name for May Day, 1 May, which marks the beginning of summer. An attractive name for a child born on this day.

Benedict: This name derives from the Latin *benedictus*, meaning 'blessed'. As a result, it was adopted by several popes and at least five saints, probably the most famous of which was the sixth-century St Benedict, who founded the Benedictine order of monks and nuns in Italy. The famous Benedictine liqueur got its name because it was developed at a Benedictine monastery in France. (*12 January, 11 February, 4 April, 11 July*)

Benjamin: From the Hebrew *Binyamin* meaning 'son of the right hand' so 'favourite son'. In the Bible, it is the name of Jacob's youngest son. It has been interpreted as meaning 'son of the south', a rather more mundane interpretation based on the fact that the original Benjamin was the only one of Jacob's twelve sons born in Canaan rather than in the north. The biblical story tells that Rachel, Benjamin's mother, died in childbirth, and so he was originally called Benoni, 'son of sorrow'. Fortunately, Jacob later changed the name. One of his brothers was the famous Joseph, he of the multicoloured coat. Short forms of the name would be **Ben** or **Benny**.

Bernard: Originally an Old German name brought to England after the Norman Conquest and formed from elements meaning 'bear' and 'hardy', so given to someone who was 'brave and strong as a bear'. This meant that it was also adopted by the Celts, who were great admirers of bears. The name is also well known today as that of a breed of dog, named after the eleventh-century St Bernard. (*28 May, 20 August*)

Bertram: A name based on two Old German words meaning 'bright' and 'raven'. In German mythology, the raven symbolised wisdom so, ultimately, the name was given to someone who was 'famous and wise'.

Bertrand: An early French form of Bertram.

Blaine: Probably from the Gaelic meaning 'narrow', although some have linked it to the word meaning 'white' or 'fair'.

Blair: Originally a Scottish surname based on the Gaelic word for 'field', so given to someone who lived near or on a field.

Blaise: From either the Latin for 'stuttering' or from the Celtic meaning 'taste'. A fourth-century doctor, St Blaise, is one well-known bearer of the name; another is the hermit magician who trained the legendary Merlin and wrote about the battles of King Arthur. (*3 February*)

Blake: A name of contradictions. It was originally a surname derived from two distinct Old English words, one meaning 'black', the other meaning 'pale'. Either way, it would have been a nickname for someone with either very dark or very fair features.

Boreas: The name of the god of the north wind in Greek mythology.

Boris: Originally from a Tartar word meaning 'small'. It is now taken to be a familiar form of longer Russian names like Borislav, which is based on two Slavonic words meaning 'battle' and 'glory' so, ultimately, 'glorious in battle'. (*24 July*)

Boyd: A Celtic name, primarily used as a surname, but sometimes as a first name. It is based on a word meaning 'yellow', so was given to someone with fair or golden hair.

Bradley: Originally a surname based on an Old English place name meaning 'broad clearing'. Now increasingly used as a first name. The short form would be **Brad**.

Bran: From an old Celtic word meaning 'raven'. The raven was sacred to the Celts.

Brandon: From a place name, which became a surname taken from the Old English words meaning 'broom' or 'gorse', and 'hill'.

Branwell: A Cornish surname meaning 'raven's well'. One of the first uses as a given name appears to be that of Patrick Branwell Brontë, the alcoholic brother of the literary Brontë sisters. It was his Cornish mother's surname that was then given to him as a second name, a fairly common means by which surnames have become first names.

Brendan: From the Celtic name meaning 'prince' or 'royal', which has been fairly common in all Celtic regions. The name was given to several saints, the most famous is the sixth-century Irishman, Brendan the Navigator. (*16 May*)

Brent: Originally a surname, which derives from a place description meaning 'hill'. There are several such places found in Devon and Somerset.

Brett: There are two possible origins of this name. The first is as a surname meaning 'man of Brittany', given to Bretons who arrived in England after the Norman Conquest. The second is a development of the Celtic meaning 'son of the ardent one'.

Brian: Probably from a Celtic word meaning 'high'. It has been a popular name in Ireland both in this form and in other forms such as **Brion** and **Bryan**. One of the most famous historical bearers of the name was the tenth-century High King who notoriously defeated the Vikings at the Battle of Clontarf in 1014, only to die of his wounds.

Brice: Possibly from the Welsh meaning 'speckled'. The name is also used in the form **Bryce**. (*13 November*)

Brodie: Originally a Scottish surname, Brodie is likely to mean muddy place or ditch, so an inspired choice by any parents with realistic expectations of where boys love to play!

Brooklyn: The name chosen by Victoria Adams and David Beckham for their son. It is based on the place name of the New York borough, which was named after the native village of its Dutch founder.

Bruce: A name taken from a Scottish surname, which itself was probably a Norman place name. Its popularity as a given name was established as boys were named in honour of the fourteenth-century Scottish king, Robert the Bruce. He is particularly famous for gaining inspiration to continue his campaign against the English from the efforts of a spider. His perseverance paid off when, against the odds, he defeated the English at the Battle of Bannockburn in 1314.

Bruno: A name taken from the simple translation of the German meaning 'brown'. (*19 June, 6 October*)

Bryn: A Welsh name meaning 'hill'.

Byron: Despite its romantic connotations, from association with the nineteenth-century poet, Lord Byron, this name has a rather more mundane origin. It comes from the Old English meaning 'at the cattlesheds' and was originally a surname given to someone who lived or worked there.

C

Caesar: This grand, historical name is of uncertain origin. It is allegedly derived from the Latin meaning 'to cut', and was given to the great Julius Caesar who, it is believed, did not have a natural birth but was born from an incision in his mother's womb (hence the term 'Caesarian section'). However, another theory has linked the name to the Latin *caesaries*, meaning 'head of hair'. The name became the title of the Roman emperors from Augustus to Hadrian, and is commonly associated with powerful rule. In fact, it gave rise to the titles *Kaiser* and *Tsar*.

Cain: Probably from the Hebrew meaning 'blacksmith', although the Bible's interpretation is 'I have forgotten'. In the Bible, Cain is the elder son of Adam and Eve, who killed his brother, Abel, in a jealous rage.

Caleb: The name comes from the Hebrew word meaning 'bold'. In the Bible's Old Testament, Caleb was one of twelve men sent on a sort of reconnaissance to Canaan, the Promised Land. While ten of his friends thought the objective of gaining Canaan for the Israelites too great a task, a lack of faith that condemned the whole people to 40 years in the wilderness until each of the ten had died, Caleb and Joshua trusted in God. They were the only two who lived long enough to enter the Promised Land, Caleb, by then, being 85 years old.

Calum: A Scottish Gaelic name that is based on the Latin *columba*, meaning 'dove', the symbol of purity and peace. The name is also spelled **Callum**.

Calvin: This was originally a descriptive surname taken from the Norman *calve*, meaning 'little bald one'. Its use as a first name dates from the sixteenth century when it was given in honour of the French Protestant theologian, Jean Calvin.

Cameron: A Scottish Gaelic name that began as an unfortunate descriptive name. It seems to be based on two Gaelic words meaning 'crooked nose'. It is the name of one of the most famous Highland clans.

Campbell: The name of one of the most famous of all Scottish clans. As such, it was originally a surname that has made its way into the list of first names. Its origins are likely to be from two Gaelic words meaning 'crooked mouth', although some have tried to find a link with the Latin meaning 'about the field of battle'.

Campion: A truly chivalrous name, meaning 'champion', which was given in medieval times to someone who would, for example, fight a duel on your behalf.

Carl: The German version of Charles, now widely used elsewhere. In Arthurian romances, Carl, one of the Knights of the Round Table, was transformed into a giant. The spell was only broken when Sir Gawain cut off his head.

Cary: Taken from a surname, fairly common in Somerset, which developed after the Celtic-named river Cary. The river's name may be based on the word meaning 'well loved'. Its popularity as a first name owes much to the fame and appeal of film star Cary Grant, who took it as a stage name in place of his actual name of Archie Leach.

Caspar: The name given to one of the three wise men in the story of the Nativity, although none of them is actually named in the Bible. The name is a Dutch form of Jasper, itself probably of Persian origin meaning 'treasurer'. Another spelling is **Casper**.

Cecil: This surname of one of the most prominent families of Elizabethan England has two possible origins. The first is from an old Welsh name meaning 'sixth', so probably given to a sixth child. The second derives from a Roman family name based on the Latin meaning 'blind'.

Cedric: Probably first used by Sir Walter Scott for the character Cedric of Rotherwood in his novel *Ivanhoe*, published in 1819. Whether he dreamed it up or based it on Cerdic, the traditional founder of the kingdom of Wessex, is not known. Its association with the main character in Frances Hodgson Burnett's *Little Lord Fauntleroy* has not done it any favours.

Cerdic: Of uncertain origin, although possibly linked to Cedric. In Arthurian legend, Cerdic is the founder of Wessex. Some, however, believe that he may have been one of King Arthur's sons.

Cerwyn: A Welsh name meaning 'fair love', which could be used for a boy or a girl.

Charles: From the Old Germanic word meaning 'free man', the same word that gave the modern word 'churlish', which did not always have the ill-mannered associations that it has today. Originally made popular by the ninth-century Holy Roman Emperor Charlemagne, or Charles the Great, it was introduced to England in the sixteenth century by Mary, Queen of Scots on her return from an upbringing in France. She gave the name to her son, Charles James, who became James VI of Scotland and I of England. The name continued with his son, Charles I, who was beheaded in 1649, and grandson, Charles II. With our current Prince of Wales also bearing the name, it seems likely that, after a break of over 300 years, England will eventually have another Charles on the throne. Both Charles and its pet form, **Charlie**, are popular choices among parents. (*7 January, 3 June, 4 November*)

Charlton: From an Old English place name meaning 'settlement of free peasants', which developed into a surname. It became used as a first name largely on the influence of the actor Charlton Heston, whose own name was taken from his mother's maiden name.

Charon: From the Greek meaning 'bright eyes', which had less to do with the fluffy rabbits of *Watership Down* film fame and more with the name of the legendary ferryman who took the dead across the river Styx to the Underworld.

Chester: From the surname based on the Latin meaning 'legionary camp'.

Christian: From the Hebrew meaning 'anointed one'. Obviously, this name has the ultimate meaning of 'a follower of Christ' and is used in this way in the Bible itself.

Christopher: From the Greek meaning 'bearer of Christ', so used for children who would, hopefully, 'bear Christ in their heart'. The name is most readily associated with the legend of St Christopher, who allegedly carried the baby Jesus across a stream and became the patron saint of travellers. (*25 July*)

Cian: An Irish name meaning ancient.

Clarence: From the Latin meaning 'of Clare'. The name developed from the royal title Duke of Clarence. This was first given, in the fourteenth century, to Lionel of Antwerp, son of King Edward III, who was betrothed at just three years of age to Elizabeth, heiress of Clare in Suffolk.

Claris: Of uncertain origin, although it is possibly the male form of Clarisse. In Arthurian legend, Claris is one of the Knights of the Round Table.

Clark: Originally an occupational surname that denoted someone who worked as a clerk – someone distinguished in the Middle Ages by their ability to read and write. Its popularity as a first name owes much to the fame of the film star Clark Gable.

Claud: From a Roman family name, which itself developed from a nickname based on the Latin meaning 'crippled'. The name is often spelled **Claude**. (*15 February*)

Clement: From the Latin meaning 'merciful'.

Clifford: From a place name based on Old English words meaning 'cliff' or 'riverbank' and 'ford'. The popular short form is **Cliff**.

Clive: From a place name based on the Old English word meaning 'cliff' or 'riverbank'. Its use as a first name developed in the eighteenth century, largely in honour of Robert Clive, 'Clive of India', the founder of British India.

Coel: Of uncertain origin, although it could be linked to Cole. Coel is a name firmly caught in the Arthurian legends. According to some sources, Coel was either the King or Duke of Colchester, and was an ancestor of King Arthur. Supposedly, the fourth-century Roman emperor, Constantinus Chlorus, besieged Colchester for three years before marrying Coel's daughter, Helena. It is likely that this Coel is the 'Old King Cole' of the nursery rhyme.

Cole: Originally a surname, possibly based on the descriptive Old English word meaning 'swarthy' or 'black as coal'.

Colin: This name has several possible origins. The most popular is as a form of the medieval name Col, itself a short form of Nicholas. However, some uses of the name may be derived from the Celtic word meaning 'chieftain' or the Gaelic words meaning 'young one'. It is possible that the use of one may have influenced the use of the other.

Conan: Possibly from the Gaelic meaning 'hound'. In Arthurian legend, some sources have Conan as one of King Arthur's ancestors, and the first ruler of Brittany. Today, however, the name is more likely to be associated with *Conan the Barbarian*.

Connor: From the Irish name meaning 'lover of hounds'.

Conrad: From the German meaning 'bold counsel'. Its use in England stems largely from the nineteenth century. In Arthurian legend, Conrad was a bishop who unsuccessfully charged Merlin with heresy. (*22 April*)

Constantine: From the Latin name Constans, meaning 'constant'.

Corey: Possibly from the Greek meaning 'maiden' or, if it is based on the Irish surname, possibly a form of Godfrey.

Corin: Probably from the Sabine meaning 'spear'. It is taken from Quirinus, an ancient god in Roman mythology, whose name was also taken by Romulus, founder of Rome, after he was deified.

Cornelius: From an old Roman family name of uncertain origin but possibly based either on the Latin word meaning 'horn' or another meaning 'hero'. (*16 September*)

Cosmo: An Italian name based on a Greek word meaning 'order' or 'beauty'. It was first introduced to England in the eighteenth century by the Scottish dukes of Gordon, who were related to the ducal house of Tuscany. **Cosimo** is a variation of the name.

Craig: From a Scottish surname meaning 'rock', which was given to someone who lived near one.

Crispin: Originally a nickname that developed into a surname. It is based on the Latin *crispinus*, meaning 'curly', as in 'curly hair'. (*25 October*)

Curtis: From the surname that began as a nickname with two quite distinct meanings. The first was given to someone who was 'courteous', based on an Old French word of that meaning. The second was given to a short person, based on the Middle English for 'short stockings'.

Cuthbert: From an Old English name meaning 'famous'. (*20 March*)

Cyril: From the Greek meaning 'lord' and taken as a name by several saints, the most famous of whom lived in the ninth century. (*14 February, 18 March, 27 June*)

D

Dale: From the surname given to someone who, surprisingly enough, lived in a dale or valley.

Damian: From the Greek name Damianos, itself probably based on the similar name Damon, meaning 'to tame'. In the fourth century, Damianos was one of two Christian brothers martyred for their faith. **Damien** is another spelling of the name. (*26 September*)

Damon: From the famous classical Greek name, ultimately meaning 'to tame'. In the fourth century BC, Damon was the

loyal friend who stood in for the condemned Pythias to
allow him home to put his things in order before he died.
The strength of this friendship and the trust it engendered
so impressed Pythias's captor, Dionysus, that he allowed
both men to go free.

Daniel: From the Hebrew meaning 'God is my judge'. In the
Bible, Daniel was a slave famed for his ability to interpret
dreams. He rose to become a powerful man whose enemies
persuaded the king to forbid prayers to anyone but himself.
Daniel's refusal to stop praying to God led to his being
thrown into a den of lions but, with God's protection, he
remained unharmed. The name became popular among the
Celts who held the ability to interpret dreams very highly.
Indeed, the short form of the name, **Danny**, is today
particularly associated with Ireland thanks to the popularity
of the song 'Danny Boy'. In Arthurian legend, Daniel is the
name of a knight who was brother to Sir Dinadan. (*10
October, 11 December*)

Darcy: Ultimately from a French surname based on the word
meaning 'fortress'. It was introduced to England after the
Norman Conquest. In Ireland, the use of the name is
certainly influenced by the Gaelic meaning 'dark-haired'.

Darius: From the Persian meaning 'he who is rich'.

Darren: A relatively modern name of uncertain origin.

Darryl: From the French place name Airelle. It was brought to
England after the Norman Conquest. Alternative spellings
are **Daryl** and **Darrell**.

David: From the Hebrew meaning 'beloved'. In the Bible,
David was a shepherd who fought the giant Goliath and
later became King of Israel. The name has several forms
including **Dai**, **Dafydd**, **Dewi** and **Tafydd**. (*1 March, 24
May*)

Dean: From a surname that has two origins. The first was
given to 'someone who lives in a valley'; the second was an
occupational name for 'someone who served as a dean'. The
name is also spelled **Deane** and **Dene**.

Declan: A Gaelic name of uncertain origin, although it may be based on words meaning 'full of goodness'.

Denis: Based on the Greek Dionysus, the god of wine. This is of uncertain origin but is probably pre-Greek, meaning 'divine son'. **Dennis** is another spelling of the name. (*9 October*)

Denzil: From the Cornish place name that developed into a surname. The origins are uncertain, although it may be based on the Celtic goddess Don or be a Celtic form of Dionysus, the Greek god of wine.

Derek: The English form of the German name Theodoric, which also gave the name Terry. It was introduced to England by the fifteenth-century Flemish cloth traders.

Dermot: One form of the several Celtic names including **Diarmad**, **Diarmait** and **Dermott**. All probably originate from the words meaning 'without envy'. It is the name of the legendary Gaelic hero who fell in love with Grainne. She was betrothed to a man with the wonderful name of Fionn MacCool, so the couple eloped.

Desmond: Originally an Irish surname given to someone who came from Deas-Mhumhan, the Irish name for South Munster.

Dirk: The Flemish and Dutch form of Derek. This version of the name was made popular in the 1960s after Dirk Bogarde, who was himself of Dutch descent.

Dominic: From the Latin meaning 'lord'. (*9 March, 8 August*)

Donald: From the Gaelic name meaning 'ruler of the world', along with its other forms **Domhnal** and **Donal**. Although still quite popular in Scotland, it lost some of its appeal because of its association with Disney's Donald Duck – a sad reality for such an aspirational name. (*15 July*)

Donovan: The English form of an Irish name meaning 'brown black', so it would have been given to someone with dark features.

Dorian: A name probably invented by Oscar Wilde for the beautiful young man who was the main character in his novel *The Portrait of Dorian Gray*, published in 1891. It is likely that he took the name from the Dorian race of Greek-speaking people. Today, it is often used as a girl's name.

Dougal: From a Gaelic name meaning 'dark stranger'. It probably arose as a means for the Irish to distinguish between the fair-haired Vikings and the dark-haired Danes. This is a far cry from its latter-day association with one of the central characters in *The Magic Roundabout*!

Douglas: From a name given to several rivers and meaning 'black water'. According to Arthurian legend, King Arthur fought four battles near the River Douglas. It is particularly associated with the ancient Scottish Douglas clan.

Drew: A name with several possible origins. While it is usually considered a short form of Andrew, it could be developed from the German name Drogo, the meaning of which is unclear, or from the Old French meaning 'favourite'. Another possible connection could be to a Celtic name meaning 'dealer in magic', which also gave the word druid, meaning 'wise one'.

Duane: From the Gaelic name meaning 'little dark one'. Other versions include **Dwane** and **Dwayne**.

Dudley: From the place name Dudley in the West Midlands, which was called 'Dudda's wood' in Old English.

Duncan: From the Gaelic name meaning either 'dark warrior' or 'princely battle'. Probably its most famous bearer was the eleventh-century Scottish king murdered by Macbeth.

Dunstan: From the Old English meaning 'dark stone'. (*19 May*)

Dustin: From the surname that has uncertain origins. It might be based on the Old Norse meaning 'Thor's stone'.

Dwight: From the surname that might have originated as a form of Dionysus, the Greek god of wine. It was made popular in the United States in honour of the President Dwight D. Eisenhower (1890–1969).

Dylan: From the Welsh meaning 'sea'; Dylan was a legendary Celtic god of the sea. Its popularity owes much to the Welsh poet, Dylan Thomas, although the recent choice of this name by Michael Douglas and Catherine Zeta-Jones for their son has certainly increase its appeal.

E

Eamon: The Irish form of the Old English name Edmund, meaning 'successful protector'.

Ebenezer: From the Hebrew meaning 'stone of help'. In the Bible, it is the place where the Israelites secured victory over the Philistines. The prophet Samuel marked the place with a stone. The name was popular among the seventeenth-century Puritans but today its use is limited thanks to its association with the notorious Ebenezer Scrooge in Charles Dickens's *A Christmas Carol*, published in 1843.

Edgar: From the Old English words meaning 'prosperity' and 'spear', so implying a 'successful warrior'. The name was made popular in the tenth century by King Edgar, known as Edgar the Peaceful.

Edmund: From the Old English words meaning 'prosperity' and 'protector', so implying someone who would 'successfully defend in battle'. Several saints have this name but the most famous bearer is probably the ninth-century King of East Anglia who gave his name to Bury St Edmunds. (*16 November, 20 November*)

Edryd: A Welsh name probably meaning 'restoring', although some have linked it to the word meaning 'storyteller'.

Edward: From the Old English words meaning 'prosperity' and 'guardian', so implying a successful protector. It has long been a popular royal name, having been borne by Edward the Confessor in the eleventh century and another seven kings (eight if you count Edward VIII, who abdicated the throne and became Duke of Windsor). (*18 March, 13 October*)

Edwin: From the Old English meaning 'prosperity' and 'friend', so implying a good friend or ally. The seventh-century King Edwin, the first Christian King of Northumbria, was killed fighting the pagans and subsequently regarded as a martyr.

Egbert: From the Old English meaning 'sword edge' and 'famous', so implying a 'skilled and successful warrior'. (24 April)

Eli: From the Hebrew meaning 'height'. In the Bible, Eli is a high priest and judge, but the actions of his sons brought God's displeasure. It was particularly popular among the seventeenth-century Puritans.

Elijah: From the Hebrew meaning 'the Lord is my God'. In the Bible, the prophet Elijah was protected by God. During a great drought, God showed him a spring that had not dried up and birds brought him food.

Elliott: Originally a surname, probably from the Old English meaning 'noble battle', although it has also been seen as a form of Elias, meaning 'the Lord is my God'. Alternative spellings are **Elliot** and **Eliot**.

Ellis: A Welsh name that is probably based on the word meaning 'benevolent'.

Elton: Originally a surname taken from the Old English male name Ella and the word meaning 'enclosure', so possibly 'Ella's enclosure'. It has been made particularly well known by the singer Elton John.

Elwin: A Celtic name meaning 'kind and fair'.

Emlyn: The Welsh form of the Latin name meaning 'rival'.

Emmanuel: From the Hebrew meaning 'God is with us'. In the Bible, it is spelled **Immanuel** in the Old Testament.

Emmet: Originally a surname based either on a medieval female name, which was a form of Emma, or on the Old English word meaning 'ant'. It is especially popular in Ireland where it is given in honour of the eighteenth-century patriot, Robert Emmet. **Emmett** is an alternative spelling.

Enoch: From the Hebrew meaning 'teacher'. In the Bible, Enoch is the son of Cain and father of the long-lived Methuselah who traditionally lived for 1,000 years!

Eric: From the Old Norse words meaning 'monarch'. One of the most infamous bearers of the name was the tenth-century Eric Bloodaxe, who killed seven of his brothers to secure the throne. (*18 May*)

Ernest: From the German meaning 'serious', in battle, that is.

Eros The god of love in Greek mythology.

Errol: Originally a Scottish place name that became a surname before transferring to a first name. Its popularity was enhanced by the swashbuckling film star Errol Flynn.

Ethan: From the Hebrew meaning 'strong'.

Euan: A popular Celtic name that comes in several forms including **Eoghan**, **Ewen** and **Owen**. Its origins are uncertain but it may derive from the Celtic word meaning 'yew tree'.

Eugene: From the Greek meaning 'well born'.

Eurwyn: A Welsh name, the male equivalent to Eurwen, meaning 'golden fair'.

Eustace: From the Greek meaning 'good' and 'ear of corn', so implying someone who would 'reap a good harvest'. In Arthurian legend, Eustace was the Duke of Cambenet who joined the rebellion against King Arthur. (*20 September*)

Evan: The Welsh form of John. The forms **Evin** and **Ewan** are also used.

Evander: From the Greek words meaning 'good man'. In Greek mythology, it was the original name of Pan.

Everard: From the Old English words meaning 'boar' and 'brave'.

Ezra: From the Hebrew meaning 'help'. In the Bible, he is a prophet who leads a group of exiles back to Jerusalem.

F

Fabian: From an old Roman family name, Fabius, based on the Latin meaning 'bean'. (*20 January*)

Felix: From the Latin meaning 'lucky' or 'happy'. It was originally a Roman nickname. One of the best-known bearers of the name was the seventh-century St Felix, the first Bishop of East Anglia, after whom Felixstowe, meaning 'Felix's place', is named. According to Arthurian legend, Felix was the name of a king of Cornwall who was grandfather to Tristan. (*14 January, 8 March, 18 May, 30 August, 24 October*)

Ferdinand: From the German words meaning either 'journey' or 'peace', and 'ready'. The name became popular in Spain as Ferdinando and was brought to England in the sixteenth century by Roman Catholic supporters of Mary I, wife of Philip II of Spain. (*30 May*)

Fergal: A Celtic name, probably meaning 'brave man'. **Fearghal** is another form of the name.

Fergus: This name has many forms including **Fearghas** and **Feargus**. Its origins are uncertain but are probably associated with the words meaning 'man' and 'vigour'. Fergus was one of the Knights of the Round Table in Arthurian romances.

Fletcher: Originally an occupational surname for someone who made arrows. Perhaps the most famous bearer of the name was Fletcher Christian, leader of the mutiny on the *Bounty* in 1789.

Francis: From the Latin meaning 'French'. Although it is popularly associated with the thirteenth-century St Francis of Assisi, famed for his love of animals and birds, this was not his original name. In fact, he was born Giovanni but came to be nicknamed Francesco because of his father's close commercial ties with France. (*24 January, 2 April, 11 May, 4 June, 13 July, 25 September, 4 October, 10 October, 3 December*)

Frank: This is not a pet form of Francis, as is popularly supposed, but originally meant someone from the 'Frankish tribe', which invaded Gaul in the fourth century. Their tribal name gave the modern country its name, France. The name has thus been in use since medieval times and was brought to England after the Norman Conquest.

Franklin: Originally a surname meaning 'free man'. In the thirteenth century, it would have been given to a landholder who was not of noble birth. It is sometimes given in honour of either the eighteenth-century statesman, Benjamin Franklin, or the former President of the United States, Franklin D. Roosevelt. The name can also be spelled **Franklyn**.

Fraser: Originally from the French place name, La Fraselière. The Scottish Frasers were originally Norman.

Frederick: From the Old German words meaning 'peace' and 'ruler', so a 'peaceful ruler', and introduced to England after the Norman Conquest. Its popularity in Victorian times probably led George Bernard Shaw to choose it as the name of the 'upper-class twit', Freddie Eynsford Hill, in his 1913 play *Pygmalion*, which became the basis of the hugely successful film *My Fair Lady*. According to Shaw's postscript, Freddie finally succeeds in marrying Eliza.

G

Gabriel: From the Hebrew meaning 'my strength is God'. In the Bible, Gabriel is one of the archangels who appears to Zacharias to announce the imminent birth of his son, who would grow up to be John the Baptist. More famously, it was Gabriel who told the Virgin Mary that she would give birth to Jesus. It is because of this latter story that the name is often given to children born on or near Christmas Day. (*27 February, 29 September*)

Galahad: One of the most famous knights in Arthurian legend, Sir Galahad is the son of Sir Lancelot. His life was spent searching for the Holy Grail. The most likely meaning of his name is 'tall Frenchman'.

Gareth: Probably from the Welsh word meaning 'gentle', although it is often associated with similar names such as Gary, Geraint and Gerard. In Arthurian legend, Gareth is King Arthur's nephew. Disguised as a kitchen hand, he saves Lyonors from the Red Knight, killing the Black and Green Knights on the way. He and Lyonors eventually marry, only for Gareth to be killed by Sir Lancelot during the latter's rescue of Queen Guinevere.

Garth: From the surname based on the Old Norse meaning 'enclosure', so would have been given to someone living near one.

Gary: From a surname that was originally based on a German word meaning 'spear'. The same element appears in names such as Gerald. The name was made particularly popular by the taken name of film star Gary Cooper, originally called Frank Cooper; the name Gary was suggested by his theatrical agent who took it from the name of her hometown of Gary, Indiana. The town itself was named after the American industrialist Elbert Henry Gary. The name is also taken as a short form of Gareth and can be spelled **Garry**.

Gavin: Although it is of uncertain origin, the name probably derives from the Celtic words meaning 'white hawk of battle'. One bearer of a related name was **Gawain**, one of the Knights of the Round Table and a nephew of King Arthur, whose strength grew as the sun rose and diminished as it went down. His name appeared in the French as Gauvain, which itself led to Gavin. One of Sir Gawain's most epic legendary adventures is told in the fourteenth-century poem 'Sir Gawain and the Green Knight'.

Gene: A short form of Eugene that is now used as a name in its own right, thanks primarily to the influence of stars such as Gene Kelly and Gene Wilder. More recently, Gene was the name chosen by Liam Gallagher and Nicole Appleton for their son.

Geoffrey: From the Germanic words meaning 'territory' and 'peace', thus suggesting a 'peaceful ruler'. The name was introduced to England after the Norman Conquest. There are several variations including **Jeffrey** and **Geoff**. (*8 November*)

George: From the Greek meaning 'earth worker', so 'farmer'. It is the name of the patron saint of England who, legend has it, slew a dragon. He was chosen as the symbol of the medieval Crusaders, through whom his fame spread across Europe. This explains why he is also the patron saint of Germany and Portugal. In the early eighteenth century, the first of six kings of England with this name arrived from Germany. With the first four King Georges reigning consecutively, the name became hugely popular. (*23 April*)

Geraint: A Celtic name that is probably of Greek origin from the word meaning 'old man'. The name is perhaps best known as that of one of the legendary Knights of the Round Table.

Gerald: From the Old German words meaning 'spear' and 'rule'. The name was introduced to England following the Norman Conquest. (*13 March, 13 October*)

Gerard: From the Old German words meaning 'spear' and 'strong'. The name was probably given to a successful warrior. (*24 September*)

Gervaise: An unusual Norman name, the origins of which are unclear. However, it may well contain the Germanic word meaning 'spear'.

Gerwyn: A Celtic name meaning 'fair love'.

Gideon: From the Hebrew meaning 'he who cuts down'. In the Bible, an angel appears to the Israelite Gideon and tells him to save Israel from the Midianites using an army of just 300 men. Although the odds were stacked against them, Gideon and his men attacked at night and won a famous victory.

Gilbert: From the German words meaning 'hostage' and 'bright'. In medieval times, hostages were often handed over to the enemy in return for some concessions. One of the most famous bearers of the name was the twelfth-century St Gilbert of Sempringham. (*4 February*)

Gildas: A name used in Celtic communities – probably a form of Giles.

Giles: From the Greek, through Latin, meaning 'young goat'. The eighth-century St Giles is one of the famous bearers of the name and his reputation caused it to be very popular in the Middle Ages. (*1 September*)

Gladstone: From a surname based on the Old English words meaning 'kite' and 'rock'. It is sometimes given in honour of the nineteenth-century Liberal Prime Minister, William Ewart Gladstone.

Glen: Originally a surname based on the Gaelic word meaning 'valley'. The form **Glenn** is used both as a male and female name. Another form, **Glyn**, has recently come into use as a first name.

Godfrey: From the Old German meaning either 'God's peace' or 'good peace'. It was introduced to England by the Normans after the Conquest of 1066.

Godwin: From the Old English name based on the words meaning 'God's friend' or 'good friend'.

Gordon: From a Scottish place name and surname meaning 'spacious fort' from either a town near the English border or one in Normandy. In origin it is probably English, but as a result of the famous clan of the name, it is now firmly associated with Scotland.

Graham: From the Scottish place name and surname that originates from Grantham in Lincolnshire and means either 'Granta's village' or 'gravelly village'.

Grant: From the French meaning 'big' or 'tall', as in the French word *grand*. It was therefore originally a nickname given to someone who was particularly tall.

Granville: From the Old French meaning 'large settlement'. It was a Norman baronial name that was brought to England after the Norman Conquest and subsequently became an aristocratic surname.

Gregor: A variation of the name Gregory.

Gregory: From the Greek, through Latin, meaning 'to watch'. It was very popular among the early Christians and was the name of many popes and saints. More recently, its

popularity benefited from the association with the film star
Gregory Peck. (*2 January, 9 March, 25 May, 25 August, 3
September, 1 October, 14 November, 17 November, 27
November*)

Guy: A Norman name based on one of the Old Germanic
names containing the element 'witu', meaning 'wood'. The
German 'w' often became the French 'gu', as can be seen
from the similar words 'wicket' and 'guichet'. (*12 September*)

Gwilym: The Welsh form of William, which derived from
Guillaume, the French version of William the Conqueror's
name.

H

Hamish: The Scottish form of the name Seamus, itself a form
of James.

Hannibal: From the Punic word meaning 'grace' and the
name of the god Baal. It was famous as the name of the
third-century general who crossed the Alps with a large
army and several elephants. More recently, it has come to be
associated with Dr Hannibal Lecter, the sinister but brilliant
murderer and cannibal in Thomas Harris's hugely
successful novel *The Silence of the Lambs*, published in 1988,
and its sequel *Hannibal*, published in 1999.

Harold: From the Old English words meaning 'army' and
'rule', so given to a 'successful leader'. However, King
Harold, probably its most famous bearer, patently failed to
live up to his name when he lost the Battle of Hastings in
1066 and died in the process.

Harry: An old pet form of Henry. It was common in medieval
times and was used by Shakespeare. It remains a popular
name today, no doubt partly influenced by its being the
choice for Prince Charles's second son.

Harvey: A name of Breton origin based on the words meaning
'battle' and 'worthy'. It was introduced to England following
the Norman Conquest. (*17 June*)

Hector: From the Greek meaning 'to hold fast'. In Greek mythology, Hector was the eldest son of King Priam of Troy, husband of Andromache and hero of the Trojan war. He was killed by Achilles who then dragged his body around the walls of Troy. The background to the English word 'hector', to shout down, developed from a character in medieval romances.

Helios: The god of the sun in Greek mythology whose chariot was pulled across the sky each day. He returned at night in a large cup on the stream of the ocean.

Henry: From the Old German words meaning 'home' and 'power' or 'ruler'. It was popular among the Normans who then introduced it to England after the Conquest in 1066. The first of the eight kings of England to bear this name was the eleventh-century Henry I, youngest son of William the Conqueror. (*19 January, 13 July*)

Herbert: From the Old German words meaning 'army' and 'famous', so implying a 'great warrior'. (*20 March*)

Hercules: From the Greek meaning 'glory of Hera' after the supreme Greek goddess. Although he was not her son by Zeus, Hera mistakenly nursed and then tried to kill him. He was a real modern-day Rambo who fought and destroyed those who stood in his way and was eventually made into a god himself. The original Greek form of the name was **Heracles**.

Herman: From the Germanic words meaning 'army' and 'man' so, ultimately, 'soldier'. It was used by the Normans, who introduced it to England after the Conquest, but died out in the Middle Ages.

Hermes: From the Greek meaning 'prop' or 'support'. In Greek mythology, he is the messenger of the gods and protector of travellers. He was originally the god of fertility and went on to father Pan.

Horace: From the Roman family name Horatius, which is of uncertain origin although it has been associated with the Latin meaning 'time'.

Horatio: A form of Horace, so with the same origin and possible meaning of 'time'. Its most famous bearer was certainly the English hero and scourge of the French fleets, Admiral Horatio Nelson.

Howard: From the surname, probably based on the Scandinavian words meaning 'high' and 'guardian'.

Hubert: From the Germanic words meaning 'mind' or 'spirit', and 'bright', so implying someone who is 'understanding and kind'. The name was popular among the Normans who introduced it to England after the Conquest. (*3 November*)

Hugh: A short form of longer Germanic names which contained the word meaning 'mind' or 'spirit'. This is another name that was popular in medieval France and brought to England by the Normans after the Conquest. The Welsh form of the name is **Huw**. (*1 April, 29 April*)

Hugo: The Latin form of Hugh that is now used as a separate name.

Humphrey: From the Germanic words meaning 'warrior' and 'peace', so implying a 'powerful person who brings peace'. The film star Humphrey Bogart was one of the most famous recent bearers of the name.

Hywel: From the Welsh meaning 'eminent'.

I

Ian: The Scottish version of John, which is also spelt **Iain**. In Wales, the same name is **Ieuan** or **Iwan**.

Idris: A Welsh name meaning 'ardent lord'.

Ifor: A Welsh form of the Scandinavian name Ivor, meaning 'archer'.

Igor: A Russian name originally from the Scandinavian name Ingvarr. This is made up of the name of the god of fertility, Ing, and the word *var* meaning 'careful'.

Illtud: A Welsh name probably meaning 'lord of all'. In Arthurian legend, he was a cousin of King Arthur.

Indra: The god of thunder and lightning in Hindu mythology.

Ira: From the Hebrew meaning 'watchful'. In the Bible, it is the name of one of King David's officers.

Irving: From a Scottish surname based on a place in what was Dumfriesshire. The place was probably named after a Celtic river name meaning 'green water'.

Isaac: From the Hebrew meaning 'he will laugh'. In the Bible, Isaac is the son of Abraham and Sarah, born when both were long past child-bearing age. In fact, Abraham was said to be 100 years old! Isaac himself was nearly sacrificed by Abraham after God had asked him to do it in order to prove his faith. Only when the young child was strapped to an altar did God call the whole thing off. The meaning of the name could refer to God's pleasure in Isaac or, more likely, to his father's amazement at the birth. (*9 September, 19 October*)

Isidore: From two Greek words, the first based on the Egyptian goddess, Isis, and the second meaning 'gift'. (*4 April*).

Ithel: From the Irish meaning 'generous lord'.

Ivan: The Russian equivalent to John, and popularly associated with the sixteenth-century despot, Ivan the Terrible. In fact, although his methods were autocratic and cruel, this first tsar of Russia's name lost a little in translation in that it meant more that he was 'awesome' than 'awful'.

Ivor: From the Scandinavian words meaning 'yew' and 'army'. As the yew tree provided the wood for bows, this name was actually given to an archer.

J

Jack: Often thought of as a pet form of James due to the similarity with the French form of that name, Jacques. However, this is actually a pet form of John. This came about from the Middle English pet name Jankin, meaning 'little Jan (John)'. It is now taken as a name in its own right and is a popular name in nursery stories, as in Jack and Jill, although at the other extreme it is also associated with the notorious Jack the Ripper. More recently, it is a name that has seen an increase in popularity after the hero, played by Leonardo di Caprio, in the blockbusting film *Titanic*. (No doubt the same is true of the name Leonardo.)

Jacob: From the Hebrew meaning 'supplanter'. In the Bible, Jacob is one of the twin sons of Isaac and tricked his blind father into blessing him as heir instead of his elder brother. In fact, the story goes that he even held on to his brother's heel as the pair were being born. He went on to have twelve sons, one of whom was Joseph of the multicoloured coat fame. It is also this Jacob whose vision of a ladder going up to heaven led to the famous 'Jacob's ladder'.

Jago: The Cornish form of Jacob.

Jake: A form of Jack, sometimes used as a short form of Jacob, and now used as a name in its own right.

James: From the Late Latin name Iacomus, a form of Jacob. In the Bible, James is a fisherman who becomes one of the apostles. More recently, the name is popularly associated with the all-action hero of Ian Fleming's James Bond stories, which have also become cult films. James continues to be one of the most popular names for boys, as does its pet form **Jamie**. (*30 April, 3 May, 15 July, 25 July, 28 November*)

Jan: A short form of either John in men or names such as Janet and Janice in women.

Janus: The god of beginnings, doors, gates and passageways in Roman mythology.

Jared: A name, popular in Ireland, that comes from the Germanic meaning 'hardy spear'. This name, and the alternative **Jarret**, are related to the names **Garreth** and **Garrett**.

Jarvis: From the surname that is based on the Norman first name, Gervaise.

Jason: Probably from the Greek meaning 'to heal', it is likely to be a form of Joshua. The name is famous as that of the

Greek mythological hero who was leader of the Argonauts and retriever of the Golden Fleece. Tradition has it that Jason was given his name by the centaur Chiron, who had taught the young man medicine.

Jasper: Probably from the Persian word meaning 'treasurer'. It is traditionally the name of one of the three wise men who brought gifts to the infant Jesus but they are not actually named in the Bible. It is also the name of a precious stone, which the apostle John saw laid in the foundations of his vision of the New Jerusalem. Other forms of the name are **Caspar** and **Gaspard**.

Jay: Originally a nickname for someone who resembled the bird or for anyone with a name beginning with the letter 'J'. It is the name of the hero in F. Scott Fitzgerald's great romantic novel, *The Great Gatsby*, published in 1925.

Jeffrey: Another form of Geoffrey, which has been in use from medieval times.

Jeremy: From the Hebrew meaning 'raised up by God'. The original name was Jeremiah who, in the Bible, was a prophet who warned the people of the overthrow of Jerusalem as a judgement for turning away from God. This led to Jeremiah being used as a nickname for particularly depressing or gloomy people.

Jerome: From the Greek name meaning 'holy name'. (8 February, 20 July, 30 September)

Jesse: From the Hebrew meaning 'gift'. In the Bible, Jesse is the father of David, famous for his one-to-one combat with a giant, who later became king.

Jesus: From the Greek meaning 'God saves'.

Jethro: From the Hebrew meaning 'excellence'. In the Bible, Jethro is the father-in-law of Moses.

Jim: A short form of James, in use since medieval times.

Job: From the Hebrew meaning 'hated' or 'persecuted'. In the Bible, he is the man forced to endure some terrible ordeals as part of Satan's attempt to prove that even the most faithful of men could be turned against God. Job put up with it all and retained his faith. His forbearance led to the common phrase 'patient as Job'.

Jocelyn: From a surname that itself was based on an Old French male name derived from the name of the Gauts, a Germanic tribe. It was introduced to England following the Norman Conquest and has since been used as both a male and female name. Another spelling would be **Josceline**.

Joel: From the Hebrew meaning 'the Lord is God'. In the Bible, he was a prophet who told of the day when evil would be judged and conquered.

John: From the Hebrew meaning 'God has shown favour'. It is one of the most enduring ancient names that, until recently, was always among the top 50 names given to children in the United Kingdom. In the Bible, there are several characters who bear this name. John the Baptist was the man chosen to prepare the way for Jesus; he was eventually imprisoned and beheaded. Another biblical John was the fisherman who became one of the apostles and author of one of the Gospels. (*5 January, 23 January, 31 January, 4 February, 8 February, 8 March, 18 May, 12 June, 16 June, 22 June, 23 June, 26 June, 12 July, 19 August, 13 September, 19 October, 21 October, 23 October, 25 October, 19 November, 26 November, 4 December, 14 December, 23 December, 27 December*)

Jolyon: A medieval version of Julian.

Jonah: From the Hebrew meaning 'dove'. In the Bible, he is the reluctant prophet who was told by God to go to a notorious pagan city and warn them that His judgement was coming. He tried to sail to a different place but when the ship was faced with a great storm he persuaded the sailors that it was his fault and they threw him into the sea. He was eventually swallowed by a 'great fish', more commonly related as a whale, and delivered safely to shore, finally ready to do God's wish. (*29 March*)

Jonas: The Greek form of Jonah.

Jonathan: From the Hebrew meaning 'God has given'. In the Bible, he is the son of King Saul and loyal friend of David, the man God intended to be Saul's heir. He was eventually killed in battle. There are several spellings of the name including **Johnathon** and **Jonathon**.

Jordan: From the Hebrew meaning 'flowing down'. It is the name of the famous river in Israel, where Christ was baptised by John the Baptist. It was originally given as a name to any child baptised in holy water from the River Jordan. Today Jordan is a popular name for boys and girls.

Joseph: From the Hebrew meaning 'he will add'. In the Bible he is the first son of Jacob and Rachel who is sold into slavery and is famed for his multicoloured coat. The New Testament Joseph, however, is perhaps the best known of all, being the carpenter chosen by God to be the father-figure to his only son. Yet another Joseph, this time of Arimathea, was the man who took Jesus down from the cross after the Crucifixion – so a Christian name in every sense of the word. Joseph remains a very popular name, while its pet form **Joe** is also frequently used. (*17 March, 19 March, 30 April, 1 May, 23 June, 25 August, 9 September, 18 September*)

Josh: A short form of Joshua that is now sometimes used as a name in its own right.

Joshua: From the Hebrew meaning 'God saves'. In the Bible, he is a close friend of Moses who took on the role of leader of the Israelites after the latter's death, and eventually led them into the Promised Land after 40 years in the wilderness.

Josiah: From the Hebrew meaning 'God supports'. In the Bible, he is the seventh-century-BC King of Judah whose faith inspired his people during a politically difficult time.

Joss: A short form of Jocelyn.

Judas: The Greek form of the name Judah, meaning 'praised'. This name has never been particularly popular, primarily because of its association with the biblical Judas Iscariot, who betrayed Jesus to his enemies for thirty pieces of silver.

Judd: A medieval pet form of the name Jordan.

Jude: A short form of the name Judas. To some extent, it has come to be associated with the central character in Thomas Hardy's dark novel, *Jude the Obscure*, published in 1895. It was also the title of a song by the Beatles: 'Hey Jude', released in 1968. (*28 October*)

Julian: From the Late Latin name Julianus, itself from Julius. The origin of the name is uncertain but it may be based on the word meaning 'fair skinned'. It was for some time used as a female name. A variation of the same name is Jolyon. (*12 February, 8 March, 16 March, 27 May Julius, 3 July Julius, 28 August*)

Jupiter: One of the main Roman gods, intially seen as god of the sky and later as god of the day.

Justin: From the Roman family name Justinus, meaning 'just' or 'fair'. (*1 June, 30 July*)

K

Kane: From the Celtic meaning either 'dark' or 'little battler'. The name is also spelt **Kain**.

Keith: From a Celtic place name in East Lothian meaning 'wood'. It became a Scottish surname before being adopted as a first name.

Kelly: A name used for both boys and girls that is probably based on an Irish surname. Ultimately, it comes from the word meaning 'church'.

Kelvin: A fairly modern name, first used in the 1920s. It is taken from the name of the Scottish River Clyde.

Kendall: From the surname that derived from either Kendal in Cumbria, which was so named because it is in the valley of the river Kent, or from Kendale, which got its name from the Old Norse word meaning 'spring'.

Kenelm: From the Old English words meaning 'bold' and 'helmet'. (*17 July*)

Kennedy: From the Irish Gaelic name meaning 'ugly head'. As such, quite possibly a name to avoid.

Kenneth: From the Gaelic meaning 'handsome'.

Kent: Originally a surname that was taken from the English county. This was based on the Celtic word meaning 'border'.

Kentigern: From the Celtic meaning 'I do not condemn you'. According to tradition, Kentigern's mother was condemned to be thrown off high cliffs when she became pregnant but she and her unborn son were saved by God. Kentigern grew up to become Bishop of Glasgow. (*13 January*)

Kermit: From the Gaelic surname meaning 'son of the one without envy'. The success of *The Muppet Show*, in which the main character is Kermit the Frog, makes this an unusual name for a child, although the related name **Kermode** may be better.

Kerry: A fairly recent name that is probably taken from the Irish county. The name of the county ultimately means 'country of the dark children'.

Kevin: From the Irish meaning 'beautiful' or 'handsome'. (*3 June*)

Kieran: An ancient Irish name meaning 'dark one'.

Killian: From the Irish name based on the word meaning 'church'.

Kingsley: From the Old English surname meaning 'king's wood'.

Kirk: Originally a surname given to someone who lived near, or worked in, a church.

Kit: Either a pet form of Christopher or, if female, of Katherine.

Kyle: A Scottish surname taken from a place name meaning either 'church' or 'narrow'.

L

Lachlan: From a Scottish surname given to Vikings and meaning (from the) 'land of the lochs'.

Lance: A short form of the name Lancelot.

Lancelot: Possibly either from the French meaning 'spear carrier', or based on a Celtic word meaning 'church'. Lancelot is a famous name from the Arthurian legends. Sir Lancelot was King Arthur's champion whose love for Queen Guinevere ultimately led to Arthur's downfall.

Laurence: From the Latin name meaning 'man of Laurentum', a city in Italy. The place itself is probably based on the Latin meaning 'laurel'. The name is also frequently spelled Lawrence. (*3 February, 21 July, 10 August, 5 September, 14 November*)

Lazarus: From the Hebrew meaning 'God has helped'. One of the characters of this name in the Bible was raised from the dead by Jesus.

Leander: From the Greek meaning 'lion man'. In Greek mythology, he loved Hero, a priestess of Aphrodite, and swam across the Hellespont every night to visit her, guided by a lighthouse. He drowned one night in a storm when the light was out, a tragedy that led Hero to throw herself into the sea. (*27 February*)

Lee: From the Old English surname meaning 'clearing in a wood', so would have been given to someone who lived there. Alternatively, it may derive from the Gaelic meaning 'poem'.

Leigh: A form of Lee.

Lennon: The name chosen by Liam Gallagher and Patsy Kensit for their son, in honour of ex-Beatle John Lennon.

Lennox: From a Scottish surname taken from a place name meaning 'grove of elms'.

Leo: From the Latin word meaning 'lion'. The name had a welcome turn in the limelight when it was chosen by Tony and Cherie Blair for their new son. (*19 April, 10 November*)

Leonard: From the Old German meaning 'strong lion'. The name can also be spelled Lennard. (*6 November, 26 November*)

Leopold: From the Old German meaning 'brave people'. (*12 May, 15 November*)

Leslie: From a Scottish surname, itself from a place name of uncertain origin.

Lester: From the surname that derived from the place name Leicester.

Levi: From the Hebrew meaning 'associated'. In the Bible, he is one of the sons of Jacob. It was also the actual name of the apostle Matthew.

Lewis: From the French name Louis, itself of Germanic origin meaning 'famous warrior'.

Liam: The Irish form of William.

Liber: The god of fertility in Roman mythology.

Lincoln: From a surname based on the city, itself probably meaning 'lake' or 'settlement'.

Lindford: From a surname based on a place name using the Old English words meaning 'lime tree' or 'maple', and 'ford'.

Lindsay: From a Scottish surname, although this was based on the place Lindsey in Lincolnshire, which has the meaning 'the wetland belonging to Lincoln'. It is now used for both boys and girls, with various forms including **Lindsey**, **Linsy** and **Lynsey**.

Linus: From the Greek name Linos, itself of uncertain origin. In Greek mythological terms, Linus is probably an unfortunate name. There were three main characters with this name: the son of Apollo, who was sent as a baby to live with shepherds and was killed by his father's dogs; a son of one of the Muses, who was killed by Apollo; and a musician, who taught music to Hercules but was killed by the latter with his lyre. It is also the name of one of the principal characters in the 'Peanuts' cartoon.

Lionel: From the Old French name meaning 'lion'. In Arthurian legend, Lionel was given the throne of Gaul by King Arthur. After Arthur's death, he was killed by Mordred's son.

Llew: A Welsh name that is either derived from the word meaning 'lion' or, more probably, from the name of the Celtic sun god, which itself meant 'radiant light'.

Llewellyn: From the original Welsh name Llywelyn, which is of uncertain origin but may be based on the word meaning 'lion'. It is best known as the name of two Gwynedd princes who fought for Welsh independence against the Norman barons in south Wales during the thirteenth century.

Lloyd: From the Welsh meaning 'grey'. Originally a nickname for someone with grey hair.

Lonnie: A name of uncertain origin, although it might be a pet form of the Spanish name Alonso.

Louis: One of the most common French names, based on the Old German words meaning 'famous warrior'. It was borne by eighteen French kings including Louis XIV, the 'Sun King', and the unfortunate Louis XVI, husband of Marie Antoinette, who, with his wife, went to the guillotine during the French Revolution. The name was brought to England after the Norman Conquest and its spelling was usually anglicised to **Lewis**. (*28 April, 25 August*)

Lucas: A form of Luke.

Lucius: Probably based on the Latin meaning 'light'.

Ludovic: From the Latin name Ludovicus, itself from the Germanic name Hludwig, which also gave Louis.

Luke: From the Greek name Loukas, meaning 'man from Lucania', a region in southern Italy. In the Bible, Luke is a Greek doctor, a friend of St Paul the apostle and author of one of the Gospels. (*18 October*)

Lupercus: A god who protected flocks, especially from wolves, in Roman mythology.

Lyall: A Scottish name of uncertain origin, but probably based on a Scandinavian name meaning 'wolf'.

Lyle: Originally a Scottish surname given to someone who came 'from the island'.

Lyndon: Originally a surname taken from a place in Leicestershire that was named from the Old English words meaning 'lime-tree hill'. In America, it is often given in honour of President Lyndon Johnson. **Lindon** is an alternative spelling.

Lysander: From the Greek meaning 'liberator of men'.

M

Madoc: A Welsh name meaning 'generous'. In some sources of the Arthurian legend, Madoc is King Arthur's brother-in-law. (*31 January Maedoc*)

Magnes: In Greek mythology, this is the name of one of the many sons of Zeus. It is probably based on Magnesia, a place rich in minerals.

Magnus: From the Latin meaning 'great'. The ninth-century Holy Roman Emperor, Charlemagne, was first recorded as being called Carolus Magnus or Charles the Great. The name was introduced to Ireland in the Middle Ages and, along with its alternative spelling **Manus**, it is still popular. (*16 April*)

Malcolm: From the Gaelic name meaning 'devotee of the dove' (Columba means 'dove'). This sixth-century saint was responsible for converting Scotland and northern England to Christianity. Malcolm remains one of the most popular Gaelic names, although its use has diminished following its association with the phrase 'being a bit of a Malcolm', meaning being a bit of a weak twit.

Manfred: From the German meaning either 'peaceful man' or 'strength through peace'.

Marc: The French form of Mark. According to Arthurian legend, Marc was the grandson of Tristan.

Marcel: The French form of the Latin name that gave Marcus.

Marcus: From a Latin name that was either based on Mars, the Roman god of war, which also gave the name Mark, or perhaps on the word meaning 'virile'.

Mark: From the Latin name Marcus, which is probably based on Mars, the Roman god of war, although some have linked it with the word meaning 'virile'. In the Bible, Mark is a friend of Paul and Peter and author of the second Gospel. According to Arthurian legend, Mark was King of Cornwall and husband to Iseult. In some sources, after the deaths of Iseult and her lover, Tristan, Mark was killed by Sir Lancelot. Others say that he was put in a cage overlooking the graves of the lovers. (*29 March, 25 April, 18 June*)

Marlon: A name of uncertain origin. The first bearer of the name may well have been the father of the film star Marlon Brando who then passed it on to his son and ensured the name a place in history.

Marmaduke: A name of uncertain origin that has been linked with the Celtic name Madoc.

Mars: The god of war in Roman mythology.

Martin: A name that originates from the Latin and is probably associated with Mars, the Roman god of war. (*20 March, 13 April, 3 November, 11 November*)

Marvin: From the Welsh meaning 'sea fort'.

Matthew: From the Hebrew meaning 'gift of God', which is also the origin of the similar name Matthias. In the Bible, Matthew, who is also called Levi, is a tax collector who was called by Jesus to follow him. Not unlike the attitude of many today, tax collectors were regarded as the lowest of the low and the fact that Jesus was ready to mix with them was the cause of some upset. Matthew went on to write one of the Gospels. (*21 September*)

Matthias: A name with the same origins as Matthew. In the Bible, Matthias is the disciple who took the place of Judas after the latter had killed himself for betraying Jesus.

Maurice: From the Latin meaning 'dark skinned'. The name can also be spelled Morris.

Maximilian: From the Latin meaning 'greatest'. The name is often shortened to **Max** or **Maxim**, the latter version being the name of the tragic husband in the book, *Rebecca*, written by Daphne du Maurier in 1938. The character was memorably played by Laurence Olivier, and it is he who is often readily associated with the name. Its short form, Max, is more popular today. (*12 March, 14 August*)

Maxwell: From the Scottish surname, itself based on a place meaning 'Magnus's stream' or 'Maccus's stream'. There was a King Maccus of the Isle of Man.

Melchior: Thought to mean 'king of the city', this is traditionally the name of one of the wise men who brought gifts to the infant Jesus. None, however, is actually named in the Bible.

Melville: From a place name meaning 'bad town', given by the Normans to a town in Scotland, which then became a surname.

Melvin: A relatively recent name that is probably a mixture of Melville and Mervyn. The form **Melvyn** is also used.

Mercury: The messenger of the gods and god of trade in Roman mythology. (*25 November*)

Merlin: From the Welsh meaning 'sea fort'. Famous as the name of King Arthur's magician and advisor.

Mervyn: This Welsh name, which is also used with the spellings **Merven**, **Mervin** and **Merfyn**, probably comes from the words meaning 'marrow' and 'thriving'. In the USA, the name is often spelled **Marvin**.

Michael: From the Hebrew meaning 'who is like God?' There are several Michaels in the Bible but the best known is probably the one who fought Satan and protected God's people from him. (*14 May, 29 September*)

Miles: Possibly taken from the name Milo, which might be based on the Slavonic meaning 'grace'.

Mohammed: From the Arabic name meaning 'praiseworthy'. It is famous as that of the seventh-century founder of Islam. The form **Muhammad** is also used.

Montgomery: From the Norman baronial name, taken from a place name meaning 'hill' and linked with a Germanic name meaning 'power of man'. The name is often shortened to **Monty**.

Mordred: Of uncertain origin, although it may be based on the Welsh words meaning 'own' and 'course', or 'host'. In Arthurian legend, Mordred is either King Arthur's nephew

or son. He rebelled against Arthur while the latter was away
fighting Lancelot. Arthur returned to fight the rebellion in
what turned out to be his last battle.

Morgan: Both an Irish and Welsh name that is given to both
boys and girls. It derives from words meaning either 'great
queen' or 'bright sea'. It is a fairly common surname that has
transferred to a first name. In Arthurian legend, Morgan Le
Fay is the half-sister of King Arthur.

Morris: A form of Maurice that was popular in the Middle
Ages.

Moses: A great name that either derives from an Egyptian
word meaning 'son' or, as the Bible has it, from the Hebrew
meaning 'to draw out'. In the Bible, Moses was hidden in
bulrushes on the River Nile to save him from the Egyptians
who were killing all the Israelite boys. He was found by one
of the daughters of the pharaoh who took on Moses's
mother as a wet nurse and then brought him up at court.
Moses famously became the great leader of the Israelites,
leading them across the Red Sea to the Promised Land.

Mungo: A pet name of the sixth-century St Kentigern. It
probably means 'dearest friend'.

Murray: From the Scottish place name meaning 'settlement
beside the sea'. This became a surname and is now fairly
commonly used as a first name.

Myron: From the classical Greek name based on the word
meaning 'myrrh', so associated with the gift brought by one
of the wise men to the infant Jesus. As such, it was popular
among the early Christians.

N

Nathan: From the Hebrew meaning 'God has given'. In the
Bible, Nathan is a prophet who passed messages from God
to King David. In one incident, he had to warn David about
his adultery with Bathsheba. It was also Nathan who
anointed Solomon as the next king.

Nathaniel: As with Nathan, from the Hebrew meaning 'God has given'. In the Bible, he is one of the first disciples of Jesus and one of those who saw him after the resurrection.

Neil: From the Gaelic meaning 'cloud' or 'champion'. It is a form of the name Niall.

Nelson: From the surname meaning 'son of Neil' or 'son of Nell'. It was probably first used as a given name in the eighteenth century, in honour of the famous Admiral Horatio Nelson. More recently, it has become associated with the eminent South African leader and hero, Nelson Mandela.

Neptune: God of the sea in Roman mythology.

Nestor: From the Greek meaning either 'journey' or 'to bring back safely'. In Greek mythology, Nestor is the oldest of the Greeks in the Trojan War and one who was known for his wisdom. He was the only one of the Greeks to arrive home without trouble, so the latter meaning is certainly the most apt.

Neville: From the Norman place name meaning 'new settlement'. It became a Norman first name and was introduced by them after the Conquest.

Niall: The Gaelic name which gives the English Neil. In a traditional story, Niall was a fourth-century king who, unlike his brothers, agreed to kiss an ugly hag guarding a water well as 'payment' for a drink. As soon as he had completed the unpleasant task, she transformed herself into a beautiful woman. Truly the stuff of which dreams are made!

Nicholas: From the Greek words meaning 'victory' and 'people', so probably 'conqueror'. It was the name borne by the fourth-century saint, otherwise known as Santa Claus, and the Bishop of Myra who is also patron saint of Greece and Russia as well as of sailors and children. (*21 March, 10 September, 13 November, 6 December*)

Nigel: From the Latin name, which was the equivalent of Neil, with the spelling altered under the influence of the word *niger*, meaning 'black'. It is an ancient name, being mentioned in the Domesday Book, and was introduced to England by the Normans after the Conquest. In later years it was brought to prominence by the publication in 1822 of Sir Walter Scott's *The Fortunes of Nigel*.

Noah: From the Hebrew meaning 'rest'. Noah is one of the best-known characters in the Bible. He was told by God to build an ark to save himself, his family and the animals from a great flood, which was going to be sent to destroy the wickedness of the world. It was a popular name among the seventeenth-century Puritans.

Noel: From the Latin meaning 'birthday'. As the French word for Christmas, which is Christ's birthday, it is often, though not exclusively, given to children born on or near Christmas Day.

Norman: From the German meaning 'Norseman', so 'man from the north'. The name was used in England before the Norman Conquest and was subsequently adopted by the Normans themselves.

Norris: From the Norman French meaning 'from the north'.

Notus: The god of the south wind in Greek mythology.

O

Oberon: A form of Auberon.

Oliver: From the Scandinavian meaning 'the ancestor remains', although it is often thought of as being the male version of Olivia and so associated with the word 'olive'. Oliver is famous in French legend as the close friend of Roland, both being knights of Charlemagne, whose story is told in the 'Song of Roland'. A slightly more recent but equally popular association is with Charles Dickens's *Oliver Twist*, published in 1838. (*1 July*)

Orlando: The Italian form of Roland. In Arthurian legend, Orlando is the lover of King Arthur's daughter Melora.

Orson: From a Norman French nickname meaning 'bear cub', which became a surname and then a first name. It is

probably particularly associated with the actor Orson
Welles.

Orville: A name invented by Fanny Burney for Lord Orville,
hero of her novel *Evelina*, published in 1778. Today,
however, it has unfortunate associations with a
ventriloquist's dummy in the shape of a large green duck!

Osbert: From the Old English words meaning 'god' and
'famous'.

Oscar: This name could be taken as either Scandinavian or
Irish in origin. As a Scandinavian name, it probably derives
from words meaning 'god spear'. The Irish, however, may
claim its origins to be in the words meaning 'friend of the
deer'. Whatever the origins, the name is associated both
with the nineteenth-century playwright and author, Oscar
Wilde, and with the statuette given annually to film stars
and makers. It is said that the statuette got its name because
it reminded one of the ceremony's officials of his Uncle
Oscar! It is also said that Napoleon Bonaparte called his
godson Oscar after the Ossian poems by James
Macpherson. (*28 February, 9 August*)

Oswald: An ancient name from the Old English words
meaning 'god' and 'power'.

Otis: From the Old German meaning 'riches'. Originally a
surname before being taken as a first name.

Owen: Probably the Welsh form of the Latin name Eugenius,
meaning 'well born'. This also gave the name Eugene. Other
Welsh variations of the name include **Owain**, **Eoghan**,
Euan and **Evan**.

P

Padarn: An ancient Celtic name taken from the Latin meaning
'fatherly'. In Celtic legend, Padarn, or Patern, was the
founder of a church in Wales who forced King Arthur to
apologise for insulting the church by making the earth
swallow him up to the neck until he did so.

Pan: The Greek god of fields, shepherds and flocks whose name comes from the Greek meaning 'all'. He was also a lover of mischief and enjoyed jumping out at people, thus causing 'panic' – which is hardly surprising considering he was half man and half goat!

Paris: From the name of a Celtic tribe, the Parisii, which itself is of uncertain origin. In Greek mythology, Paris is the prince of Troy and son of King Priam, and is also known as Alexander. Here the name is possibly based on a word meaning 'pouch'. The name Paris had come to prominence more recently as the name chosen by *James Bond* star, Pierce Brosnan, and his wife Keely Shaye-Smith for their new son.

Parry: A Welsh name meaning 'son of Harry'.

Patrice: The medieval French form of Patrick or Patricia. In modern France it is a male name but elsewhere it can be used as a female name.

Patrick: From the Latin meaning 'patrician', so a member of the aristocracy. It is most famous as that of the fourth-century saint who was responsible for converting the people of Ireland to Christianity. Other forms of the name include **Padraic**, **Padruig** and **Padrig**. (*17 March*)

Paul: From the Latin meaning 'little', it was originally used as a nickname and then developed into a family name. In the Bible, St Paul was converted to Christianity on the road to Damascus and is now regarded as one of the founders of the Christian Church. (*15 January, 25 January, 6 February, 7 March, 12 March, 26 June, 29 June, 10 October Paulinus, 19 October*)

Pax: From the Latin meaning 'peace' and, as such, an appropriate aspirational name for today.

Pearce: From the name Piers, the spelling being altered on transfer to Ireland. In some cases, it could represent the meaning 'son of Piers'.

Percival: Possibly from the Old French meaning 'piercing the valley'. In Arthurian legend, he is one of the Knights of the Round Table and in some versions the name is spelled

Perceval. It is also quite possible that the name is a version of the Celtic Peredur, which probably means 'spear'.

Percy: Originally a place name in France, it became a Norman personal name and in post-Conquest England became the name of one of the most aristocratic families. Whereas one of its associations is with the infamous Scarlet Pimpernel, Sir Percy Blakeney (from the novel by Baroness Orczy, published in 1905), more recently it has less heroic connotations, being primarily linked with the phrase 'point Percy at the porcelain'!

Peregrine: From the Latin meaning 'wanderer', a word that also gave the English word pilgrim. It was popular among early Christians.

Perry: Originally a surname given to someone who lived near a pear tree.

Peter: From the Greek meaning 'stone' or 'rock', a word which also gave petrified. The French version of the name, Pierre, is exactly the same as their word for stone. In the Bible, St Peter was one of the twelve disciples. Originally a fisherman, he became a true believer in Jesus although it was he who denied Him three times. However, Jesus forgave him after the resurrection and he went on to become one of the founders of the Christian Church before being crucified himself. The name was made particularly popular after the publication in 1904 of J. M. Barrie's classic children's story, *Peter Pan*. (*10 January, 28 January, 21 February, 28 April, 8 May, 19 May, 2 June, 29 June, 30 July, 3 August, 9 September, 19 October, 26 November, 9 December, 21 December*)

Philip: From the Greek meaning 'lover of horses'. In the Bible, the most prominent bearer of the name was one of the twelve apostles. Its short form of **Pip** was used by Charles Dickens for the central character in his novel *Great Expectations*. (*9 January, 3 May, 26 May, 23 August, 22 October*)

Phineas: From the Egyptian meaning 'black', so would have been given to someone with 'dark skin' or 'dark features'. In the Bible, the name is said to be based on the Hebrew meaning 'oracle'.

Phoenix: A mythological name meaning 'blood red'. It occurs both in Greek legend, where he is the tutor of Achilles, and, more famously, in Egyptian mythology, where the phoenix is a bird that burns on a fire and rises again from the ashes.

Piers: A form of Peter.

Pius: From the Latin meaning 'dutiful', a meaning that then developed to 'holy'. The name has been taken by several popes.

Pluto: God of the Underworld in Greek mythology and, in contrast, the name of one of Disney's most famous dogs!

Poseidon: God of the seas and waters in Greek mythology.

Preston: From the Old English words meaning 'priest's enclosure'. Originally a place name, then surname.

Priam: Famous as the last King of Troy in Greek mythology, whose name probably means 'chief'.

Q

Quintin: From the Latin, through French, meaning 'fifth'. It was a popular name in Victorian times for a fifth child, although with today's mostly smaller families it would be equally appropriate for a child born on the fifth day or during the fifth month.

R

Rabbie: The Scottish pet form of Robert and the name by which Scotland's famous poet, Robert Burns, is most commonly known.

Ralph: From the Old German meaning 'wolf counsel'. **Rafe** and **Ralf** are variations of the same name.

Rama: From the Sanskrit meaning 'black' or 'dark'. In Hindu mythology, Rama is the name of an incarnation of the god Vishnu, which he used when he was asked to vanquish the demon Ravana. Rama married Sita, who was abducted by Ravana, and the pair were only reunited after an epic battle in which Ravana was killed. They then lived happily together for 10,000 years before Rama rejected his wife. She died broken hearted, and Rama lived on alone for another 1,000 years.

Ramsay: From the Old English meaning 'wild garlic island'. Although it is mainly a Scottish name, originally a surname, it was in fact introduced to Scotland from the place Ramsey in Huntingdonshire. An alternative meaning, that of 'raven's island', has been argued, particularly with reference to the place name Ramsey on the Isle of Man. The raven was regarded as a sacred bird by the Celts. Probably its most famous bearer was Ramsay MacDonald, who became the first Labour Prime Minister in 1924.

Randall: From the medieval name Rand, which has been linked to the name Randolph. However, it could also have been given to someone who lived on the edge of a village, from the Old English meaning 'edge'.

Randolph: From the German name Randulf, meaning 'edge (of a shield)' and 'wolf'.

Ranulf: From a Viking name meaning 'wolf advice', that was introduced to Scotland in the early Middle Ages.

Raphael: From the Hebrew meaning 'God has healed'. In the Bible, it is the name of the angel who heals the blind Tobit. (*29 September*)

Ray: A name that could have several origins. Some have linked it to the Old French word meaning 'king', others to the Old English for 'roe deer' and others still to the place name Rye. Take your pick.

Raymond: From the Old German words meaning 'advice' and 'protector', it was brought to England at the time of the Norman Conquest. An alternative spelling is **Raymund**. (*7 January Raymund, 31 August Raymund*)

Rayner: Originally a surname based on the words meaning 'advice' and 'army'.

Rees: Along with its other variations including **Reece**, this is a form of the Welsh name **Rhys**, meaning 'ardour'.

Reginald: From a Latin name that was itself based on Reynold, from the Old German words meaning 'advice' and 'ruler'.

Reuben: From the Hebrew meaning 'see, a son'. In the Bible, Reuben was the eldest of Jacob's twelve sons and brother of the famous Joseph. It was he who persuaded his other brothers not to kill Joseph; he was sold into slavery instead. The name was popular among seventeenth-century Puritans.

Rex: From the Latin meaning 'king'. It was not used as a personal name until the nineteenth century but then quickly came to public attention through the actor Rex Harrison and, in a less likeable way, through the unfaithful and self-important character Rex Mottram in Evelyn Waugh's hugely successful novel *Brideshead Revisited*, published in 1945.

Reynard: From an Old French name based on the German words meaning 'advice' and 'brave'. It was introduced to England following the Norman Conquest.

Reynold: From an Old French name based on the German words meaning 'advice' and 'ruler'. This is another of the many names introduced to England by the Normans after 1066.

Rhett: Originally a Dutch surname from the word meaning 'advice'. Its best known association is with the infamous Rhett Butler, hero of Margaret Mitchell's *Gone with the Wind*, published in 1936. The character will forever be linked with the actor Clark Gable, who played him in the massively successful film of 1939, and the memorable phrase, 'Frankly, my dear, I don't give a damn.'

Richard: From the Old German meaning 'brave ruler', it was introduced to England by the Normans after the Conquest. The short form of **Dick** (which today has a very different association!) probably came about because the English found it difficult to pronounce the Norman 'r'. (*3 April*)

Rigel: From the Arabic meaning 'foot'. Rigel is the brightest star in the constellation Orion and is thought to mark the giant's left foot.

Riley: From the Gaelic meaning 'courageous'. It was originally a surname and, to a large extent, is still used as such although it is beginning to be used as a first name. Others have linked it to the Old English words meaning 'rye' and 'clearing'.

Riordan: From the Gaelic meaning 'king's poet'. **Rearden** is another variation. It is mainly used as a surname although it is beginning to be given as a first name.

River: Another name, like Sky and Rainbow, that became popular in the 1960s.

Robert: An unusual name inasmuch as it derives from the Old German words that mean 'famous'. It was the name of William the Conqueror's father and was introduced by the Normans after the victory over the English in 1066. It is also often associated with Robert the Bruce who, in the fourteenth century, won Scotland's independence from the English, having been inspired by the efforts of a spider. In Scotland, it is often used as Rabbie, while the shortened version of **Bob** is very common. The form **Bobbie**, however, is mainly used for girls. (*17 April, 29 April, 7 June, 17 September*)

Robin: A pet form of Robert that is now used as a given name in its own right. Two of the most common associations are with the legendary medieval hero and scourge of bad King John, Robin Hood, and the young sidekick of Batman. In recent years, the name has also been used for girls, probably as an association with the bird, and is often respelled Robyn.

Rocco: The name chosen by Madonna and Guy Ritchie for their new son. The origins are uncertain.

Roderick: From the Old German words meaning 'fame' and 'power'. The popularity of the shortened versions **Rod**, **Roden** and **Roddy** is based on its association with the Irish meaning 'strength'.

Rodney: From the place name in Somerset that means 'Hroda's island'. As with many place names, this developed into a surname before becoming a first name.

Rogan: From the Gaelic meaning 'red haired'. The name is used fairly widely outside the Celtic areas.

Roger: From the Old German words meaning 'famous spear'. The name was introduced to Britain by the Normans following the Conquest. A variant spelling is **Rodger**.

Roland: From the Old German meaning 'famous in the land'. It was introduced to England following the Norman Conquest. One of the most famous bearers of the name was the legendary Frankish hero, who was one of Charlemagne's knights killed in battle in the eighth century. A variation of the spelling is **Rowland**.

Rolf: A short form of the name Rudolf.

Rollo: The Latinised version of Roul, itself the Old French version of Rolf.

Romeo: This endlessly romantic name originated as a medieval name for someone who had made a pilgrimage to Rome. It will always be associated with the lover of Juliet in Shakespeare's *Romeo and Juliet*, written in 1595. Today it is often used to describe either a lover or, less attractively, a gigolo.

Ronald: From the Scandinavian name based on the Old Norse words meaning 'advice' and 'ruler', so implying a 'wise ruler'.

Ronan: From the Irish meaning 'little seal'. According to legend, sea women could take the form of seals and were sometimes able to live with men. Any offspring were therefore 'little seals'.

Rory: A popular Scottish and Irish name, Rory is based on either the Celtic word meaning 'red haired' or that meaning 'red king'. It was the name chosen by Bill Gates and Melinda French for their son.

Ross: This is one of those names that has several possible origins. It could be based on a place in France, which means 'clearing', being introduced to England after the Norman Conquest; it could be based on one of the many places in England or Scotland called Ross, meaning 'headland'. Some have linked it to the Old English word meaning 'horse', in which case it might have been given to someone who bred horses or even someone who looked like a horse!

Rowan: An ancient Irish name based on the Gaelic meaning 'little red one'.

Rowland: In Arthurian legend, Rowland is one of King Arthur's sons. His sister, Ellen, was abducted by the King of Elfland and two of his brothers tried and failed to rescue her. Rowland, however, followed the instructions of Merlin to the letter and eventually rescued his sister and the two captured brothers. (See also Roland)

Roy: A Scottish name, which began life as a nickname, from the word meaning 'red', so applied to someone with red hair or a ruddy complexion. It has also come to be associated with the Old French word for 'king'.

Rudolf: From the Old German words meaning 'fame' and 'wolf', this name also gave the name Rolf, which is more popularly used in English-speaking countries. **Rudolph** is an alternative spelling.

Rufus: From the Latin meaning 'red' or 'ruddy'. It would originally have been used as a nickname before being absorbed into the list of given names.

Rupert: The German form of Robert that is now used as a name in its own right. (*27 March*)

Russ: The short form of Russell.

Russell: From the Norman French nickname given to someone with 'red hair'.

Ryan: A short form of an Irish surname meaning 'descendant of the devotee of Riaghan'. Others have linked the name with the word meaning 'king'. Its popularity certainly increased under the influence of actor Ryan O'Neal, star of the hugely successful film *Love Story*.

S

Samson: From the Hebrew meaning 'sun'. In the Bible, he is
the incredibly strong man who divulged the source of that
strength, his hair, to Delilah. She had his hair cut and
betrayed Samson to the Philistines, who then sentenced him
to death. Just before they executed him, Samson's strength
returned and he brought down the pagan temple where
they were holding him, killing himself in the process. It is
interesting that Delilah's name may be based on the Hebrew
meaning 'night', in total contrast to Samson. (*28 July*)

Samuel: From the Hebrew meaning 'asked of God'. In the
Bible, Samuel's mother had longed for a child and in her
prayers to God she promised that should she have a boy he
would be brought up in service to the Lord. He gave her
Samuel, so he was truly 'asked of God'. His mother kept her
word and Samuel was the prophet whom God told to
anoint first Saul then David as kings of the Israelites.

Sandy: A pet form of Alexander as well as a descriptive name
for a person with sandy-coloured hair.

Sasha: A Russian pet form of Alexander or Alexandra.

Saturn: The god of agriculture in Roman mythology. He was
also father of Jupiter, which is the next planet along in the
solar system.

Saul: From the Hebrew meaning 'asked for'. In the Bible, it is
St Paul's name before he converted to Christianity and the
name of the first King of Israel, anointed by Samuel.
However, this king so ignored God's will that God rejected
him and had Samuel anoint David as king in his place.

Scott: An ancient personal name either meaning 'painted
warrior' or a name that was given to someone 'from
Scotland'.

Seamas: The Irish form of James, although it is now regarded
as essentially an Irish name in its own right. Alternative
spellings include **Seamus** and **Shamus**, while the Scottish
version is Hamish.

Sean: The Irish version of John which, along with its variants including **Shane**, **Shaun** and **Shawn**, is now used outside Ireland. The popularity of the name has been boosted in recent years by association with the actor Sean Connery, one of the most famous of the James Bonds, and a champion of Scottish independence.

Sebastian: Meaning 'man from Sebastia', a town now in Turkey, although it has been linked to the Greek meaning 'reverenced'. It was made famous by the third-century saint. (*20 January*)

Selwyn: The origins of this name are unclear. It has been linked to the Old English words meaning 'prosperity' and 'friend', and to the Latin meaning 'wood'.

Seth: From the Hebrew meaning 'appointed'. In the Bible, Seth was the third son of Adam and Eve, given to them after Cain had murdered Abel. It is said that he lived for over 900 years.

Seymour: Originally a Norman baronial name taken from the place Saint-Maur in Normandy.

Sheldon: Originally a surname based on several places with this name, such as those in Devon and Derbyshire, each of which have different origins.

Sheridan: Originally a surname either meaning 'descendant of Siridean' or based on the words meaning 'eternal' and 'treasure'.

Sholto: A Scottish name based on the Gaelic meaning 'sower'.

Sidney: From the surname that stemmed either from Saint-Denis in northern France or from the Old English meaning 'wide land by the marsh'. The name is also spelled **Sydney**.

Siegfried: From the Old German words meaning 'victory' and 'peace'. In German mythology, Siegfried is the son of Sigmund and kills a dragon guarding treasure. It is commonly associated with the 'Siegfried Line' of German fortifications during the Second World War.

Sigurd: From the Old Norse words meaning 'victory' and 'guardian'. Very similar to the German Siegfried, Sigurd is the hero of Norse mythology who kills a dragon and wins treasure.

Silas: This is another one of those names with several possible origins. It could be based on the Aramaic meaning 'to borrow', or from either of the Latin words that mean 'snub nosed' or 'wood'. In the Bible, Silas is a friend of Paul and both are imprisoned together. Perhaps more usually, however, the name is associated with Silas Marner in George Eliot's book of the same name, published in 1861. Here, Silas is a weaver who loses his beloved pot of gold but finds a young child and brings her up as his own. (*13 July*)

Silvanus: The god of agriculture in Roman mythology.

Silver: A name taken from the precious metal, so implying beauty and value.

Silvester: From the Latin meaning 'of the woods'. An alternative spelling is **Sylvester**. The name has become more popular in recent years thanks to the fame of the actor Sylvester Stallone.

Simeon: From the Hebrew meaning 'God has heard'. In the Bible, it is the name of two characters, the best known of whom was the old man told by God that he would not die until he had seen Christ. When he saw Mary and Joseph with the infant Jesus, he recognised him at once and took him in his arms. (*5 January, 1 July*)

Simon: The more usual form of Simeon. There are several characters of this name in the Bible. It was the original name of the apostle Peter as well as that of one of Jesus's brothers. (*16 May, 28 October*)

Sinclair: Originally a surname taken from the place Saint-Clair in northern France. It was a Norman baronial name that became a Scottish surname and, along with the given name, is now completely associated with Scotland.

Solomon: From the Hebrew meaning 'peace'. In the Bible, he is the son of King David and succeeded his father to the throne of Israel. On his accession, he asked God for the gifts of a 'listening heart' and wisdom.

Somnus: The god of sleep in Roman mythology – perhaps a good second name for a child from parents who hope to get some!

Spencer: Originally an occupational name given to someone who worked in the pantry of a manor house or monastery from which food was 'dispensed'. It transferred from a surname to a personal name and became well known through the film star Spencer Tracy.

Spike: This name is usually a nickname for someone with 'spikes' of hair and has become particularly associated with the member of the brilliant Goons team, Spike Milligan.

Stanley: Originally a surname based on a place name taken from the Old English meaning 'stone clearing'.

Stephen: From the Greek meaning 'crown' or 'garland'. In the Bible, Stephen was the first martyr. He was stoned to death and prayed for God's forgiveness for his tormentors as he died. **Stephan** and **Steven** are alternative spellings. (*17 April, 26 April, 16 August, 28 November, 26 December*)

Sterling: Originally a surname from a town in Scotland, itself of uncertain origin. It has been linked by some to the Middle English meaning 'little star' and may also be given as a name because of the quality, as in 'sterling effort'. **Stirling** is an alternative spelling of the name.

Stewart: Originally an occupational name for someone who worked as a steward. The French spelling of **Stuart** is far more commonly used.

Storm: A modern name taken from the vocabulary word.

Stuart: French spelling of the surname Stewart. This form was introduced to Scotland in the sixteenth century by Mary Stuart, Queen of Scots, who had been brought up in France.

T

Taliesin: A well-known Welsh name meaning 'shining brow'.

Tancred: From the German words meaning 'thought' and 'counsel'. It is the name of the Norman hero of the First Crusade in the late eleventh century.

Tarquin: A name of uncertain origin. It was the name of several early Roman kings, the two most famous being Tarquinius the Old and Tarquinius the Proud.

Taylor: From the Old French meaning 'to cut', this was originally an occupational surname for someone who, not surprisingly, worked as a tailor. It is now used for both boys and girls.

Terence: From the Latin meaning 'to wear out' or 'to polish'. The name is popular in Ireland where the alternative variation of **Torrance** is also found. It is not, as is commonly supposed, the original source of the name Terry, although this is now the usual short form. **Terrance** and **Terrence** are variations of the spelling.

Terminus: God of boundaries and frontiers in Roman mythology.

Terry: Although this is often used as a short form of either Terence or Theresa, it is a medieval name in its own right and originated from the same Old German name that gave Derek.

Thaddeus: Possibly from the Greek meaning 'gift of God'.

Theobald: From the German meaning 'brave people', where the spelling of the first part of the name was influenced by the Greek word Theo, meaning 'God'.

Theodore: From the Greek meaning 'gift of God'. The female name Dorothea is based on exactly the same two elements used in reverse. (*22 April, 19 September, 9 November, 11 November*)

Thomas: From the Aramaic meaning 'twin'. In the Bible, Thomas is one of the disciples who came to be known as 'doubting Thomas' because he did not believe in the resurrection until he had seen Jesus for himself. The name is also associated with the twelfth-century saint, Thomas à Becket, who was murdered in Canterbury Cathedral by Henry II's knights, and with the unlucky public-schoolboy in Thomas Hughes's *Tom Brown's Schooldays*, published in 1857. In Ireland, the form **Tomas** is also used. (*28 January, 22 June, 3 July, 22 September, 3 October, 29 December*)

Timothy: From the Greek meaning, in its Christian sense, 'honouring God'. It is based on the words meaning 'worth' or 'honour', and 'god'. In the Bible, Timothy is a friend and companion of St Paul. (*26 January*)

Tobias: From the Hebrew meaning 'God is good'.

Toby: The anglicised form of Tobias. It has a few unfortunate associations: from the 'Toby jug'; to Shakespeare's appropriately named Sir Toby Belch in *Twelfth Night*; and the name of the dog in the Punch and Judy puppet show.

Todd: From the Old English word meaning 'fox'. It was originally a nickname for someone who had either the features or the cunning of a fox.

Travis: From the French *traverser*, meaning 'to cross'. It was originally an occupational surname given to someone who collected tolls on bridges or roads.

Tremaine: Originally a Cornish surname taken from a place name meaning 'stone homestead'.

Trevor: Originally a Welsh surname taken from a place meaning 'big village'. In Wales, the spelling **Trefor** is also used.

Tristan: The French form of Tristram. **Trystan** is an alternative spelling. In Arthurian legend, Tristan is a Knight of the Round Table and lover of Iseult. Their love affair was ill-starred and after their deaths it is said that they were buried side by side. A vine grew out of Tristan's grave and a rose from Iseult's. Both plants grew towards each other and were forever entwined.

Tristram: The origins of this name may lie with the Celtic word meaning 'noise', but it is more popularly linked to the Latin and French words meaning 'sad'.

Troy: Probably from a surname taken from the place name Troyes in France. Many, however, associate it with the ancient city of Troy.

U

Ultan: An Irish name meaning 'Ulsterman'.

Uranus: God of the sky in Roman mythology and source of years of sniggering over the pronunciation!

Uriah: From the Hebrew meaning 'God is my light'. In the Bible, Uriah is a warrior killed on the orders of King David who had made Uriah's wife, Bathsheba, pregnant. It is also, negatively, associated with the cringing Uriah Heep in Charles Dickens's *David Copperfield*, published in 1850.

V

Valentine: From the Latin meaning 'healthy' or 'strong'. It is strongly associated with the third-century saint, whose association with valentine cards and declarations of love came about only because his feast day, 14 February, happened to fall on the same date as an existing pagan fertility festival! (*14 February*)

Vaughan: Originally a Welsh surname that developed from a nickname meaning 'small'.

Vernon: From the French meaning 'place of alders'. It was originally a place name from northern France that transferred to a surname and then to a first name.

Vertumnus: The god of fertility in Roman mythology.

Victor: From the Latin meaning, hardly surprisingly, 'conqueror'. It was popular among the early Christians who used the name to symbolise Christ's victory over sin. (*8 May, 21 July*)

Vincent: From the Latin meaning 'to conquer' and so of the same origin as Victor. (*22 January, 5 April, 25 September, 27 September*)

Vulcan: The god of fire in Roman mythology whose name gives the word volcano.

W

Wallace: From the Old French surname meaning 'foreign'.
The name is especially popular in Scotland where it was,
and is, given in honour of the thirteenth-century warrior
William Wallace of *Braveheart* fame. He was particularly
successful in fighting against the English, who took their
revenge by hanging, drawing and quartering him after he
was betrayed and arrested.

Walter: From the Old German meaning 'military leader', itself
from the words meaning 'rule' and 'army'. It was brought to
England by the Normans following the Conquest of 1066. It
is popularly associated with the daydreaming lead character
in James Thurber's *The Secret Life of Walter Mitty*, published
in 1939. The character proved so popular that daydreamers
today may still be referred to as 'a real Walter Mitty
character'.

Warren: From the Norman baronial surname that was partly
based on the place in Normandy called La Varenne,
meaning 'the game park', and partly from an Old German
word meaning 'guard'. It was introduced to England after
the Norman Conquest. The film star Warren Beatty is one of
the most famous bearers of the name.

Wayne: From an occupational surname based on the Old
English meaning 'waggon', which would have been given to
someone who worked as a cartwright. It was made
particularly popular by the actor John Wayne, whose name
is synonymous with westerns, in almost every one of which
is the perfectly relevant cry, 'Waggons roll!' His real name
was, incongruously, Marion, and he took his stage name
from the American Revolutionary general, Anthony Wayne.

Webster: From the occupational surname based on the Old
English meaning 'web', which was given to someone who
worked as a weaver.

Wesley: From the English place name meaning 'western wood
or clearing'. It is frequently given in honour of the

eighteenth-century clergyman John Wesley, founder of the Methodist Church.

Wilfred: From the Old German meaning 'peace lover'. **Wilfrid** is an alternative spelling of the name. (*12 October*)

William: From the Old German words meaning 'strong protection'. It is one of the most popular names to have been introduced to England after the Norman Conquest. Indeed, it was the name of the Norman leader, William the Conqueror. It has been borne by four English kings and, with the current Prince William one day likely to ascend to the throne, there will be another one to add to that list. Liam is the Irish form of the name while **Bill** and **Billy** are short forms. (*26 March, 6 April, 25 April, 23 May, 8 June*)

Wilmot: Originally a surname that was based on a pet name for William.

Winston: From either the Old English words meaning 'joy' and 'stone', or from the place name meaning 'friend's farm'. Certainly one of the best-known bearers of the name was Sir Winston Churchill, who guided England as Prime Minister during World War II. This family name came about after one of his seventeenth-century ancestors, Sir Winston Churchill, was named after his mother's maiden name.

Woody: A name that started life as a pet name or nickname, and is perhaps best known through the film director Woody Allen. More recently, it was chosen by Zoë Ball and Norman Cook as the name for their son.

Wynford: An anglicised form of the Welsh name meaning 'fair lord'.

Wynn: A popular Welsh name meaning 'fair'.

X

Xavier: Probably from the Basque word meaning 'new house', which was originally a surname. One of the most famous bearers of the surname is Francis Xavier, the sixteenth-century founder of the Jesuits.

Y

Yestin: The Welsh form of Justin, which is also spelled **Iestin**.

Z

Zachary: From the Hebrew meaning 'God has remembered'. In the Bible, Zachary, or Zechariah, was the father of John the Baptist. The short form **Zack** is now sometimes used as a name in its own right. (*22 March Zacharias, 5 November*)

Zebedee: From the Hebrew meaning 'God has given'. In the Bible, Zebedee was the father of James and John, two of Jesus's disciples. More recently, the name has come to be associated with the character in the children's television programme, *The Magic Roundabout*.

Zephyrus: God of the west wind in Greek mythology.

Zeus: Supreme ruler of the gods in Greek mythology. He had many children by goddesses and mortal women alike.

BIBLIOGRAPHY

Attwater, Donald with John, Catherine Rachel, *Dictionary of Saints*, Penguin, 1965

Beal, Andrew, *The Independent Book of Anniversaries*, Headline, 1993

Coghlan, Ronan, *The Illustrated Encyclopaedia of Arthurian Legend*, Element, 1995

Dunkling, Leslie, *The Guinness Book of Names*, 1995

Gardner, Paul and Gardner, Joy, *Bible Names for Your Baby*, Marshall Pickering, 1996

Gibson, Clare, *The Ultimate Birthday Book*, Chancellor Press, 1998

Goring, Rosemary (Ed), *Larousse Dictionary of Literary Characters*, 1994

Gruffudd, Heini MA, *Welsh Names for Children*, Y Lolfa Cyf, 1980

Hanks, Patrick and Hodges, Flavia, *A Concise Dictionary of First Names*, Oxford University Press, 1992

Harrod, Jacqueline, *The New A–Z of Babies' Names*, Elliot Right Way Books, 1995

Philip, Neil, *Myths and Legends*, Dorling Kindersley, 1999

Room, Adrian, *Brewer's Dictionary of Names*, Helicon Publishing, 1993

Room, Adrian, *Who's Who in Classical Mythology*, NTC Publishing Group, 1996

Todd, Loreto, *Celtic Names for Children*, O'Brien Press Ltd, 1998

The New English Bible, Oxford University Press, 1970